Moving Figures

EDINBURGH STUDIES IN EAST ASIAN FILM
Series Editor: Margaret Hillenbrand

Available and forthcoming titles

Independent Chinese Documentary
Dan Edwards

The Cinema of Ozu Yasujiro
Woojeong Joo

Eclipsed Cinema
Dong Hoon Kim

Moving Figures
Corey Kai Nelson Schultz

Memory, Subjectivity and Independent Chinese Cinema
Qi Wang

Hong Kong Neo-Noir
Edited by Esther C. M. Yau and Tony Williams

edinburghuniversitypress.com/series/eseaf

Moving Figures

Class and Feeling in the Films of Jia Zhangke

Corey Kai Nelson Schultz

EDINBURGH
University Press

Edinburgh University Press is one of the leading university presses in the UK. We publish academic books and journals in our selected subject areas across the humanities and social sciences, combining cutting-edge scholarship with high editorial and production values to produce academic works of lasting importance. For more information visit our website: edinburghuniversitypress.com

© Corey Kai Nelson Schultz, 2018

Edinburgh University Press Ltd
The Tun – Holyrood Road
12 (2f) Jackson's Entry
Edinburgh EH8 8PJ

Typeset in 10/13 Chaparral Pro by
IDSUK (DataConnection) Ltd

A CIP record for this book is available from the British Library

ISBN 978 1 4744 2161 4 (hardback)
ISBN 978 1 4744 2162 1 (webready PDF)
ISBN 978 1 4744 2163 8 (epub)

The right of Corey Kai Nelson Schultz to be identified as author of this work has been asserted in accordance with the Copyright, Designs and Patents Act 1988 and the Copyright and Related Rights Regulations 2003 (SI No. 2498).

Contents

List of Figures	vi
Acknowledgments	viii
Introduction	1
1 The Worker Class: From Leader to the Margins	20
2 The Peasant and the *Mingong*: From Empathy to Sympathy to Looking Back	48
3 The Soldier: From Degraded Reproduction to Avenging Hero	84
4 The Intellectual: Power and the Voice	109
5 The Entrepreneur: From Crook to "New Reform Model"	136
Notes	163
Filmography	177
Works Cited	178
Index	195

Figures

I.1	Yin, Hong and Ke Da (尹洪, 大可). "Chinese Are Amazing!" (中国人了不起). Hubei: Hubei Meishu Chubanshe, 1996. ChinesePosters.Net	1
I.2	Anonymous. "The Industry Learns from Daqing, Agriculture Learns from Dahai and the Whole Country Learns from the People's Liberation Army" (工业学大庆农业学大寨全国学人民解放军). Shanghai: Shanghai Renmin Chubanshe, 1971. ChinesePosters.Net	11
1.1	Anonymous, "Greet the 1970s with the New Victories of Revolution and Production" (用革命和生产的新胜利迎接七十年代). Shanghai: Shanghai Renmin Meishu Chubanshe, 1970. ChinesePosters.Net	23
1.2	Qi Shuyan, Political Work Group of the Revolutionary Committee of the Railroad Factory Collective Work (戚墅堰; 铁路工厂革命委员会 政工组供稿). "Use and Study Chairman Mao's Glorious Philosophical Thought in a Big Way" (大学大用毛主席光辉哲学思想). Shanghai: Shanghai renmin chubanshe, 1971. ChinesePosters.Net	23
1.3	Huang Baomei in *Huang Baomei*	27
1.4	Huang Baomei's photograph in *Huang Baomei*	27
1.5	Factory exterior from *Huang Baomei*	28
1.6	Factory interior from *I Wish I Knew*	29
1.7	Ruin in *24 City*	31
1.8	The manager's office in *Still Life*	32
1.9	He Xikun in *24 City*	36
1.10	Couple in *24 City*	37
1.11	Xiao Hua in *24 City*	37
2.1	Anonymous, "Greet the 1970s with the New Victories of Revolution and Production" (用革命和生产的新胜利迎接七十年代). Shanghai: Shanghai Renmin Meishu Chubanshe, 1970. ChinesePosters.Net	53
2.2	Cats catch big fish, every year good luck increases in *Xiao Wu*	55
2.3	Wang Hongwei in *Xiao Wu*	57

2.4	First POV shot in *Xiao Wu*	63
2.5	Second POV shot in *Xiao Wu*	64
2.6	Third POV shot in *Xiao Wu*	64
2.7	The final POV shot – the crowd gazes back in *Xiao Wu*	67
2.8	Dockworkers in *I Wish I Knew*	69
2.9	Workers in *Still Life*	71
2.10	Still from *Dong*	72
2.11	*Mingong* in *24 City*	80
2.12	Final gaze in *A Touch of Sin*	81
3.1	Sex workers dressed as PLA soldiers in *A Touch of Sin*	91
3.2	Factory 420's stage in *24 City*	93
3.3	Zhao Gang and his father in *24 City*	94
3.4	Fine Arts Section of the Chinese Revolutionary Army Museum (中国人民革命军事博物馆美术组). "Charge the Enemy to the Last Breath" (生命不息，冲锋不止) Shanghai: Renmin Meishu Chubanshe, 1970. *ChinesePosters.Net*	97
3.5	Dahai in *A Touch of Sin*	98
3.6	Close-ups of Dahai's first murder sequence of Liu	102
3.7	Dahai's stunned expression after his second murder in *A Touch of Sin*	102
3.8	Close-up of the blood in *A Touch of Sin*	103
3.9	Dahai after the final murder in *A Touch of Sin*	105
4.1	Liu Xiaodong interviewed in *Dong*	119
4.2	Ma Ke interviewed in *Useless*	120
4.3	The miners in *Useless*	123
4.4	Wang's father in *Dong*	126
4.5	The upset widow in *Dong*	128
4.6	Factory employees in *Useless*	130
4.7	Ma Ke's atelier in *Useless*	131
5.1	Yin, Hong and Ke Da (尹洪, 大可). "Chinese Are Amazing!" (中国人了不起). Hubei: Hubei Meishu Chubanshe, 1996. *ChinesePosters.Net*	139
5.2	Argument in the manager's office in *Still Life*	142
5.3	Coffee table with guns in *Mountains May Depart*	145
5.4	Shoppers at Louis Vuitton in *Useless*	148
5.5	Shoppers at Louis Vuitton in *Useless*	149
5.6	Su Na's face emerging from the debris in *24 City*	152
5.7	Su Na in her car in *24 City*	153
5.8	Su Na's gaze in *24 City*	155

Acknowledgments

My sincere thanks to Professor Chris Berry, Dr. Margaret Hillenbrand, Professor Harriet Evans, Professor Tom Gold, Dr. Gareth Stanton, and the Department of Media and Communications at Goldsmiths (University of London). And, of course, to Jia Zhangke.

The Chinese propaganda posters in this book are reproduced with the permission of the International Institute of Social History (IISH) and the Stefan R. Landsberger Collections.

Introduction

This poster, titled "Chinese are Amazing!" (1996), was one of four "'Amazing' Educational Propaganda Posters" produced for primary and middle schools in compliance with the Chinese Communist Party (CCP) Propaganda Department's "Outline to Implement Patriotic Education."[1] It features the following figures: in the foreground from left to right, we have the Maoist figures of the

Figure I.1   "Chinese Are Amazing!" (中国人了不起). Yin, Hong and Ke Da (尹洪, 大可). Hubei: Hubei Meishu Chubanshe, 1996. *ChinesePosters.Net*. (1996). Accessed February 10, 2011. http://chineseposters.net/gallery/e13-747.php

soldier, worker, and peasant, and in the background, also from left to right, an athlete, an intellectual, and a business manager. Starting from this image, this book analyzes the class figures of the worker, peasant, soldier, intellectual, and entrepreneur in the films of the contemporary Chinese director Jia Zhangke. Every chapter is structured around a class figure, and in each one I examine a figure's socio-historical and cultural contexts, its representation in the films, the cinematic tropes that are attached to it, and the feelings that are evoked. These five figures were chosen because they are the contemporary descendants of the five traditional classes of the craftsmen, peasants, soldiers, scholar gentry, and merchants[2]: the craftsmen (工), who became the worker class in the Maoist period; the peasants (农), who have also become the *mingong* (民工) rural-to-urban migrant workers; the soldiers (兵), who became the People's Liberation Army (PLA) soldiers; the scholar gentry (士), who are now the intellectuals; and the merchants (商), who are now the managers and entrepreneurs.

These figures have been socially, politically, and culturally significant throughout China's modern history. As the nation has transitioned from a planned to a market economy during the Reform Era (1978 to present), old social classes have been dissolved and new ones have been created – or, in some cases, have re-appeared from China's pre-Communist past. For instance, during the Maoist period (1949–76), the idealized classes of the worker, peasant, and soldier (工农兵) were exalted in Chinese art, literature, film, and performance. They were seen as the vanguards of the revolution, and as potent Maoist symbols that could inspire Socialist behaviors in the viewer, and therefore create a socialist utopia; thus, these "mimetic models" were therefore "designed as much to project a socialism of the future as to provide exemplars for the present."[3] Conversely, during the Cultural Revolution, the intellectuals were called the "stinking number-nine," and people in business were known as "capitalist roaders," and both groups were despised.[4] During the Reform era's Four Modernizations Campaign (四个现代化, beginning 1978), intellectuals and businesspeople were rehabilitated and re-conceptualized as "working class," and were advanced by the Party to develop the nation through science and technology.[5] However, during this period, the Maoist figures concurrently lost their former status, and now live in the shadow of their past glories. This situation is reflected in Jia's films; the workers are becoming extinct and their factories are in ruins; the peasants have been uprooted from their rural environments and have become migrant workers who wander the nation in search of employment; and the soldiers have vanished and, in their disappearance, so too has their protection. Conversely, compared to these Maoist figures, the intellectual and entrepreneur figures are depicted in the films as having largely benefited during the Reform era; the intellectual figure is represented as an important figure that has resumed its traditional role of speaking for society, and the entrepreneur, although often a threatening figure, sometimes becomes a *rushang* (儒商), a businessperson with an intellectual's temperament who is the Reform era's new model of success.

The title of this book is *Moving Figures: Class and Feeling in the Films of Jia Zhangke*. I have selected "moving figures" because I argue that the class figures are not only "moving" via the medium of the "motion picture," but are also "moving" emotionally. The title also contains the words "class" and "feeling" not only to connect with the Maoist concept (阶级感情), but also to highlight my main argument about how these class figures are being "felt" in the films, through examining how they create what Raymond Williams termed "structures of feeling" – feelings that concretize around particular times, places, generations, and classes, which are sometimes captured and evoked in art and culture.[6] By using this concept, I will be combining cognitive analysis ("thinking") with affective analysis ("feeling"), by examining not only how the figures are represented, but also how their representational power is affective. Specifically, I will interrogate how the figures' representations and the specific cinematic tropes associated with them produce structures of feeling that evoke the "felt" experience of China's contemporary social and economic transformation over the past forty years. Furthermore, there is not one feeling but several; the films do not offer a singular emotional trajectory, and thus it is this complexity and variance that captures the contradictions of the Reform era. This period is confusing, it is contradictory, and has been experienced and felt by different class groups in various ways, thus producing complementary as well as contradictory structures of feeling. I examine how this changes over time in the films – from anxiety over the threat of Reform, to decrying its negative effects, to welcoming its opportunities, to finally demanding solutions to the problems it has caused. For instance, in the film *Xiao Shan Going Home* (1995), there is excitement for the opportunities that the era brings, but this is also juxtaposed with the protagonist's growing disillusionment with this era as the film progresses. This contradiction is also found in *Xiao Wu* (1997), where economic reforms are eagerly anticipated by some, yet dreaded by others for the negative effects that have already materialized. Although this dread is ultimately magnified in the massive destruction featured in *Still Life* (2006), other films such as *Useless* (2007) and *24 City* (2008) mourn the past but also embrace the future. The Reform era becomes a time of opportunity for the entrepreneurs in *Words of a Journey* (2011), but their success contrasts sharply with the era's destructive effects found in *A Touch of Sin* (2013) and *Mountains May Depart* (2015). Thus, the films are neither a trajectory of horror nor success, but rather chart the changing structures of feeling of this period of momentous transformation, a time that has left some class figures wretched and living in the echoes of their past glories, but has given others hope and unimaginable opportunities.

I have chosen the medium of film because it constructs and evokes an era's structure of feeling – it is both a cultural product and a producer of culture, and communicates not only consciously, but also emotionally, in that it offers both a way of thinking as well as a way of feeling. It is a medium that is engaged in moments of economic, social, and historical crisis, and provides unique and new ways to observe, interpret, and articulate social and cultural transitions. While making specific observations on Jia's films, including his shorts, documentaries, and narrative films, this book also sheds light on broader issues. First, it adds to the scholarship about China's massive transformation by considering how it has been "felt" through examining a cultural product – Jia's films. Second, it grounds itself securely in how these classes have been analyzed in the social sciences and in the arts, before considering how film as film creates meaning through its engagement with theories of film phenomenology and affect, and by analyzing specific cinematic forms that are attached to these class figures. Third, it examines each class figure's structures of feeling, and interrogates how they differ between classes and generations, and change during the course of the Reform era.

Approach to Feeling

To examine further the concept of structures of feeling, Raymond Williams wrote about it in various texts, including *Preface to Film* (1954), *The Long Revolution* (1961), *Drama from Ibsen and Brecht* (1973), *Marxism and Literature* (1977), and *Politics and Letters* (1979). In these works, he expanded on several of the concept's recurring elements: how it analyzes the meanings, values, and sense of a specific time and place, as it has been developed by different classes and generations; how it is captured and evoked in culture and art; and its use as a method to examine feeling and emotion in cultural products. In the section titled "Structures of Feeling" found in *Marxism and Literature* (1977), he expands more on this concept than in any of his other works, yet the section still amounts to little over seven pages. In this work, he uses both the singular and the plural terms of "structure of feeling" and "structures of feeling," thus stressing that it is not a single feeling, but can be several feelings that can contradict or support one another. He argues that different classes can have different structures of feeling, as can generations, because "no generation speaks quite the same language as its predecessors."[7] He elaborates further on this concept, often repeating keywords such as feeling, affective elements, and social experience, found in descriptions such as: "a particular quality of social experience and relationship, historically distinct from other particular qualities, which gives the sense of a generation or period"; "affective elements of consciousness and relationships"; "meanings and values as they are actively lived and felt"; "social experiences" that are emerging *"changes of presence"* that "do not have to await definition, classification, or rationalization before they exert palpable pressures"; "as social experiences in solution, as distinct from other social semantic formations which have been *precipitated* and are more evidently and more immediately available"; and "not feeling against thought, but thought as felt and feeling as thought."[8] Finally, he argues that structure of feeling is not only a concept, but is also a methodology, which is "derived from attempts to understand such elements and their connections in a generation or period, and needing always to be returned, interactively, to such evidence."[9]

The concept, though slightly amorphous, can be described as the feeling and sense of a specific time and place, which originates from how it is experienced by specific classes and generations; a social experience that has not yet been defined or labeled, but is rather captured and evoked in cultural products; and as a methodology, which offers an approach to analyzing feeling and the emotions – the often non-conscious affective elements of human lives. Structures of feeling examines how social change has been felt, and thus advocates for meaning-making through analyzing feeling. It is also intimately connected to class. As Williams states:

> At times the emergence of a new structure of feeling is best related to the rise of a class (England, 1700–60); at other times to contradiction, fracture, or mutation within a class (England, 1780–1830), when a formation appears to break away from its class norms, though it retains its substantial affiliation, and the tension is at once lived and articulated in radically new semantic figures.[10]

A structure of feeling's importance to a specific time and place is elaborated further by Ben Anderson, who writes, "epochs are often defined in terms of a dominant public feeling: an emotion that when named expresses something about what it feels like or felt like to live in that particular period of time."[11] He argues that they help define a "collective mood" of an age, and thus "are shared between people, dispersed and distributed across sites and come to condition emotions and feeling."[12] This feeling for a specific time and place is examined further by Jennifer Harding and E. Deidre Pribram, who refer to structures of feeling as "specific deployments of emotion at specific historical junctures with particularized effects . . . [that] refer to the ways an emotion or emotions manifest at a distinct place and point in time . . ."[13] Jonathan Flatley describes structure of feelings as "orient[ing] one toward a specific social class or context," explaining that, for example, although depression is a feeling/mood, "we might describe the particular depression of the Russian peasant in the steppe in the 1920s as a structure of feeling, or the depression of the residents of a decimated New Orleans after Katrina as a structure of feeling."[14] Finally, structures of feeling associated with the past can also be evoked in the present; as Laura Podalsky argues, films not only "speak," but also "deploy emotion" and invite us to "feel" through evoking the "affective legacies" of the past.[15] Thus, the concept is intimately tied to class and class figures during times of social change – in this instance, the fall of the worker, peasant, and soldier, and the rise of the intellectual and entrepreneur figures during China's Reform era.

Additionally, there is not one homogenous structure of feeling attached to an era or a figure; rather, there can be multiple and sometimes contradictory structures of feeling. In Kathleen Woodward's analysis of Williams's *Politics and Letters*, she notes that he describes mid-19th century British Middle Class structures of feeling as "an anxious oscillation between sympathy for the oppressed and fear of their violence," and therefore constitutes "an emotional spectrum anchored by two related – and opposite – feelings about something."[16] An era can thus generate many disparate structures of feeling. Such a range is found in Jia's films in that some of the class figures have been made wretched during this period (such as the workers, peasants, and soldiers), while others have benefited from it (the intellectuals and entrepreneurs). This situation is also reflected in Jia's mixed feelings surrounding economic reforms: "I do have positive feelings about this economic change in China. Society becomes well-off and also more open. On the other hand I also start to notice the other kind of change brought by economic development. Often, the common people cannot really benefit from the economic (boom) . . ."[17]

Class in China

In order to provide a foundational understanding to the arguments raised throughout the book, this section will examine the socio-historical and cultural context of class in China, and will review the importance of the class figures in Chinese visual propaganda. Class and the class figures have been of paramount importance in the history of modern China, politically, sociologically, ideologically, historically, and culturally. The traditional Chinese class structure was heavily influenced by Confucianism, which advocated a hierarchal class system and prescribed rules of proper behavior and social conduct in order to promote social harmony. There were five major classes: scholar gentry (士), landlord and peasant (农), craftsmen (工), the merchant (商), and the soldier (兵).[18] These classes were not grouped by wealth, but by their sources of income: landlords and peasants due to their reliance on agriculture, and merchants and craftsmen due to their dependence on the market and trade. The scholar gentry, as controllers of the bureaucracy, were the ruling elites, and below them were the peasants who provided the "sustenance to the kingdom," followed by the craftsmen "who make the necessities for life," the merchants (due to their dependence upon money and trade, even though their wealth could buy them status),[19] and finally the soldiers, who were traditionally recruited from the underclasses and were frequently feared as criminals.[20] Although the Confucian class system was rigid, it did not form castes because there was a possibility of social mobility, such as that found in the Imperial Examination (科举), established in the Qin dynasty and finally dissolved in 1905. Although official positions were sometimes purchased or inherited, it was by and large a meritocracy based on the success of the test, as passing the exam led to entry into the scholar gentry class.[21]

This five-class structure existed for centuries, and was drastically changed only after the Communist Revolution in 1949. Mao Zedong (1893–1976) was the founder and leader of the People's Republic of China (PRC) until his death in 1976. He was inspired by the historical-materialist philosophies of Marx and Lenin that argued classes were formed from society's economic situation and historical circumstances, but he also believed that classes were further differentiated by their attitudes towards the Communist Revolution. Hence, Mao began his *Analysis of the Classes in Chinese Society* (1926) by asking the following questions: "Who are our enemies? Who are our friends?".[22] These questions set the tone for the text, and described the classes as something to be viewed in polarized terms – friend from enemy, revolution from counter-revolution, and right from wrong – and divided the groups between those who would support the future Communist Revolution, those who would oppose it, and ways in which the ones in the middle could be swayed. In this text, Mao listed six classes: the landlord/comprador; the middle bourgeoisie; the petty bourgeoisie (peasants with land, craftsmen, and intellectuals); the semi-proletariat (such as peasants, small handicraftsmen, shop assistants, and peddlers); the proletariat (industrial workers, coolies, and farm laborers); and the lumpenproletariat (landless peasants and unemployed craftsmen).[23]

After the revolution ended in 1949 with the CCP's victory, the state consolidated total economic control by collectivizing property and industry. During this time, the state announced that there were thirteen classes, which included: landlords, capitalists, enlightened gentry, rich peasants, middle peasants, intelligentsia, the self-employed, religious professionals, small handicrafts people, small business operators, poor peasants, workers, and the poor and migrant workers.[24] As the CCP controlled the political, economic, and social spheres, the populace became dependent on it for income, employment, and status.[25] Thus, as a result of this social transformation, the capitalists and bourgeoisie disappeared, and the new socialist classes of cadres, workers, intellectuals, and soldiers were championed.

The state instigated three policies that had enormous and lasting effects on the social system: forming the *danwei* (单位), the work unit; establishing the *hukou* (户口), the household registration system; and initiating the *chengfen* (成分), the class classification of every resident. First, there were three types of work units: government agencies, state enterprises, and non-profit state institutions, which were categorized by economic sector and ownership (state or collective) and supervised by central or local governments.[26] Many urban residents were assigned a work unit and each of these units was responsible for employment, housing, health insurance, medical facilities, education, and pensions, and also provided employment opportunities for spouses and children.[27] In addition to providing material and welfare resources, they also provided social status and political mobility via CCP membership.[28] Thus, the *danwei* functioned "as parent, caretaker, mediator," and even determined whether or not their employees could get married, divorced, or have children.[29]

Second, each person in the country was registered to a *hukou*, which specified whether they had urban or rural status and where they could live. It was used to track the populace and prevented large-scale rural-to-urban migration, thus ensuring that the peasants stayed in the countryside to produce food so that the urban residents could focus on heavy industrialization.[30] Children received their status via the maternal line, and thus, since women traditionally lived with their husbands' families, this policy was also effective in blocking rural to urban migration, until the law was changed in 1998 to allow *hukou* inheritance from either parent.[31] During the Maoist era, rural property was collectivized and these collectives, not the state, provided benefits and social services. Because the state kept the cost of farm products low to support urban development, rural services were naturally not as well supported and therefore were inferior to those available to urban residents.[32] The *hukou* therefore increased the rural-urban divide,[33] and became a "badge of citizenship" that "determined a person's entire life chances, including social rank, wage, welfare, food rations (when these were in use), and housing."[34] For rural residents tied by the *hukou* household registration system, mobility was possible only via the military, through marriage or higher education,[35] but if they permanently left their collective, they were forced to surrender their inherited right to the land.[36]

Third, the *chengfen* (meaning both "composition" and "family background") was initiated during the post-Revolution land reforms. It was defined by the

Chinese Academy of Social Sciences as a "social role," and was often combined with "class" (阶级) to form "class role" (阶级成分").[37] The three main class groupings and their subcategories during this period included: laboring classes (revolutionary cadre, soldier, and martyr; worker; poor/lower–middle peasant); other (upper–middle peasant; small proprietor; white-collar employee; independent professional); and exploiting classes (capitalist, rich peasant, and landlord).[38] The Party published definitions of the various class categories in the press so that both the cadres doing the labeling and the citizenry being labeled would understand these new categories, thus reinforcing both this bureaucratic system as well as promulgating its underlying Marxist ideology. Furthermore, although social role could change (for example student and worker), social origin remained inherited. Because class was viewed in property-based classificatory terms that were derived from an individual's source of income and livelihood during the first few years after the Revolution, such labels could easily be incongruous with the person's current situation. This label stayed with each person and their descendants, and everyone was required to report it on school, work, and promotion applications until its abolition in 1979.[39]

These labels were later used to politically mobilize the masses during the 1950s and 1960s. For instance, during the "Four Cleanups Campaign" (四清运动, 1963–6), cadre work teams organized "Remember the Bitterness" sessions to remind the peasants of the poverty and misery of the pre-Liberation period. During these meetings, the peasants were inculcated with the belief that their suffering (or, if too young to have personally experienced the era, the suffering of their parents and grandparents) had instilled in them a superior quality, one that connected them with "China's Savior" – Chairman Mao – and gave them the mission "to usher in a better future for China and the world."[40] This "subaltern consciousness" also became one of the factors used to create the nation's "new socialist subjects,"[41] thus initiating a structure of feeling of pre-Maoist suffering in order to mold the populace.

Inculcating the correct "class feelings" was seen as necessary component to becoming a good Socialist citizen.[42] This notion of "class feeling" (阶级感情), also referred to as "class affection" (阶级友爱) and "proletarian feeling" (普罗感情), was prominent during the Maoist period, and defined the dominant structures of feeling of patriotism and proletarian solidarity that defined the era. It was promoted alongside class struggle during the Maoist period in media, politics, and culture, and was prevalent in political discourse, cultural representation, and public practice.[43] Originally advanced by Mao at Yan'an when he urged intellectuals to go into the countryside so that they could obtain both "perceptual knowledge" as well as learn to identify with the peasantry's "class feelings" in order to reach "a higher level of knowledge,"[44] class feeling became particularly important during the Cultural Revolution (1966–76). For example, it was one of the main motivators of the Red Guards, who were instructed to "with profound class feeling, earnestly criticize and repudiate (the reactionaries') shortcomings and mistakes,"[45] and propaganda teams were sent to universities to stimulate the teachers' and students' "class feeling of profound love for Chairman Mao."[46]

An example of its discursive use was illustrated in the article "Study Chairman Mao's Works with a Profound Class Feeling," which was printed in the *People's Liberation Army Daily* (June 6, 1964), and reprinted in the *Guangming Daily* (June 8, 1964).[47] The editorial describes "proletarian feeling" as "a noble feeling which shows unlimited fervent love for the Party, the class and the people ... [and] unlimited loyalty for the revolutionary cause of the proletariat," and declares that this feeling is necessary in order to study and truly understand Mao Zedong Thought.[48] Furthermore, it warns that if this proletarian feeling is not inculcated, it will be replaced by corrupt influences, stating "If one does not bear the thought and feeling of the proletariat, one will bear the thought and feeling of the bourgeoisie or other classes."[49] The feeling was not only a sentiment, but a moral requirement imposed on the socialist citizens, in order "to accept and practice truth."[50] Thus, it was a state-constructed feeling, created through propaganda, which emphasized feelings of patriotism and proletarian solidarity, which became the dominant structure of feeling associated with the era and that still echoes today.[51]

This feeling was a necessary element of "self-remolding," which was necessary not only to "transform" the members of the "exploiting classes," but also the proletariat so that they could defend themselves from the corrupt classes.[52] During the Maoist period, art and culture served as educational and propagandistic vehicles to mold society. According to Mao, art and literature should be a component of the "revolutionary machine," and function as "powerful weapons" that unite and educate the people so that they could "fight the enemy with one heart and one mind."[53] He urged artists and writers, whom he referred to as "workers in art and literature," to make literature and art for the proletariat.[54] To assist in constructing "good" classes, the Party produced a worker-peasant-soldier aesthetic to inspire the populace and instill in them the desire to build the envisioned socialist utopia. During this period, the intellectual class disappeared (thus implying "the integration of learning and application, or the combination of mental and physical labor"), as did the merchant class (whose function was taken over by the redistribution power of the state).[55]

Class Figures and their Effects

Figure I.2 is characteristic of a typical Maoist-era propaganda poster. This example features idealized representatives of the worker-peasant-soldier in the foreground and an enthusiastic crowd of followers in the background. These figures "pledged allegiance to the Communist cause, or obedience to Chairman Mao Zedong, or were engaged in the glorious task of rebuilding the nation . . . [and] glorified work and personal sacrifice for the greater well-being."[56] They were used to support a variety of political campaigns to mobilize the population, and became the preferred medium of propaganda because they did not require a literate viewer,[57] as illiterate rural residents were used to "reading" messages pictorially through such media as shop signs and religious imagery.[58]

Class figures have historically been potent icons in Chinese visual culture. Initially advanced by the Confucian gentry, the belief in the instructive power of class models was found throughout Chinese history, and was later absorbed into Mao Zedong Thought.[59] Models were referred to as *mofan* (模范), meaning "an

Figure I.2 "The Industry Learns from Daqing, Agriculture Learns from Dahai and the Whole Country Learns from the People's Liberation Army" (工业学大庆农业学大寨全国学人民解放军). Anonymous. Shanghai: Shanghai Renmin Chubanshe, 1971. *ChinesePosters.Net*. Accessed February 10, 2011. http://chineseposters.net/gallery/e12-604.php

exemplary thing, pattern for emulation, model, standard ideal."[60] The concept of the model exemplar was entwined with the Confucian notion of *xiushen* (修身) – "to fix the self" (修 "to fix," 身 "the self"). This is part of the four elements that make up the Confucian model of moral growth, the *xiu-qi-zhi-ping* (修齊治平): *xiushen* (修身) "morally cultivating the self'"; *qijia* (齊家) "regulating the family"; *zhiguo* (治国) "managing the state"; and *pingtianxia* (平天下) "harmonizing the world."[61] It stemmed from Confucius's (551–479 BCE) conviction that "role modeling" through "persuasion and education would be more effective than the use of force or punishments in achieving a state of social harmony," and was later promoted by the philosopher Mencius (372–289 BCE) to "automatically" inspire people "to modify their own behavior when confronted with examples of impeccable moral qualities."[62] It was based on the concept "that correct ideas stem from proper, or correct, behavior," and thus the models served as both the "embodiment of abstract moral principles," as well as "moral examples" that "present[ed] behaviour, values and attitudes which the leadership wants the masses to emulate."[63] This belief in the use of models for the masses' "moral edification"[64] was considered not to be just a way to educate and inspire the masses, but was accepted as "by far the most efficient way, and one could inculcate any virtuous behavior in people by presenting the right model."[65]

Class models were used to advertise political changes, criticize institutions and attitudes, and motivate the people to follow Party ideologies and projects, thus influencing people "by indirect, participatory means."[66] Socialist imagery was designed not to represent existing reality, but rather offered "an idealised future *based* on a recognisable reality that may have existed."[67] Thus, such idealized icons wed with utopian imagery "not only showed 'life as it really is', but also 'life as it ought to be', stressing the positive and glossing over anything negative."[68] The models therefore functioned as "vehicles of socialization" and "a means of social control," and were believed "to provide social cohesion by establishing a shared body of beliefs, and to adapt society to new needs and situations."[69] The representation of such an idealized society was believed to "magically affect one's sense of reality," because "it invites one to participate in the play of appearances, which for the moment becomes the reality."[70] This was seen as a necessary action by Mao, to be undertaken by the state, society, and the individuals themselves. As he remarked:

> In the course of building a socialist society, everybody needs to be remolded. The exploiters must be remolded, and the working people must also be remolded ... The working class must remold the whole society in the class struggle and the struggle against nature. At the same time, they must also remold themselves.[71]

The worker-peasant-soldiers were represented in Chinese art, literature, film, and performance as models for mass social emulation; or, as Evans and Donald argue, "designed as much to project a socialism of the future as to provide exemplars for the present."[72] These models not only symbolized ideal behavior, but were intended to invoke it – or, in other words, to bring about this change in others, in order to inspire the viewer's development into what was described as a "New Socialist Human" – a figure of Socialist perfection that was believed to be attained through emulation[73] – which was believed to result "in the creation of a convincing new socialist person from the inside out."[74] This concept arose when Liu Shaoqi, the president of the PRC from 1959–68, added the Confucian belief in "self-cultivation" to the Soviet Union's concept of "New Man" (described by Trotsky as a Communist "superman"),[75] and thus "To become a 'New Man', or a good communist, the cultivation of the self would follow the model of the words, deeds, work and qualities of the founders of Marxism and Leninism."[76]

These models were believed to create a transformational "experience." Stefan Landsberger theorizes that this belief in the emulatory power of models was based on the idea that "processes of knowing and believing were accompanied by promptings to act," and thus became a continuous struggle towards perfection.[77] He explains that the model functioned as a "conveyor belt" that was believed to transmit Party information to the masses based on the following principles:

First, models are able to illustrate abstract universal values because, by seeing the particular, the universal will be understood. Secondly, a model is more effective when he or she not only is able to pinpoint public attention to a single aspect of a problem, but is also able to suggest a solution. Thirdly, a model demonstrates how this solution can be concretely executed.[78]

During the Maoist period, these figures were ubiquitous in visual propaganda, specifically the mass media of propaganda posters and film. As Jia has remarked, "many people who are familiar with revolutionary art are still being influenced by it. This kind of art uses the most popular form to disseminate the voice of those people who are in power."[79] This power was found in their omnipresence both in private and in public visual spheres, in that they essentially became part of the populace's quotidian lives and subconscious. Propaganda posters were "carriers of political meaning," and they were carefully controlled and edited in order to be ideologically correct.[80] For instance, propaganda posters were particularly pervasive, because they had print runs that ranged from single digits to tens of millions,[81] and were found in private and public environments, including schools, work, government offices, and stores.[82] They were not only consumed by the masses, but were also created by them in that people could also learn how to produce them in community "mass art centres."[83] Their popularity and omnipresence made them a component of everyday social life and discourse,[84] and "created a socialist *imaginaire* and an imagined society shared by millions,"[85] which "penetrated" the lives of the masses and formed part of the era's "historical subconscious."[86]

In addition to the class figures' perceived affective qualities in propaganda posters, they also were believed to have the same qualities in film. During the Maoist era, film was never simply a medium of entertainment, but one that was seen "as a vehicle for intellectual, moral, and political uplift," and by the 1960s, film had become a major "shaper" of mass culture.[87] Class was emphasized through onscreen inequality and conflict in order to create a "proletarian cinema,"[88] which emphasized "revolutionary-minded proletarians."[89] They became the "Proletarian nobility" that "share[d] a righteous conviction that their cause will triumph, a belief that allows gestures of revolutionary nobility," thus emphasizing patriotism and self-sacrifice.[90] Film was viewed by the Party as having the ability to transform people through its emotive power, facilitate character identification, and produce politically-oriented emotion, because it was not limited by low levels of literacy, was mass produced and could circulate widely, and was assumed to invoke stronger responses than music, literature, or performance.[91] The Party believed that film was a "transformative" medium that could create an "emotional mass experience," which would ideologically influence the audience's "individual and collective identity" through viewer identification, in order to create a new nation and a new national subject.[92] Furthermore, the Party provided a specific "political language" for the audience to use to engage with the films; for instance, during the 1950s and 1960s, the journal Popular Cinema (大众电影) included articles on "how one should *feel* following a cinematic experience," which "recorded officially sanctioned reviews while it conditioned responses to film by supplying the language and emotions appropriate to the experience."[93] Thus films' political messages were not only conveyed through representation (which was dependent upon the viewer's consciousness), but also affectively (subliminally via the viewer's unconsciousness), which "reproduced subjects of the state affectively rather than discursively."[94]

During the Cultural Revolution (1966–76), class contradictions were exaggerated, and class struggle in films was used as a synecdoche for political power struggles.[95] Model films (样板电影) were made based on model operas (样板戏) that highlighted the heroics of workers, peasants, and soldiers and glorified the Revolution.[96] Aesthetics during the Cultural Revolution also emphasized the "Three Prominences" (三突出) in the visual arts, literature, and the performing arts, which stated: "Among all characters the positive characters must stand out; among all positive characters the heroic characters must stand out; and among all heroic characters the major heroic characters must stand out."[97] In the films, the focus was on the "good" characters who were usually brightly-lit and towering in the foreground,[98] while the "bad" characters were darkly-lit and were filmed "from behind, above, and at an angle, thereby cutting them down to size."[99]

After the Cultural Revolution ended, in 1978 Deng Xiaoping instigated economic reforms that introduced the market economy, thus beginning the Reform era. As part of the reform process, the Party announced that class struggle was no longer necessary because the "bad" elements had been rehabilitated,[100] and all the negative class labels were reclassified as "commune members" or "workers," a decision which ushered in an era of social, political, and economic reform, while also strengthening the economy and consolidating political power.[101] These economic reforms changed the way that wealth was concentrated, as previously the state controlled all wealth and redistributed it to the population. Regionally, economic reform privileged the "Special Economic Zones" initially located in the coastal southern cities over the rest of the country, because these zones did not require the authorization of the central government for trade and investment.[102] Reforms also re-introduced class polarization in rural areas, and created a situation in which the poorer peasants began working for the richer ones, thus returning to pre-Revolutionary practice.[103] This period led to the creation of the "new rich" (新富, 新贵, 大款),[104] but also increased the number of the urban unemployed, as previous workers at state-owned enterprises (SOEs) became unemployed after their factories were disbanded and sold.[105] However, in response to whether or not China was becoming capitalist, Deng declared:

> The crux of the matter is whether the road is capitalist or socialist. The chief criterion for making that judgment should be whether it promotes the growth of the productive forces in a socialist society, increases the overall strength of the socialist state and raises living standards.[106]

By the 1990s, however, the economic reforms had restructured the social hierarchy, and were blamed for a range of problems. As David Goodman and Xiaowei Zang point out, China's Gini coefficient, a scale used to measure economic disparity between incomes in society in which 0 is perfect equality and 1 is complete inequality, had changed remarkably from an extremely egalitarian score of 0.22 in 1978, to a very unequal rating of 0.496 by 2007, equivalent to countries such as Brazil and Uganda.[107] In 2012, it was still at 0.49, a measure that according to the World Bank rubric signified "severe income inequality."[108] The state has been blamed for a range of problems, such as corruption, abuse, exploitation, moral infractions, lay-offs, increasing taxes, land seizures, and the decline in living standards, and it is believed that, unless checked, this inequality will continue and the gap between rich and poor will exponentially increase.[109]

In order to mitigate social tensions while still ensuring the continuation of economic development,[110] the Party has advanced the concept of "harmonious society" (和谐社会), which has the goals of creating "common prosperity" (共同富裕) and a "well off society" (小康社会).[111] First introduced by Hu Jintao when he became General Secretary of the Communist Party in China in 2002, Hu describes it as a society that was "democratic and ruled by law, fair and just, trustworthy and fraternal, full of vitality, stable and orderly, and maintains harmony between man and nature."[112] The concept was later incorporated into the state's 11th Five-Year Plan (for 2006–2010) and the country's constitution, and a white paper on the nation's future development was issued by the Information Office of the State Council in December 2005.[113] Simply put, in order for economic reforms to continue smoothly, social divisions and the growing gap between the rich and the poor must somehow be smoothed over – not addressed, per se, but mitigated just enough so that reforms can continue unabated.

Chapter Outlines

Chapter 1 analyzes the representation of the worker figure. This was the class that was created in the Maoist period to develop the nation and serve as the "vanguard" of the Maoist state, but now its members are wretched and are in the process of being replaced by migrant workers (*mingong*) without the former worker figure's previous status, skills, or power. I examine the feelings that the figures stimulate in the films, which range from pride to shame, adulation to pity, development to ruin, and progress to decay. I note how their previous status as "builders" of the nation is juxtaposed with the films' depictions of the ruin, a motif that is attached specifically to this class, in that the ruin is often that of factories and worker housing. I analyze the feelings that arise from these repeating images of ruin, and examine how it evokes contradictory structures of feeling, due to how it has been symbolized over the centuries in Chinese visual culture. Then, I argue that *24 City* commemorates the factory and the worker class by, as the verb entails, "bringing it to remembrance" through its use of "portraits in performance" and "memories in performance" that, although they commemorate the factory and its members, produce a structure of feeling of nostalgia that ultimately elegizes this group's irreversible decline and disappearance in the Reform era and resigns them to the past. I conclude by arguing that the films emotionally commemorate this class, which positions the worker figure as being in and of the past, because they, similar the Maoist past, are to be mourned but not resurrected.

Chapter 2 analyzes the representation of the figure of the peasant and its contemporary incarnation as the *mingong*. I begin by examining the representation of the peasant and the *mingong* in Jia's early films. Then, I analyze the structures of feeling of empathy and hope that concretize around the *mingong* figure in these films, but contrast these feelings with contradictory structures of feeling found in the later films that produce a hopeless and sacrificial figure of sympathy. I explore the structure of feeling of precariousness that has crystallized around this figure in the more recent films, and how the figure has been made subaltern, wretched, and rootless. I examine two cinematic forms associated with this figure – the point-of-view (POV) shot and the observational shot, positing that the POV evokes empathy while the observational shot creates sympathy. Then, I focus on the *mingong* mass that replaces the individual *mingong*, and argue that the *mingong* have been commodified and made expendable. I conclude with a cinematic form associated with this group – the *mingong* gaze. This gaze, directed at the viewer, exists as a reminder, watching and, in its presence, remaining, thus showing that this figure has not disappeared, while also demanding that the viewer acknowledge the *mingong* and their current state.

In chapter 3, I analyze the figure of the soldier. The active soldier does not appear in the films, per se, but "appears" in memory and inferior reproduction, and its presence is therefore still "felt." I examine the positive structures of feelings of honor and bravery that were associated with this figure during the Maoist era, which emphasized the army's spirit of "serving the people" and the benevolent protection of the state. I argue that the absence of this lauded figure, seen as a protector of the people, hope for social advancement for the poor, and symbol of the state's guardianship in everyday life, serves as a potent reminder of the disappearance of these noble qualities and feelings in contemporary society. Then, I analyze the figure's "appearance" in simulacra in the films – the police officers, security guards, and entertainers who dress up as soldiers – and argue that these imitation and substitute figures become increasingly degraded in the films, as they shift from naïve and ineffectual police offers to thieving security guards to sex workers who dress up as soldiers in order to entice their clients. This debased representation contrasts with their Maoist depiction and the structures of feeling that it engenders, thus emphasizing the loss of these noble Maoist qualities in the Reform era. I briefly examine the death of this figure in *Mountains May Depart*, and conclude by analyzing the soldier hero in *A Touch of Sin*, arguing that this heroic, vengeful figure symbolizes the immediate need to address social and economic disparity, and heralds a shift in Jia's oeuvre from mourning the demise of the Maoist classes to demanding redress for their plight.

In chapter 4, I analyze the representations and feelings associated with the figure of the intellectual, as primarily found in the documentaries *Useless* (about the fashion designer Ma Ke), and *Dong* (about the artist Liu Xiaodong). I examine this humanitarian figure and the structures of feeling that are associated with it, which include patriotism, altruism, and a sense of mission, and the desire to save the nation and its people. This chapter is based around the voice – the power of the voice, the class that has it, and its effects. I argue that, in the Reform era, the intellectuals have reassumed their pre-Maoist position as a lauded class; they are no longer the despised group of "Stinking Ninths" that they were during the Cultural Revolution, but have resumed their traditional role and moral obligation of speaking for the masses and serving society. I analyze what this voice says, such as its anxiety for the future, the predominance of patriotic feelings, and the desire to speak for the people, and argue that the power of the voice granted to this figure creates a structure of feeling of humanistic concern. I examine how this figure in Jia's films connects to a larger contemporary middle class Chinese structure of feeling that emphasizes humanistic anxiety and sympathy for the lower classes, but I argue that this in effect "Others" them, and therefore emphasizes the intellectual's power in the Reform era in that, although they speak for the masses, they do not share their problems. Finally, I examine the "voice" of the camera, which I interpret as the voice of another intellectual, that of Jia Zhangke, and how it switches from a passive "observatory lens" to an engaged "exploratory lens," in that it breaks its orbit around these figures to examine other people and environments. I argue that although this trope gives limited agency through depiction, it does not give them a voice because the subjects mostly remain mute, and thus the focus on the peasantry reinforces feelings of sympathy for the peasants.

In chapter 5, I conclude by analyzing the contradictory representations and structures of feeling associated with the entrepreneur figure. In many of Jia's films, this figure is a threatening criminal who represents and evokes the anxiety surrounding market reforms in the early Reform era, and produces a structure of feeling that embodies the confusion, economic abuses, and fear of changing to a market economy. However, some of the films also present the figure of the *rushang* (儒商), who is a businessperson imbued with traditional Confucian characteristics, and is advanced as the era's new model for emulation. This figure is depicted as philosophical, friendly, and inspirational, and is tempered by traditional Confucian values, such as filial piety, patriotism, and anti-materialism, making it a figure to be lauded, not feared. These benign entrepreneurs have adapted to the new economy and are thriving because of it, but are also altruistic towards the common people and thus serve as inspirational models, which produces a different structure of feeling concretized around this figure. This feeling of inspiration through personal development and improvement is complemented by advertising-like cinematography, which focus on facial close-ups that emphasize the inspirational speakers' faces and that punctuates the homilies they declare during their interviews. The *rushang* is not the "New *Socialist* Human" that was the aspiration for the previous Maoist period,[114] but is rather a "New *Reform* Human" for the Reform era. This figure symbolizes construction from the destruction of the Maoist state and thus indicates a new structure of feeling for this new era.

Chapter 1

The Worker Class: From Leader to the Margins

Introduction

In this chapter, I examine the figure of the worker and the feelings that it stimulates, which range from pride to shame, adulation to pity, development to ruin, and progress to decay. The worker class was once the vanguard of the Maoist state and society's most idealized class, but Jia's films deliberately juxtapose this iconic figure with what it has become in the contemporary era – an unemployed and ruined group whose factories and housing are also in ruin. I note how the films chart the class's downward trajectory – from the model worker heroine, Huang Baomei, in *I Wish I Knew*, who epitomizes the highpoint of this class during its Maoist heyday, to the class's role as "engine" of the nation during the socialist era in *24 City*, to its mass layoffs and decline in the Reform era in *Unknown Pleasures* and *Still Life*, and finally to the class's replacement by the *mingong* (migrant workers) who have traveled from the rural areas to manufacturing centers in search of employment.

In the first section, I discuss the history of the worker class and how it was conceptualized and created as the epitome of the Maoist social order and viewed as the agent that would modernize and develop the nation. Then, I analyze the representation of the workers in Jia's films, specifically how they have been dethroned and made irrelevant during the Reform era. I show how the films contrast this once iconic class with images of what it has become – namely, a class in ruin, redundant in the new economy, and in the process of disappearing. I examine the environment of ruin associated with it in the films, arguing that ruin represents the worker class, the Maoist state, and the collapse of the state's moral responsibility towards the people. I analyze the feelings that arise from the repeating imagery of factories in ruin, and how that imagery evokes contradictory structures of feeling, due to how it has been symbolized over the centuries in Chinese visual culture. The ruin in Jia's films evokes feelings of loss and fear; not only are the Maoist structures in ruin, the state's moral responsibility towards the populace has also been decimated, thus forming a new structure of feeling for the worker figure in the Reform era. Finally, I analyze *24 City*, which examines the history of "Factory 420" and its workers. I examine the cinematic trope of the "moving portrait" that is associated with the workers in the film, before examining their interviews and the film's "performative documentary" elements. I argue that the loss of the positive structures of feeling associated with the Maoist era is emphasized and evoked by the film, which, although it commemorates the factory and its members, produces a structure of feeling of nostalgia that ultimately elegizes this group and resigns them to the past. This positions the group as being in and of the past, and therefore of no use in the present or future.

History of the Class

The Chinese worker class originated from Mao Zedong's definition of the proletariat, which he described as the industrial workers in the railway, mining, transport, textile, and shipbuilding industries whose members, albeit few in number, were believed to be the vanguard of the impending Communist Revolution.[1] After the revolution in 1949, one of the main goals of the CCP was to develop the nation and increase industrial and agricultural growth. Because the urban proletariat was small, the state produced an entire class of workers in order to fuel industrial development and technological modernization,[2] and generated a class ideology that reinforced their new position in society. As Andrew G. Walder notes, "It is commonly remarked, and with obvious justification, that the working class did not make the Chinese revolution. An equally justified remark is rarely heard: that the revolution, on the contrary, has made the Chinese working class."[3] It was believed that they were "the most progressive force of history and the embodiment of the most advanced forces of production," and, along with the peasants, were considered "the 'masters of the country' and constituted 'the regime's only, or surely, most legitimate, political actors.'"[4] In Maoist state discourse, workers were referred to as the period's "labor aristocracy" because, similar to the cadres, they had permanent employment, free medical insurance, and subsidized housing.[5] Thus, the worker class was created by the Party both physically as well as ideologically, not only to industrialize the nation but also to serve as a symbol of the progressive Socialist state.

During the Reform era, however, this paragon of Socialist citizenry has now lost its previous status, and millions of workers have become unemployed.[6] The previous "backbone of the socialist market economy" has thus "become a disadvantaged grouping, a burden to the government, and a source of instability and unrest."[7] Furthermore, the worker class was not only materially disenfranchised, but also ideologically deposed. During this time, the state press began to proclaim that because they were paid the same rate regardless of the quality or quantity of production, their work performance was poor, and also linked them to the political extremism and chaos of the Cultural Revolution period.[8] Finally, although the workers still appeared in propaganda alongside the peasants, soldiers, and intellectuals during the Reform era, they "were nothing but a weak echo of previous propaganda practices."[9]

Increasing unemployment in the Reform era has affected the worker class not only materially but psychologically as well, and now to be a member, in the words of Dorothy Solinger, "is to be among the *excluded*, the abandoned."[10] This state has created a new structure of feeling for this figure, which is based on exclusion, marginalization, and degradation. Such a feeling is referred to in Jia's book about *24 City*, titled *A Collective Memory of Chinese Working Class*. He writes that although these workers were laborers, their technical skills made them members of that time's "leading social class" (领导阶级), and that this social standing, coupled with the factory's material bonuses such as increased pay and food rations, gave them an "inner pride in their social class" (阶级的内心骄傲).[11] Later, he describes how the factory's closure caused such "leaders" to lose their social status and become marginalized, working odd jobs to support themselves, a demotion that many were unable to accept (心理的落差).[12] This view is also echoed by political scientist William Hurst, who writes that, "[n]o longer bound together through their common labor on the production line or through shared 'ways of life' and dispositions forged over decades together in workers' housing compounds and work unit activity centers, and increasingly denied the ability to mobilize in their class interest, laid-off workers in particular became decoupled from any class identity or membership they may once have had."[13] This rapid status degradation has therefore not only impacted this class's social status and pride, but also atomized the group, weakening it as a cohesive force.

Representation

The worker figure was particularly idealized during the Maoist period. Although the worker-peasant-soldier figures were equal in theory, they were not equal in practice, as regularly mentioning the workers first in state discourse gave them "preferential status," mainly due to the fact that the government had prioritized industry.[14] Because of the state's focus on industrializing and modernizing the nation, the worker became both the vehicle to accomplish this as well as the symbol of its ideological success. Figures 1.1 and 1.2 above illustrate how propaganda posters represented the worker during this time. As Paul Clark describes, "Workers almost always appeared with the accoutrements of

The Worker Class 23

Figure 1.1 "Greet the 1970s with the New Victories of Revolution and Production" (用革命和生产的新胜利迎接七十年代). Anonymous. Shanghai: Shanghai Renmin Meishu Chubanshe, 1970. *ChinesePosters.Net*. Accessed December 29, 2011. http://chineseposters.net/gallery/e12-744

Figure 1.2 "Use and Study Chairman Mao's Glorious Philosophical Thought in a Big Way" (大学大用毛主席光辉哲学思想). Qi Shuyan, Political Work Group of the Revolutionary Committee of the Railroad Factory Collective Work (戚墅堰; 铁路工厂革命委员会 政工组供稿). Shanghai: Shanghai renmin chubanshe, 1971. *ChinesePosters.Net*. Accessed December 29, 2011. http://chineseposters.net/gallery/e13-706.php

work: overalls, a wicker safety helmet, a tool of some sort in hand or nearby if the hand clutched a political tract. A small white towel knotted at the neck, to absorb the sweat generated by hard work, was a standard trope."[15] The first poster includes representatives of the urban and rural proletariat – the worker (left) and the peasant (right). They hold "Mao's Little Red Book" in their left hands and tools of their trade in their right hands – the worker, a wrench, and the peasant, a scythe. Their fists and their arms are huge, almost as thick as their heads, emphasizing their raw power and strength, a force that has been tamed and funneled through their tools. They are young, virile and handsome, with perfect, dazzling smiles. They are gazing up and outside the picture frame, a three-quarter gaze full of joyful anticipation, directed at something wonderful lying outside the poster's borders. This is an iconic gaze found in numerous Cultural Revolution era posters, which Chris Berry describes as gazing "over and past the camera (and us) into the mists of the future perfect."[16] In the background are the fruits of expanding industry (to the left) and the successful irrigation and terracing of agricultural land (to the right). And finally, there is a rifle barrel poking over the worker's shoulder and what appears to be the butt of another rifle over the peasant's shoulder. Thus, not only do they have the tools of productivity, but they also possess the weapons to defend it. In Figure 1.2, three uniformed workers in their factory are listening to the older worker read from Mao's "Little Red Book." While the older worker (and most prominent figure) mimics the three-quarter socialist-realist gaze of the first image, looking out of the poster towards the glorious future, the other two younger workers – a man and woman – direct their gazes towards the older man. Chris Berry refers to this type of socialist-realist composition as the "Chinese chorus," arguing that it serves to emphasize the heroism of specific figures – in this particular case, the older worker.[17] In their adulation, the chorus reveres him as a model for emulation, while also guiding the gaze of the viewer towards him, and therefore he is not only a model for the poster's other two characters, but also for the viewer.

This glorious and heroic representation, however, is not repeated in Jia's films. Rather, the workers are depicted as wretched, and what were once the lauded figures of the socialist state have now been dethroned. Jia's films incorporate multiple generations of the worker class. But rather than glorify them, they chart their downwards trajectory in the Reform era, contrasting what the class once was to what it now is – a ruined group. This contrast not only reflects the socio-economic condition of this class in the Reform era, but also symbolizes the decline of socialism during this time. Although these depictions are largely pitiful, this social shift is represented as something that cannot be stopped or avoided; the past cannot be reconstructed, only mourned. The result is elegiac, lamenting the past and the changes that Reform has brought.

The worker figure first appears in *Unknown Pleasures* as the mother of one of the film's protagonists, Bin Bin. She is a state factory worker, and they appear to live in a factory-provided housing development. When another character learns where Bin Bin lives she is impressed, as state industry is still seen as providing security. But this is later revealed to not be the case when we learn of the mother's redundancy and her factory's closure. Near the conclusion of the film, she is shown sitting at the kitchen table with her chin cupped in her hands and staring forlornly at the table. Bin Bin sits down and asks what the problem is. She opens a metal tin, revealing stacks of 100 Yuan bills, and he teasingly asks if she robbed a bank. She tells him that she has taken early retirement and says woodenly "Twenty years of work, 40,000 Yuan." She also states that "no one informed against me, but I have no connections," implying that she was not forced to retire due to poor work performance, but because she did not have the necessary social and political connections. Bin Bin sadly congratulates her, proclaiming "That's great, you're free now" (很自由了), but their attitudes are anything but euphoric. Her early retirement not only means that she has lost her position, but also that she cannot pass on her job to Bin Bin via the *dingti* (顶替) policy that granted children positions in their parents' former workplaces after they retired.[18]

Instead of celebration, there is a moment of pregnant silence, as the characters look numbly at the tin of money. Their forlorn demeanor is enhanced by this silence, which interjects what Andrew Abbott refers to as "tensed time." He analyzes Henri Bergson's concepts of "tensed time" and "ordered time," stating: "Tensed time is what we live; ordered time what we narrate."[19] He explains this further: "the best representations of historical passage as a phenomenon are not plots, not sequences of events, but rather the momentary Bergsonian durations of tensed time, which are always centered on a particular, indexical present."[20] I would like to use this concept to consider the pause in the film as a duration of tensed time, which emphasizes the conflicting emotions that the scene evokes. On one hand, this financial windfall heralds her retirement, but on the other, it signifies the end of her employment and represents the meager accumulation of twenty years of labor, which hints at anxiety about the future for both of them – she retired and he remaining unemployed. In this duration of tensed time, sound, narrative, and movement are stilled, therefore accentuating the significance of what has transpired. This poignant silence also emphasizes that Bin Bin and his mother have been estranged from society, he by his recent diagnosis of having Hepatitis B, which prevents him from a career in the military as well as complicates future intimate relationships, and she by her redundancy which exiles her from the worker collective body, as a result not of her work ethic but of her lack of connections. Thus, the worker in this film has been made redundant, no longer relevant, and impotent in the new economy, and is represented as a class that will not reproduce and therefore has no future.

The worker next appears in *Still Life*, and the layoffs that started in *Unknown Pleasures* appear to have been completed. One of the protagonists, Shen Hong, is searching for her missing husband whom she has not seen for several years. During her search, she visits the factory where he once worked after he was demobilized from the military, and discovers that it has become bankrupt and is now in the process of being dismantled and emptied by its few remaining employees. She locates his locker but it has become rusted shut. She finds a hammer – a tool of the worker class – and breaks the lock, unearthing a time capsule containing his work ID and other miscellanea left behind when he vanished. In this scene, the worker class has mostly disappeared – they have been dispossessed of the factories they once occupied, and now the few that remain facilitate the factory's demolition. They are as rusted as the lock.

24 City focuses specifically on the worker class, and is structured around interviews with workers or their family members who lived and/or worked in Factory 420 (which will be analyzed later in this Chapter) since it was founded in 1958. The film is a study of the past generations of post-1949 Chinese workers: the founding generation that helped build the early Communist state, who are now elderly and retired; the second generation that grew up in the factory complex but have been laid off in the 1980s, and have been forced to find alternative employment; and their children who have grown up in the Reform era but have chosen other career paths. Thus, this film covers the entire spectrum of this group, from its creation after the Communist Revolution, to its glories during the Maoist era, to its layoffs and slow extinction during the Reform era.

Jia's films not only examine the degradation of the worker class, but also the figures that replace it, such as the *mingong* migrant workers who do similar labor but lack the benefits and status of this former Maoist iconic group (which is examined in Chapter 2). Furthermore, at the same time as rural migrants were venturing into urban areas in search of employment, millions of urban workers were being laid off, and these two groups began to merge as casual labor.[21] Thus, these unemployed urban workers are downwardly mobile whilst rural-to-urban migrants are (or are hoping to be) upwardly mobile – a flow between the two classes, and a social system in transition that will ultimately lead to the disappearance of the Maoist worker class.

I Wish I Knew features an interview with the model worker Huang Baomei. She explains that she was awarded the title of "model worker" several times,

Figure 1.3 Huang Baomei in *Huang Baomei* (screenshot from *I Wish I Knew*)

Figure 1.4 Huang Baomei's photograph in *Huang Baomei* (screenshot from *I Wish I Knew*)

had a personal meeting with Mao Zedong, was sent by the Party to attend the "World Youth Festival" in Vienna in 1959, and was the subject of her own film – *Huang Baomei* (Xie Jin, 1958). Clips of that film are shown during her interview, which describe her as "a humble person who had suffered oppression . . . [who became] a national model worker respected by others," and record her carefully tending the factory's machinery. Such model workers were proffered by the Party as social exemplars, due to their work ethic, communal spirit, and self-sacrifice, thus fulfilling the Party ideal of being "red" (supportive of the Party) and "expert" (proficient in her field).[22] In his speech "We Must Learn to Do Economic Work," Mao Zedong stated that model workers, the "heroes of labor," must be three things: "initiators" to raise standards and inspire others; the "backbone" to propel the Party onwards; and act as a "bridge" to communicate between the people and the Party.[23] A close-up in *Huang Baomei* seen in Figure 1.3 shows her as a quintessential model worker as imaged in a propaganda poster, with a gaze similar to the workers in the propaganda posters (Figures 1.1 and 1.2). Her smiling face is centered in the composition, and she is radiant, looking up and away from the viewer to what is perceived as the arrival of something glorious over the horizon, and this gaze is repeated in her award portrait shown later (Figure 1.4). In the clip from *Huang Baomei*, two other workers come up to her in awe, asking if she really is Huang Baomei, idealizing her on screen as well as in screen, like the gazes of the younger worker towards the older worker in the poster discussed previously, thus producing a model of emulation for both the characters in the film as well as the viewer watching the film. Thus, unlike the "future perfect" emerging in the social realist gaze, she is the concretized future perfect – specifically, the socialist future made perfect in the film's present.

When she visits the factory during the later part of her interview, however, it is revealed to be in ruin. The factory is shuttered, and weeds have grown in

Figure 1.5 Factory exterior from *Huang Baomei* (screenshot from *I Wish I Knew*)

Figure 1.6 Factory interior from *I Wish I Knew* (screenshot)

the cracks in the walls and the pavement. A long shot records her walking slowly through one of the empty manufacturing halls – sections of the roof have collapsed, and wire and bits of metal are hanging from the beams above. As she walks steadily towards the camera, we hear the crunch of the rubble under her feet while her voiceover narrates her history with the factory. The interview includes a clip from *Huang Baomei* that shows the factory's active smokestack, which is a triumphant angled shot that signifies the factory's dynamism and production (Figure 1.5). This image, however, is later contrasted with a shot of one of the factory's smokestacks, now silent. The camera then explores Huang touring the now-abandoned factory that lies in ruins, the triumphant soundtrack to her film still echoing in the background (Figure 1.6). But instead of a dynamic industrial space, the factory is a decrepit shell in ruins, and is occupied only by an elderly worker who reminisces about the past in the ruin of the present.

In addition to the ruined factory in *I Wish I Knew*, the ruins of factories and worker housing are also found in *Unknown Pleasures*, *Still Life*, and *24 City*. These buildings were once workplaces and homes to hundreds, if not thousands of people, but in the films the structures are in ruin and decay. Thus, they are no longer the production centers of the nation, but instead exist as the lingering fragments of past industry and the former Maoist state. These ruins echo Mao's earlier endorsement of "no construction without destruction" (不破不立), words uttered to support the destruction of traditional feudal society in order to construct a socialist utopia.[24] The ruins in the films, however, are not of the feudal past but are in fact factories and worker housing constructed during the Maoist era of nation building; thus, it is the Maoist "construction" that is being destroyed to create a "modern" industrial nation. China's economic reforms therefore have destroyed the very society that they were meant to improve, thus countering the teleological notion of a positive economic trajectory of modernization.[25] Furthermore, the ruins not only reflect the changes that economic reforms have brought to the urban landscape, but also express the disintegration of the worker class and Maoist society, in that the films associate the ruins with both. Thus, they evoke a structure of feeling of loss for this group.

In modern Chinese state discourse, ruins are viewed as signs of development, because the old and useless was being replaced by the new and useful. In traditional Chinese art history, however, the ruin had a different connotation. The art historian Wu Hung writes about the "taboo" surrounding the motif of the ruin in Chinese art, explaining that "although abandoned cities or fallen palaces were lamented in poetry, their images . . . would imply inauspiciousness and danger."[26] Ruins represented the chaos and destruction of China's "century of humiliation," when foreign armies invaded the nation during the mid-19th to the mid-20th century.[27] To illustrate this, Wu refers to the Yuanming Yuan (also known as the Old Summer Palace) that was destroyed by the British and French armies in 1860, calling it the "most important modern ruin in China," one kept as a monument "to national shame."[28]

During the Maoist era, the ruin heralded development and advancing modernity in the aforementioned belief in "no destruction without construction." In Chinese contemporary art, however, the ruin has become a popular motif that critiques economic reform and its transformation of Chinese society. Wu Hung argues that these contemporary images of the ruin and destruction in the wake of modernization inspire different affects than the previous century's image of "human tragedies," arguing that the sheer scale witnessed in modern China has profoundly impacted the people, because it has kept major urban centers "in a state of perpetual destruction and disruption."[29]

This destruction is expressed in *Still Life*, when Shen Hong's search for her husband takes her to the state-owned factory where he once worked. As she approaches the complex, the film records the environment in several takes, examining a landscape overgrown with weeds and piles of corroded machinery, and then focuses on discarded tools and the corroded metal of the factory building itself. Shen Hong passes by a handful of laborers disassembling the factory but, on closer inspection, the entire scene is a pantomime; the laborers are not attempting to disassemble the factory by removing bolts, prying off panels, or

Figure 1.7 Ruin in *24 City* (screenshot)

cutting into the structure, but are simply ineffectively beating the structure with tools – more of a performance of dissecting rather than the actual act. Similar to this futile labor, the factory itself is impotent and is no longer producing; rather, it is a structure advancing into rust and decay.

Another factory in ruin appears in *24 City*. Similar to the factory in *Still Life*, it was also one of many state-led projects established to develop the nation's industry and to serve as a symbol of China's growing strength and the nation's positive historical progression. In the film, however, the factory is being demolished and its lands redeveloped for the private market, as it is in the process of being replaced by a luxury shopping and residential complex. In one scene, a slow pan records a group of aged ex-factory workers singing the Communist hymn "The Internationale," and the scene fades to a long take of one of the factory's buildings seen from a distance. As the workers sing the lyrics "arise ye toilers of the earth," the structure collapses, and a dust cloud of debris rises and moves towards the camera, eventually obscuring the landscape (Figure 1.7). The factory is no more.

The films' representations of factories in ruins and unemployed workers are not just metaphorical, but also illustrate the workers' actual socio-economic situation. For example, when Shen Hong in *Still Life* arrives at the factory manager's office to enquire about her missing husband, she discovers a group of laid-off employees who are accusing the manager of bankrupting the factory

Figure 1.8 The manager's office in *Still Life* (screenshot)

and selling the enterprise, at a reduced rate, to a private businesswoman from Xiamen. This was a common occurrence in the Reform era, and was one of the popular "exit" strategies to liquidate a State Owned Enterprise (SOE).[30] For instance, from 1993 to 2006, over 60 million jobs were lost in SOEs and collective enterprises through such processes as privatization and economic liberalization.[31] In this scene, a man and his sister are also in the office arguing with the manager and threatening to sue the factory. On the wall overlooking the manager's desk are framed portraits of Marx, Engels, Lenin, Stalin, and Mao, which have been placed in the office as reminders of the state and the Party (Figure 1.8). Similar to the socialist realist portraits of the posters discussed earlier, they are in three-quarter profile and are staring into the "future perfect"; but, because of their position high up on the wall, they seem disconnected from the present, looking away from the events below, perhaps looking not into the future but into the socialist past. The brother and sister are arguing with the factory's manager underneath these portraits, and are declaring that the factory has a moral responsibility to help him, because he was an employee of the SOE and was forced to leave when the factory went bankrupt and to find alternate employment in another factory where he unfortunately lost his right arm in an industrial accident. The manager's emphatic refusal and dismissal of their claim, however, indicates that whatever moral or legal responsibility the factory once had to its workers is now a thing of the past. This poignant scene reflects a larger shift that occurred during the Reform era, one in which Solinger argues that the past "covenant" shared between the urban state workers and the state was broken, in that the state "fail[ed] to fulfill the paternalistic role they had always, and seemingly properly, assumed before."[32] Thus, not only is the manager failing to fulfill his "paternalistic role" to take care of his ex-employees, so too is the state. In his analysis of industrial ruins, Dylan Trigg argues that "A derelict factory testifies to a failed past but also reminds us that the future may end in ruin."[33] As he explains, "ruins shatter the myth of rational progress and permanency, in their abundance and in their necessity. Whereas the capitalist logic classifies things in terms of their productive value ... the logic of the ruin contests this assumption."[34] In this light, the ruin is a *memento mori* – a reminder that death and destruction will ultimately prevail – and the ruin therefore not only questions the failed Maoist past and its dreams of modernity, but also casts doubt on the Reform era's present and its promised future. For instance, *Unknown Pleasures* is set in Datong, an industrial city in northeastern Shanxi province with an economy based on coal mining and industry, which Jia describes as "exist[ing] in a state of desolation ... In one sense it is truly a city in ruins and the people who inhabit the city very much live in a spiritual world that reflects their environment."[35] Economic reforms promised to develop and improve the city are only partially realized – new buildings remain unfinished, as does a highway, which ends in the middle of nowhere.

This ruined "spiritual world" connects to Wu Hung's argument about the affect of urban ruination on the populace, specifically how it changed the residents' emotional connection with their environment to the extent that "they no longer belonged to one another."[36] These two notions – a ruined spiritual world and a rejected emotional environment – connect to the concept of psychogeography, which Guy Debord defined as "the study of the precise laws and specific effects of the geographical environment, whether consciously organized or not, on the emotions and behavior of individuals."[37] In these films, the ruin produces a structure of feeling of spiritual desolation, which emotionally rejects its former and current inhabitants. The ruin embodies structures of feeling of loss and fear; not only are the Maoist structures in ruin, the state's moral responsibility towards the populace has also been decimated, thus forming a new structure of feeling for the present-day worker figure – a class in ruin.

Cinematic Tropes: Moving Portraits and Interviews

24 City continues this elegiac tone by commemorating the worker class or, as per the definition, "bringing it to remembrance."[38] It is structured around interviews with people who have lived or worked in Factory 420, a military airplane manufacturing factory in Chengdu,[39] which during the course of the film is being razed and redeveloped into a luxury high-rise office and apartment complex named "24 City." The factory was an SOE founded in 1958 during the Maoist era, and in its prime employed more than 20,000 workers.[40] Factory 420 was a work unit, which not only allocated employment but also was responsible for providing a range of services, including education, housing, and social welfare programs, and thus had "responsibility for (and control over) most aspects of workers' lives."[41] Therefore, the Factory 420 complex not only included industrial buildings, but also residential, medical, educational, and recreational facilities. It was not only a workplace, but also the workers' self-contained "universe" – or, as Jia writes, "birth, and old age, sickness and death, all could be completed in this place" (生老病死都可以在这个院子里完成).[42]

Between several of the film's interviews are filmed portraits that are fixed long-take close-ups of the human face that last from 6 to 22 seconds. Although the composition of these portraits is similar to that of portraits in photography and the other visual arts, these long-take portraits also add the element of time. They create what I have termed a "moving portrait" – a portrait that is moving in film as well as moving emotionally.[43] These long-take moving portraits combine time, face, and presence to create "portraits in performance" that project the "essence" of the portrait subjects over a period of time.

The affective qualities of the film's interviews and moving portraits offer an intimacy with the viewer; first, they present members of this class for extended observation, and second, their emphasis on face, memory, and emotion produce a feeling of intimacy with an empathetic viewer. In this way, the film creates "portraits in performance" and "memories in performance" which use history, memory, and emotion to construct a felt history of the worker class on the eve of its extinction. This creates a structure of feeling that ultimately commemorates and elegizes this group's irreversible decline and disappearance in the Reform era, and mourns the class by placing it in the past.

The film's commemorative qualities are first encountered in the opening scene of *24 City*, when workers wearing blue uniforms congregate in Factory 420's assembly hall for the transfer of land ceremony from the Chengfa Group (the factory's owners) to China Resources Land Limited (the property developer). During the ceremony, the workers sing the patriotic anthem "Singing for our Nation," which includes the lyrics: "The five star red flag flutters in the wind. How glorious our song of victory! Sing for our beloved motherland as she prospers and grows strong!" This scene is operating on two levels. On one hand, it is a commemoration ceremony, an event created "to make memories" by ritualizing the closing of the factory and the transfer of land. On the other hand, the propagandistic content of the ceremony, such as this patriotic song, is contrasted with later scenes that depict the factory in ruins, thus questioning the alleged progress created by these state-led economic reforms.

After this scene, the viewer is introduced to the film's first moving portrait – close-up long-take of an older man standing by a window. Jia has elaborated on his reasons to include such long takes in an interview, declaring:

> When it came to *24 City*, I had people sit in front of the camera which I let run continuously for fifty minutes in silence. This is nothing like taking still photos. For the most important thing is that, in that silence and through the camera, we are trying to capture the subtle changes of expression, to display the intense activities of the inner world . . . I felt as if we were mourning silently for the lives and the stories of the past.[44]

This statement "mourning silently" describes the overall elegiac mood of the film. After all, portraits and portrait-like shots are powerful triggers, and have been analyzed for their affective and emotional qualities. For example, Béla Balázs wrote that facial close-ups had the power to reveal minute details of emotion that, although subtle, had a profound impact, because "good close-ups are lyrical; it is the heart, not the eye, that has perceived them."[45] In *Cinema 1*, Gilles Deleuze wrote of the capacity of images – in particular the face or "facial equivalent" – to affect the viewer, terming it the "affection image," which he defined as a "Power or Quality . . . [that] is something expressed."[46] Finally, Max Kozloff writes that the portrait conveys "the allure and meaning of the human presence – a psychic presence that extends beyond the body."[47] These three quotes emphasize the affective qualities of the face, not only in terms of depiction but also their potential to impact viewer emotions.

Long takes extend the portrait's presence and construct a "living" portrait. They provide a cinematic contemplation in time, a respite from the narrative of the film during which the portraits appear to live and breathe until the takes end. The moving portraits allow the viewer to spend time (virtually) with the person – a time of stillness that allows the viewer to observe the portrait subjects, thus creating a duration of tensed time similar to that found in the scene from *Unknown Pleasures* with Bin Bin and his mother, discussed earlier. These moments, freed from the action of the narrative, connect with Deleuze's "time-image." In *Cinema 2*, he describes the "movement-image" as one in which time was subordinate to movement and was therefore distorted to conform to the action of the film's narrative,[48] and contrasts it with the "time-image" – a segment of "real time" that was not edited or otherwise manipulated, and therefore presents to the viewer "*time itself*."⁴⁹ Thus, these portraits combine tensed time with the time-image and the human face to enhance their affective power.

The addition of time to portraiture has the potential to intensify observation and allow for an increasing absorption into the visual subject. Walter Benjamin argues that "the painting invites the spectator to contemplation; before it the spectator can abandon himself to his associations. Before the movie frame he cannot do so. No sooner has his eye grasped a scene than it is already changed. It cannot be arrested."⁵⁰ Long takes, however, lengthen the shot's duration and therefore extend the moment of observation. According to film theorist Donato Totaro, the long take allows the audience "the freedom to direct his/her own control over the viewing process, including what to look at, in what order, for how long, and to make their own synthesis of that viewing process"⁵¹ Long takes therefore offer a controlled freedom, in the sense that even though we know that the take will end, we still have time to explore the scene. In the case of the moving portraits, this extra time has the effect of heightening the portrait's powers.

This intimacy is further enhanced by the types of portraits. There are three types of portraits: formal (Figure 1.9); snapshot (Figure 1.10); and contemplative (Figure 1.11).⁵² Take, for instance, the first moving portrait of the film, which precedes the interview with He Xikun (Figure 1.9). He stares directly

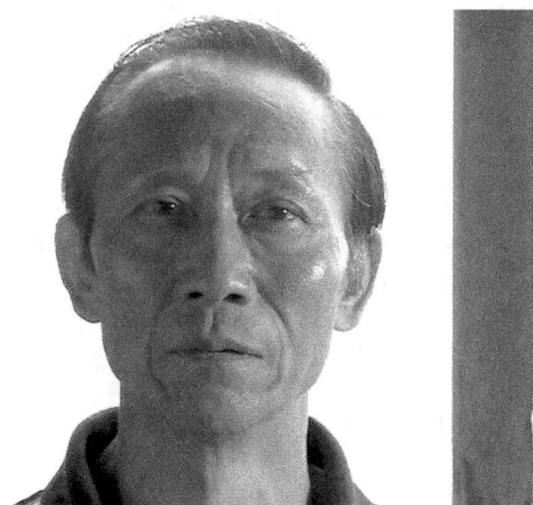

Figure 1.9 He Xikun in *24 City* (screenshot)

Figure 1.10 Couple in *24 City* (screenshot)

Figure 1.11 Xiao Hua in *24 City* (screenshot)

into the lens, frowns, and swallows. By looking into the lens, it is as if he is looking directly at the viewer, and is positioned in the viewer's personal "space." The long take allows the viewer to contemplate his almost-stillness, to study the lines and curves of his face, while at the same time presenting to the viewer the figure of the worker for an extended period of intimate observation. In the second, the example of the unnamed couple (Figure 1.10) has a more vernacular feel, as if they are snapshot photographs – everyday pictures in a family photo album that also happen to be living and breathing. In this type of photograph, the subjects look into the lens and smile, as if composing themselves for a snapshot, and their positions and smiles are held as if they are anticipating the shutter to fire and the photograph to be taken. These vernacular qualities generate intimacy with the viewer, as we have all been the subject of such personal photographs and have undoubtedly taken them of our friends and family as well, and because positioning the viewer as viewer/photographer enhances intimacy further; not only do the portraits individuate the workers, but this particular cinematic presentation positions them as personal intimates of the viewer. The third type is the contemplative portrait, termed because of the portrait subject's contemplative gaze (Figure 1.11). It is unlike the first two, which see the subjects stare directly into the lens and are "in" the viewer's space, in that the viewer is not confronted by but rather is invited to view the subject in an act of contemplation as the take unfolds over time. Those with the contemplative gaze look downwards and away from the lens and the viewer, a pose that, with its downward focus, is the antithesis of the social realist gaze into the "future perfect" discussed in the previous chapter. It appears to not look towards a "future perfect," but rather towards a "past memory," and thus offers a moment of introspection. There is an aura of thoughtfulness in the contemplative gaze, which can be seen as inviting the viewer to also adopt a contemplative gaze upon the scene.

The second commemorative trope along with the moving portrait is the interview, which records the workers' memories for posterity. Each interview is composed of long takes that record thoughts and reminiscences as they unfold, a form that allows the speaker's narrative and its accompanying emotions to slowly build, thus easing the transition from memory to memory and from emotion to emotion. In these segments, the characters are being interviewed by someone off screen, behind the camera. The interviewees are filmed in their working, living, and recreational environments, and intertitles with additional information about the interviewee, such as place of birth, age, and occupation, and photographs and ID cards are often interjected as well, which further historicizes them. The characters do not stare into the camera during their interviews, and the camera is treated as if not really there; in fact, it seldom moves – it may fade to black and then resume, but it remains silently observing as the narrative unfolds.

In an interview, Jia discussed his decision to create a film about the demise of Factory 420 as a memory project: "It was a typical case of urbanization in today's

China. I went there, saw the conditions, and it occurred to me that in five or ten years this story would be forgotten. So my aim is to use the medium of film to keep their story from disappearing."[53] Jia's self-proclaimed desire to capture this past connects with Pierre Nora's concept of "sites of memory" (*lieux de mémoire*), which he differentiates from "environments of memory" (*milieux de mémoire*), arguing that sites of memory are created when the environments that once fostered memory have disappeared.[54] Sites of memory are thus the conscious capturing of memory, or what he describes as "where memory crystalizes and secretes itself," in that they are the "remains" of a past "memorial consciousness . . . that calls out for memory because it has abandoned it."[55] Sites of memory are created due to a feared loss of memory, and a desire to stop this loss – or, in other words, are the "will to remember."[56]

Memory is a prominent theme in Jia's films, which are celebrated as recording the rapidly vanishing memories, environment, and people,[57] as well as the "disappearing forms of human life or communities that are being destroyed by global capitalist modernization."[58] His films are part of a larger "memory wave" in Chinese cinema, which began in 2005 and focused on "a past lost in memory and neglected in representation."[59] Jia has been referred to as "the historian of China's transformation,"[60] and his films have been lauded as acting as a "witness" to the era, and recording non-official individual collective and cultural memories before they vanish. As he famously stated in an interview, "I'm most interested in emphasizing cinema's function as memory, the way it records memory, and how it becomes a part of our historical experience."[61]

Thus, *24 City* can be seen as part of this memory wave and also as a "site of memory," in that it was created in order to capture these memories and stories before they disappeared, as well as make these personal and private memories public. The danger of imminent memory loss is felt in the film. Many of the interviewees are elderly and retired and, while most of the interviewees have no difficulty remembering, others do. An example is Master Wang, who appears in He Xikun's interview. He Xikun was Master Wang's apprentice decades earlier, and when he speaks to him, it is not clear if Wang always understands what He Xikun is saying, as he appears to be in a state of dementia. As he declares "my brain's rusty . . . too slow . . . I used to remember things well but now I don't." Thus, there is a sense of urgency in recording these interviews before they, like Factory 420, are ruined.

To return to Nora, he also writes about the ontological difference between memory and history, arguing that "Memory is a perpetually actual phenomenon, a bond tying us to the eternal present; history is a representation of the past."[62] He states that "memory is life" and "remains in permanent evolution, open to the dialectic of remembering and forgetting, unconscious of its successive deformations, vulnerable to manipulation and appropriation, susceptible to being long dormant and periodically revived," and compares it to history, which he explains "is the reconstruction, always problematic and incomplete, of what is no longer."[63] In this paradigm, memory and history are fundamentally different, in that memory is an event in constant change, while history is a specific depiction of the past. This difference connects with the title of the film (24 成记), which uses the word 记 (*ji*) meaning "memory" as opposed to 历史 (*lishi*), meaning "history." *Lishi* is an "official" record, while *ji* is to remember. Therefore the title itself emphasizes memory over history, choosing the more subjective term of "memory," which has more emotional and narrative connotations.

Jiwei Xiao examines the film's use of memory, arguing that it "convey[s] the texture, rhythm, and psyche of everyday life – the reality of ordinary people which is at the core of Jia's realism."[64] This notion connects to Svetlana Boym's argument that memory "describe[s] the phenomenology of human experience,"[65] a concept that allows us to consider how the past was experienced, lived and, by extension, "felt." As Maurice Halbwachs writes, collective memory differs from history because memory "still lives" in the group consciousness.[66] In this way, the individual memories in the film form a collective, "living" history of Factory 420's workers and, by extension, the larger worker class, "collecting" their memories before the group and its members disappear.

Constructing a collective history through personal memory has long been practiced in oral history-based research. For example, Ching Kwan Lee conducted interviews with workers and described their "memory narratives" as "the discursive expressions of worker identity and interest," which were "less about an objective chronology of the past than visions of the collectively experienced past."[67] This sentiment is echoed in Gail Hershatter's interviews with rural women in China, who describes collective memory as "formed in the recounting of a shared time … it is the memory of a life within a collective, a social formation that structured daily work, politics, and personal interactions."[68] The importance of the collective resonates in the interviews, but the interviews also illustrate how the emotions about the collective differ, particularly in regards to generational differences. The issue is not whose memories and emotions are true, but rather the singularity of all memory and emotion.

Regarding these differences, the Maoist generation expresses sentiments of communal solidarity and personal sacrifice for the collective, while the younger generation emphasizes independence and personal success. Karl Mannheim writes that generations are "similarly located" by their historical and lived experience,[69] an idea that resonates with structures of feeling, as both emerge from a specific time, place, and generation. *24 City* deliberately juxtaposes the generations and their particular emotional experiences, thus revealing the contradictory structures of feelings generated in the film, and the generations' varying reactions to the Reform era. For example, the older generation includes Master Wang, who, during the Maoist period, stopped He Xikun from throwing a used scraper away, telling him: "You know that this small thing has come into our hands through those of many others. It can still be used." He then sharpened it so that it could be used again. This statement is a metaphor for the collective and communal solidarity, a lineage that connects the workers and their labor across generations in building the nation-state. This solidarity, however, contrasts with the last two interviewees, Zhao Gang (b. 1974) and Su Na (b. 1982), who were brought up during the Reform era. They are the beneficiaries of market reforms, as Zhao Gang has become a television news reporter and Su Na operates her own private business. They describe the factory and factory labor not as "communal solidarity" but as boring and depressing, and see themselves as being fortunate to escape the fate that befell their parents. For instance, although a daughter of workers, Su Na never became a worker in the factory herself, although she grew up in the factory residence and attended the factory's school. In her interview, she recalls searching for her mother at work one day and not being able to recognize her, as all the workers wore the same blue uniforms, and were hunched over their machines and laboring in deafening noise. In her appalled recollection, the uniform strips the employees of their identities.

Similarly, Zhao Gang narrates that during his apprenticeship training, he left his factory position after only one day due to boredom and monotony. He explains that, as a child, he had always admired this father's work uniform, because "work uniforms meant high-status." But after he began his apprenticeship and received a uniform to wear, he soon discovered that it no longer offered a high social position and became disillusioned. He narrates that he knew he could not continue when, after preparing 50–100 identical components, more were given to him to prepare. His supervisor presented this as a Sisyphean task of repetition, stating: "Don't worry . . . if you can't finish this morning, you can go on with it in the afternoon . . . If you don't finish them today there's always tomorrow." As he says in his interview, "Your status isn't the same. You've been a student – now you're wearing worker's uniforms, but it's not the same." The picture he paints of the work environment is one that is conformist and depressing, one that he quit because "it was no fun," and left in such a hurry that he did not even retrieve his luggage. His comments echo the larger social and cultural decline of the worker class in the 1990s, in which the class not only experienced increasing unemployment but had also suffered a reduction in status.

Although the interviews can be viewed as presenting segments of "real memory" of "real people," there is one complication – some of the interviews are not "real" but are scripted fictional narratives that are performed by professional actors. Thus, the film is not entirely a documentary, but partially a pseudo-documentary that combines both authentic and fictional interviews. As Jia has remarked, "From my point of view, history is built with facts and fabulation."[70] Furthermore, the film's press kit divides the interviewees into two groups: "starring" (for the actors) and "interviewees" (for the non-actors), and in Jia's book about the film, the enacted interviews are referred to as "made up figure interviews" (虚构人物访谈) while the nonfictional interviewees are called "worker interviews" (工人访谈).[71]

The combination of fiction and truth in the film has been argued as an element that "performatively produce[s] new perspectives of interpreting history,"[72] which "enables him to explore aspects of lived time that the historical narrative cannot reach."[73] It has been hypothesized this "aims to provide *a* version of history – a personal, alternative version – to supplement rather than to replace the official version,"[74] and that it counters the state's official history by using personal stories of "individuals caught up in the experiences that official history cannot explain or deal with."[75] Furthermore, it is also posited that the combination of fiction and truth creates a "political cinema" that offers "a model of resistance structured around a series of fabulations," which "expose[s] the fictional moment at the heart of the real, collapsing the distinction between factual and fictional."[76] In a previous article, I argued that both the real and the fictional interviews created the same emotional meaning, regardless whether their sources were real or fake, thus emphasizing the importance of emotion in memory.[77] I argued that the real and scripted interviews in 24 City were affective because they recorded the act of remembering as well as its recitation, asserting that this produced an emotional past that was remembered, retold, and performed in the present, and thus commemorated the emotional histories of the workers and their families. I connected this to Abbott's concept of "lyrical sociology," in which emotion was proposed as an alternative to narrative.[78] As he explains, it "aims to communicate its author's emotional stance . . . rather than 'explain' that object."[79] Lyrical sociology is based on the word "lyric," "to express emotions," and is described as being an "alternative to 'story' thinking" that "communicate[s] a mood, an emotional sense of social reality"; thus, narrative focuses on the progress of events, but lyricism "make us feel reality through concrete emotions."[80] In this paradigm, narrative is an account of events to explain what occurred, while lyricism is the emotions and feelings behind it as constructed by the creator's emotional response; thus, narrative attempts to "show reality" while lyricism tries to make the audience "feel reality."[81] I concluded by arguing that these real and scripted interviews have the same goal and effect – to feel reality through emotion. Thus, the film captures these memories and the emotions that they evoke in their retelling and, like the moving portraits, "personalizes" the interviewees as people rather than disembodied "facts," emphasizing the emotional history of the worker class, and creating a structure of feeling that commemorates it.

Nostalgia is a particular emotional pattern found in many of the interviews with members of the older generation, who often describe the past as a period of hardship, but also as a time of communal solidarity and willing self-sacrifice for the larger collective. Nostalgia for this "golden" Maoist past is thus part of the structure of feeling connected to the older generations of workers. Not only is it part of the memory "process," it also creates an environment that encourages contemplation and mourning, in that both authentic and fictional interviews "perform" nostalgia by reminiscing about the past during their interviews. Nostalgia can be seen as a symptom of dissatisfaction with the present condition and concern for the future, and its presence an indirect condemnation of the current state of society and the growing rich-poor divide. Similar to the ruin, it also questions the teleological progress of market reforms and marks the wane of the socialist state and the worker class, while at the same time communicates the message that the past can never be reconstructed in the present. Thus, it works in tandem with the elegiac tone of the film and its commemoration of the worker class by placing the class in the past and making it of the past.

Jiwei Xiao writes that nostalgia not only "fill[s] the spiritual and cultural void left by the simultaneous retreating of socialist idealism and the official ban on historical investigation and public debate on the Cultural Revolution," but also supports "the unpleasant and inconvenient truth about today's China . . . and its new (capitalist) ineptitude in distributing social welfare and economic benefits to the working class and peasants."[82] Such nostalgia is also reflected in Lee's aforementioned interviews with Chinese workers, where "remembered socialism has turned into a powerful moral and social critique of the present, revealing the historicity of the 'market' economy and society."[83]

This nostalgia is not only a fearful reaction, it also comforts. As Dai Jinhua argues, nostalgia "rebuilds a kind of imagined link between the individual and society, between history and the present reality, in order to provide a rationale for our contemporary struggle and to impart to us some sense of comfort and stability."[84] Furthermore, Rey Chow writes of nostalgia as "no longer an emotion attached to a concretely experienced, chronological past; rather, it is attached to a fantasized state of oneness," and as "a condition of togetherness . . . that can never be fully attained but is therefore always longed for."[85] That is to say, the nostalgia in the film is nostalgia for an emotional state associated with the past, and forges a link between the alienated modern individual and the social collective.

The nostalgic longing for a socialist past in a not-so-socialist present has been a subject of research in modern ex-Communist states, and provides a useful approach to help understand the postsocialist Chinese condition. Of particular note is the concept of "*Ostalgie*," a neologism of the German words for the east (*Ost*) and nostalgia (*Nostalgie*), formed to describe the nostalgia for the ex-German Democratic Republic (GDR, the former East Germany). Paul Cooke describes *Ostalgie* as idealizing the communist past, representing the GDR as "a land where, for example, there was no unemployment and a strong sense of community existed."[86] Sheldon Lu connects nostalgia and Ostalgie to the Chinese word for nostalgia (怀旧), arguing that it is a critique of postsocialism that "addresses the sensitive zones of affect, memory, and sentiment in regard to the socialist legacy."[87] But, although nostalgia offers this communal solidarity, it must be pointed out that *24 City* does not focus on the worker collective as a collective. Rather, it mostly depicts individual members of the worker class in moving portraits and interviews, and thus emphasizes the individual over the collective. Furthermore, this atomizes the collective – they are no longer a powerful group, per se, but have been individuated.

To return to an earlier point, this nostalgia is not only evoked in the interviews but also by the persistent imagery of the ruin, a motif that Andreas Huyssen describes as "an especially powerful trigger for nostalgia."[88] Nostalgia, like the motif of the ruin, indicates a rupture with the past, and both are symptoms that something has irrevocably changed for the worse. In this way, both critique the Reform era and question the dismantling of the socialist state and the introduction of the market economy that has drastically restructured society. Nostalgia is therefore a form of dissidence, a subtle condemnation of the present Reform period. For example, in *24 City* the interviewees never come forth and directly criticize the changes that economic reforms have caused; rather, their dissatisfaction is implied through their nostalgia for "the good old days," and the emotions experienced during that time. Thus, this dissidence remains passive and does not become a political polemic to demand change.

In her analysis of nostalgia, Svetlana Boym describes two types, which she calls "restorative" and "reflective." While restorative nostalgia seeks to reconstruct the past, reflective nostalgia dwells more on the ideas and emotions associated with the past.[89] She states: "Restorative nostalgia evokes national past and future; reflective nostalgia is more about individual and cultural memory," and concludes that, while both utilize memory and symbols, they do so differently in that restorative nostalgia is more collective while reflective is more individualistic.[90] I find this concept useful in the sense that Jia's films focus on the modern "Chinese condition" – society and the very landscape itself has undergone incredible change in the last thirty years of economic reform, conveyed through the films' focus on social transition. But, to use Boym's terms, *24 City* is more reflective than restorative. The mood in *24 City* is elegiac, in that it mourns the past, but it is not a political polemic that demands a return to socialism; rather, like the interviewees who avoid blaming the state for its abandonment of socialist polices, the film mourns the loss of socialism but does not seek to reconstruct it.

Dai Jinhua considers the social environment necessary to produce nostalgia, arguing that it is also a symptom of a larger condition; namely, a transformation that occurred during the 1980s and 90s whereby the "collective dream of nationalism" was replaced by the "individualist dream of wealth."[91] She argues that, at this time, nostalgia was used for promotional purposes, stating "[t]he representation of history, infused with nostalgic sentiments and revisions, once again regains harmony and continuity in the name of the individual, or consumerism."[92] This connection between nostalgia, individualism, and consumerism – a "marketized nostalgia" – is found in the last two interviews with Zhao Gang and Su Na. Su is literally an agent of consumerism, working as a personal shopper for the wealthy, and Zhao is filmed in the act of consumption, shopping for a luxury apartment in the factory's redevelopment. Furthermore, the film itself was produced by China Resources Land Limited, which is the property developer who had purchased the site, and is named after the housing and entertainment complex that will replace it ("24 City") and not after "Factory 420" that it replaces.[93] As such, the film can be seen as using this marketized nostalgia to advertise the complex and sell housing (a situation that I will examine further in the chapter on the entrepreneur).

Memory is not only about remembering history, but also about remembering emotion. Memory and emotion are inseparable. There has been a long history of using memory and emotion for political purposes in China. For example, during the Maoist period, "Remember the Bitterness" campaigns were organized by communist work teams to ensure that the citizenry remembered the poverty of the past – not only the history of it, but also the emotions associated with it. As Jonathan Unger explains, the people "were told that their former sufferings (or those of their parents or grandparents) had granted them a superior moral value, with sacred responsibilities. They were the 'revolutionary masses' – the former wretched of the earth who had been entrusted with a mission to usher in a better future for China and the world."[94]

Although the film's interviews and the "Remember the Bitterness" campaign are both emotional, the emotions that they generate are very different. The campaigns were held to continue the revolutionary sentiment by stoking the embers of anger, resentment, and righteous indignation, but such emotions are conspicuously absent in *24 City*. Even though some of the interviewees in the film recall traumatic personal histories, they are not angry or filled with resentment, even though some of their personal sacrifices could have possibly been avoided. Thus, unlike the interview subjects in Lee's previously-mentioned study of Chinese workers whose "memory narratives" were sometimes marked by "intense rage and despair" and who "express[ed] intense moral indignation and outrage against injustice most vividly in recalling and contrasting the past with the present,"[95] the film's interviewees are mournful, but neutered of anger. They do not demand justice or retribution for their suffering; rather, they just accept it.

For example, in her interview, the repairwoman Hou Lijun explains that because of her family's migration with the factory, they were unable to see their relations that were left behind for fourteen years, thus sacrificing their external family and filial responsibilities for the larger collective. After she and her coworkers were laid off in 1984, they begged the directors of the factory to take them back. She stresses that they were not let go because they failed at their jobs, but because the factory was downsizing and needed fewer workers. There is no bitterness about her plight and her suffering in the face of economic reforms. Instead, she avoids answering the question about whether the layoffs were a political decision, replying that the factory just could not afford such a high number of employees and that "In fact, nobody was in the wrong . . . there was less work [and the factory was] earning less money. They couldn't support such a large workforce. The company had to pay its own way . . ." This theme of sacrifice for the collective, so much a part of the structure of feeling of the Maoist worker class, is continued in the interview with Hao Dali, played by the actress Lü Liping. She, however, surrendered more than family relations; she also sacrificed her only child. When the factory moved from Shenyang in northeastern China, the workers went with it, but during this migration, she and her husband became separated from their three-year-old son during the boat's stop in a riverside town to collect supplies. Because they were employed by the military during the time when it was feared that the Nationalist troops were going to invade China from Taiwan, they had no choice but to abandon the search and leave with the rest of the workers on the boat, and the child was never found. Her sacrifice and years of labor have not left her with sufficient financial support, unfortunately, and her extended family that she supported earlier has now begun to send her money after learning that the factory was being decommissioned. Thus, like other workers in the film, her sacrifice for national development has not been rewarded; rather, it has resulted in the concrete and metaphorical redundancy of her class.

Furthermore, although it is obvious from their representation that the older members of this class have been mistreated in the new economy, the film is not a political polemic that demands justice; rather, the workers remain a hapless group that is in no danger of rising up. As mentioned above in the interviews with Hou Lijun and Lü Liping, blame for their mass unemployment and redundancy in the new economy is deflected away from the state, the organ that introduced the economic reforms and that theoretically controls the Chinese economy. In the film, the worker class is not threatening but accepts its pitiful position, while those who have successfully adapted and have taken different career paths are valorized. In this way, the film acknowledges what Reform has lost (namely, communal solidarity and sacrifice) but also what has been gained in the new economy – wealth and individual opportunity. The Maoist period has ended and cannot be resurrected – like the ruin, the worker class is a state that cannot be reconstructed, and can only be commemorated and mourned. In these representations, therefore, society has irredeemably changed, and the film commemorates these emotions and this class for posterity.

I conclude by returning to one of the film's final long takes that records a field of rubble. The factory's ruins have been completely destroyed and it is impossible to tell what the structures once were. This represents the shift from ruin to rubble; ruin still indicates what once was, but rubble is an index of a complete and utter obliteration. China's social structure and the worker class are also in the process of being deconstructed at the same time that they are being reconstructed, but in an inferior reproduction. Like the Maoist axiom of "no construction without destruction," a new society cannot form unless the old one has been destroyed. The worker class and, by extension, the earlier Maoist period, is no more; like the rubble, it can no longer be reconstructed back into what it once was. Its structure of feeling of what it once it was, however, still remains.

Chapter 2

The Peasant and the *Mingong*: From Empathy to Sympathy to Looking Back

Introduction

This chapter analyzes the figure of the peasant (农) and its incarnation as the rural-to-urban peasant migrant worker, referred to as the *mingong* (民工), a cross between *nongmin* (农民, "peasant") and *gongren* (工人, "worker"). Although Jia's films deal with many kinds of migrants – middle class economic migrants, student migrants, migrant entertainers, and even a migrant serial killer – this chapter focuses specifically on the peasant migrant, and how their representation in the films transitions from an individual *mingong* with agency (albeit frustrated), to a sacrificial individual *mingong*, and finally to a wretched mass.

In order to understand this transition, I begin by analyzing the little-seen peasant figures in the films. I argue that they are represented as elderly relics of the Maoist era, but without their previous power and authority, and that this retrograde state seemingly returns them to their traditional Confucian representation as docile and naïve. Next, I examine the *mingong* as individual agent, and how this figure is represented in the early films as a figure to identify and empathize with, but later becomes an object of sympathy. I compare two different representations of individual *mingong* protagonists that appear in the films – the characters played by Wang Hongwei in *Xiao Shan Going Home* and *Xiao Wu*, who are figures with agency whom the viewer can identify and empathize with, and contrast them with the sympathetic and sacrificial *mingong* figure played by Han Sanming in *Platform* and *Still Life*. Then, I examine how the *mingong* becomes a nameless mass that is embodied and commodified, as evidenced in the (male) nudity in *Still Life*, *Useless*, and *Dong*, and the twinning of the *mingong* body with the neoliberal motif of money in *Still Life* and *The World*. This commodification has made the peasant body disposable, therefore emphasizing their subaltern status as the nation's precariat, who have been physically and metaphorically deracinated, and wander the ruins of postsocialist China in search of employment.

The *mingong* in the earlier films migrate to the cities out of hope, freedom, and adventure. But during the course of the films, this hope wanes and is replaced by hopelessness, as the previous dreams of migration for advancement have instead become a need for migration to support bare and precarious life. This creates a structure of feeling of precariousness that is intimately associated with this group during the Reform era. This feeling solidifies further into a permanent state of hopelessness in the later films, as the *mingong* lose their agency concurrently with their individuality, and become a subaltern and commodified mass. Entwined with these feelings of hope and hopelessness associated with the *mingong* is another set of feelings evoked by this state in the viewer – empathy and sympathy, with sympathy dominating in the later films. The viewer shifts from empathetically identifying with the *mingong* ("I feel for and share the feelings of the *mingong*") to a sympathetic patronization of the *mingong* ("I pity the *mingong*"). However, I conclude by considering the direct gaze emitted by the *mingong* in some of the films. This gaze is not proud, vengeful, threatening, pitiful, or dejected; rather, it is looking back, thus reminding the viewer of this group's continuing presence, and creates a feeling and an awareness of the vastly different power dynamics between what the class once was and now what it is, thus preventing a completely patronizing view.

History of the Class

During China's recent history, the conception of the peasantry has shifted from a Confucian perception of them as a placid group that needs to be taken care of, to people who must be modernized for the sake of the nation, to a group whose very existence represented the proletariat's right to rule, to an unthreatening and subaltern group during the Reform era. In her analysis of this figure, Yi-tsi Mei Feuerwerker describes the peasant as "a site or metaphor, a blank page on which various political visions and ideological agendas have been inscribed, articulated, and contested."[1] Before the modern era, the peasantry was seen as "connected" to the earth and "timeless." Later, they became a symbol for the nation and tradition, but these attributes were also believed to be incompatible with a modern, industrial, urban present. Feuerwerker writes that Lu Xun described the peasantry's representation in Chinese poetry as "Unknowing and unaware ... placid as the flowers and birds."[2] This grew out of a concept by the philosopher Mencius (fourth century BCE) who wrote that those who used their muscles were ruled by those who used their minds (劳心者治人, 劳工者治于人),[3] thus placing the peasantry at the bottom of the social hierarchy. In the Mencian paradigm, "the mandate to rule was deserved only if the people's economic and moral welfare were properly attended to," and thus the people functioned "as a yardstick for evaluating governmental success."[4] During the May Fourth period (1915–21), however, the concept of the peasantry changed and they became symbols of "backwardness" that were seen as preventing China's evolution into a modern nation.[5] This perspective again shifted in the Maoist period when their "backwardness" was viewed as "progressive" and they became "the vanguard for the revolution," the "carrier of salvational hope," the "embodiment of 'proletarian consciousness,'" and Chinese Communism's "motive force."[6] For example, in his speech "Introducing a Co-operative" (15 April 1958), Mao Zedong declared the peasantry to be "poor and blank," elements that he believed were good qualities, because "Poverty gives rise to the desire for change, the desire for action and the desire for revolution. On a blank sheet of paper free from any mark, the freshest and most beautiful characters can be written . . ."[7] By making the masses "blank," Mao was attempting "to wipe the historical-cultural slate clean," an iconoclasm that was believed to create a new Chinese culture "unmarred by historical blemishes."[8] Thus, like their earlier position as "yardstick" that measured the right to rule, the situation of the peasant in the Maoist period became a gauge that justified the CCP's political, moral, and ideological authority, and they became, by their very existence, the "agents of socio-historical transformation."[9]

Along with the worker class, the peasantry symbolically commanded the state, and were viewed as half the leading agents to transform the country into a Socialist utopia. In the Reform era, however, society has been re-structured and they compose the lower strata of society, and thus they have regressed from being the nation's leaders to being the market economy's fuel, returning to their earlier subaltern state as voiceless and powerless. These migrant workers are not "workers" in the Maoist sense; rather, they are *peasant* migrants, largely uneducated and unskilled, and are a group that has not emerged from the Worker class, nor will they become this group with its few remaining rights and privileges. They are *mingong*, a "hybrid" of *nongmin* (农民, "peasant") and *gongren* (工人, "worker"), neither belonging to the cities where they work nor the rural areas from which they hail.[10] The nation's *mingong* population is massive. In 2006, it was estimated at 200 million people, a number representing 17.4% of the total population, 31.1% of the total workforce, and 38.21% of the rural workforce,[11] and according to China's National Statistics Bureau, by the end of 2015 the number of rural migrants had increased to 247 million.[12] Although this class has been present throughout modern Chinese history, their numbers have grown exponentially during the Reform era, when they started migrating to urban areas to work as temporary labor seasonally, casually, or through short-term contracts. They migrate for money, for education, training and skills, to improve their life chances, and "see the world,"[13] or, as one *mingong* character states in *A Touch of Sin*, because she "wants a change of environment" (我想换环境). Many, however, migrate because there are simply no jobs in their hometowns, and they are encouraged by their family members and friends to go to the city to earn money so that they can send remittances to support those back home.[14]

Although the *mingong* have come to work in the cities, they have no permanent right of residency and therefore stay as peasants, both legally on their *hukou*, and conceptually in the minds of the urban residents. Even though many perform work similar to the "official" urban workers (and sometimes alongside them), they are treated very differently; they are not protected by state employment policies, are ineligible for health, retirement, injury, employment, or other welfare benefits, work longer hours for less money, have no employment guarantees or permanent labor contracts, are strictly disciplined, and cannot form unions to negotiate with their employers.[15] Furthermore, in 2006, the All-China Federation of Trade Unions (ACFTU) reported that 65% of migrant workers were working in the "Three D Jobs" (which stands for dirty, dangerous, and demeaning), and a report on *XinhuaNet* that same year also claims that migrant workers account for more than 90% of workplace deaths and more than 50% of incidences of occupational illness.[16]

Migrant workers are often viewed with suspicion and hostility in the press, and are seen, by both larger society and the state, as a menace that threatens to overwhelm the urban residents. Government officials, urban residents, and TV and film programs describe rural migrants to the city as being "stupid, dirty, lacking in breeding, and without any sense of shame,"[17] and local urban residents assign "negative ethnic labels" to migrant communities, such as "paradise of thieves and robbers," "camps for prostitutes," and "retreats of hunted criminals,"[18] and migrants are seen as "sex-starved," the men as potential rapists and the women as sex workers.[19] Note the use of negative ethnic categories that are applied to these migrant workers; in these descriptions, they are no longer fellow compatriots but have been made foreign, strange, and unwelcome. Chinese dysphemisms for this group include *liudong* (流动, "flowing from place to place"), *mingong chao* (民工潮, "tidal wave of peasant migrant workers"), and *mangliu* (盲流, those who "blindly float"), which describe this group as if they were natural disasters that mindlessly "flood" the country.[20] Regarding the description *mangliu*, Pai points out that during the 1980s–1990s, the media used this term to evoke the "irrational, senseless and out-of-control migration of labour into the cities . . . [that] has long shaped public views and sentiments towards rural migrants and further deepened the prejudice against them."[21]

Furthermore, newspapers in the 1990s emphasized the social problems caused by the presence of these *mingong*, such as crime, pollution, and overburdening urban infrastructure.[22] During this time, opinion polls of (legal) urban residents indicated a fear of the migrants' impact on employment and society, and a desire for local governments to better control migration.[23]

This belief in the "underdevelopment" of the migrants is also found in state discourse, and this emphasizes their subaltern status. For instance, in his analysis of government handbooks made for *mingong*, Felix Wemheuer writes that they "instruct the peasant workers how they should behave, dress and talk in the cities."[24] They are seen as being inherently "low quality" because of their relationship with the land, a connection with the earth that "seems to prevent farmers from achieving a high cultural and social level,"[25] a concept that has also been reinforced by the *hukou* restrictions, which has privileged the urban residents over the rural due to the urban area's superior resources,[26] which have made the peasantry "a separate, inferior class or status group"[27] with "second-class citizenship."[28]

As mentioned in the Introduction, the state has been promoting the concept of "harmonious society" (和谐社会) in order to arrest the growing gap between rich and poor through improving the labor rights of migrants, as well as emphasizing that rural workers are "citizens" due to their contributions to the nation's growth.[29] In this discursive shift, the migrants are sometimes portrayed in the media as "sacrificing" themselves for the nation, emphasizing that "they pay with their 'sweat and blood' (*fuchu xuehan*) and 'offer their youth respectfully' (*fengxian qunchun*)," which echoes descriptions of the "sent-down youth" of the Cultural Revolution period.[30] This language describes the migrant workers as uncomplaining martyrs who are sacrificing themselves to build the nation, thus contradicting the dangers posed by their representation in other media. Therefore, two very different structures of feeling have formed around this figure – on one hand, fear of them, but on the other, gratitude for their sacrifice.

Representation

Unlike their heroic representation as found in the propaganda poster opposite (Figure 2.1), that I also analyze in Chapter 1, Jia's peasants are not the peasant models with beaming smiles or gazes of firm defiance, nor are they the aforementioned "agents of socio-historical transformation." Instead, they are elderly and seemingly ill equipped to adjust to the market economy. For example, they are seen in *Xiao Wu* when the eponymous protagonist returns to his village to visit his (peasant) parents and when the (peasant) parents of Little Sister in *The World* come to Beijing to collect the body of their son, who was killed on a

Figure 2.1 "Greet the 1970s with the New Victories of Revolution and Production" (用革命和生产的新胜利迎接七十年代). Anonymous. Shanghai: Shanghai Renmin Meishu Chubanshe, 1970. *ChinesePosters.Net*. Accessed December 29, 2011. http://chineseposters.net/gallery/e12-744.php

construction site, and receive the cash settlement from his employer. Peasants also appear in *Dong*, when the artist Liu Xiaodong and his camera crew visit the family of a *mingong* who was killed working in the Three Gorges Dam area, and in *Words of a Journey*, when Pan Shiyi visits a village and is filmed interacting with the local peasantry. Finally, they also appear in *A Touch of Sin*; one of the film's plots is set in a rural mining village, and another features a serial killer who returns to his home village for his mother's birthday. Similar to the workers, the peasants are in decline, and, although deposed from their previous social standing, are in no danger of rising up and reclaiming their power. Thus, the elderly remain in the countryside as peasants, while their children and grandchildren have become *mingong* migrant workers, and have left their rural homes to pursue economic opportunities in the city.

In these depictions, the peasants appear as relics of the past who had difficulty adapting to the present day. For example, Xiao Wu gives his mother a gold ring that he had bought for a woman he loved, but who has since left him. His father asks to see it and, during his examination of it, remarks "We've been poor peasants for three generations. Is it made of gold or copper?" (你落子活了三辈子贫农就连个是金是铜也人不得). Xiao Wu angrily retorts that it is gold, but the father's question lingers. Earlier, there was a pride in this subaltern state, which was described as a Party-inspired "credential of superiority," one in which people "proudly traced the purity of their poor and lower-middle peasant ancestry" through the generations in order "to establish a 'bloodline' . . . of 'naturally red' pedigree."[31] But the father's pride in his subaltern status – three generations of being poor peasants – is inflected with his inability to discern if the ring is made of copper or gold, a basic capacity to distinguish material wealth that is needed in a market economy.

This point about the difficulties of poor peasants adjusting their values and skills in the new and more materialistic era is emphasized further in the film after Xiao Wu's father assembles his adult children and asks them to contribute 5,000 Yuan each to their brother's upcoming wedding, a monetary gift that the father obviously cannot produce by himself. They try to avoid discussing their father's request, until finally the eldest retorts that he simply cannot afford such a gift, and Xiao Wu quickly agrees. During this conversation, Xiao Wu is sitting under a new year's poster, and when he gets up to leave the camera remains fixed on it, examining it in one long take (Figure 2.2). The poster is brightly colored and features a white cat and two white kittens, one with black stripes and the other with orange stripes. The cat is using a fishing rod in an attempt to catch a large goldfish that is jumping into the air. The message reads: "Cats catch big fish, every year good luck increases" (猫钓大鱼年年好运). The goldfish is a traditional symbol of fortune and wealth, and is commonly found in New Year prints, because "fish" (鱼) shares the same pronunciation as the word "abundance" (余).[32] But the depiction of the cats (white and black) and the accompanying text probably refers to Deng's now famous declaration, "It doesn't matter whether a cat is white or black as long as it catches mice" (不管黑猫白猫，能捉老鼠的就是好猫). This statement was seen as advocating for the use of whatever means – socialist or capitalist – to improve the economy. Although Deng originally uttered it in 1962, it was later re-invoked to herald the beginning of the Reform era, and thus has become synonymous with it.[33] The unmoving long take that records the poster, however, also includes the dirty wall and the cracked and peeling paint, and one really wonders what wealth will be "caught" by the family, if any. Rather, the peasants appear to not even have the ability to distinguish wealth (gold from copper), and any fortune or good luck has yet to concretize for this peasant family, as Xiao Wu chases a fortune that never materializes, and his father likewise appears to believe that his children will be able to produce money seemingly from thin air.

Figure 2.2 Cats catch big fish, every year good luck increases in *Xiao Wu* (screenshot)

In addition to the poverty associated with Figure 2.2, the environments that they have come from have also not benefited from Reform but appear as inaccessible backwaters that are stuck in poverty. For instance, in *Xiao Wu*, the village and Xiao Wu's family appears quite poor; the dirt roads are heavily rutted, his parent's house is lit by a single electric bulb, and the only water pump is found in the yard. Likewise, the peasant village that Liu Xiaodong visits in *Dong* is also represented as being remote and in poverty, which he travels to by walking along mountainous unpaved tracks. Finally, there are two villages depicted in *A Touch of Sin*; one is home to a successful mine, but it appears not to have benefited from it since its roads are rutted, its ancient walls are crumbling, and a general mood of poverty pervades the town, while the second village appears threatened by a city that is expanding ominously in the distance.

The elderly peasants in the films are also often dressed in the blue Mao suit (中山装), the former "uniform" of the proletariat that now appears as a relic of the past. For example, Xiao Wu's father, Little Sister's father, and Han Sanming are all depicted in this iconic outfit, which marks them specifically as peasants. The Mao suit was designed by Sun Yat-sen as a Chinese alternative to the Western suit during the Republican period, and became a potent symbol with strong revolutionary and patriotic meaning. For instance, the four pockets were believed to represent the "fundamental principles of conduct" found in the *Book of Changes* (propriety, justice, honesty, and a sense of shame), the five center buttons were believed to symbolize the Republic's constitution, and the three cuff buttons were the Three Principles of the People (naturalism, democracy, and livelihood).[34] Furthermore, the Mao suit has long been associated with Maoism and the leadership of the proletariat. During the founding ceremony for the People's Republic of China on October 1, 1949, Mao wore a modified version of the Mao suit, and from this point onwards, it transformed into "a symbol of proletarian unity" and became the daily uniform of both men and women.[35] Thus, this style of clothing was ubiquitous during the Maoist period, and is still popular in rural China today, particularly amongst the elderly.[36] In the films, however, these aged peasants dressed in their Mao suits appear not as dynamic ruddy-faced proletarian leaders, but rather as pitiful relics of an earlier period, which is further emphasized by their faded regalia that depicts how far they have fallen. The uniform, like the class, has been demoted, a point that is emphasized in the opening scene in *Xiao Wu*, when the protagonist is filmed pickpocketing a peasant wearing a Mao suit whom he sits next to on the bus – a poignant metaphor for the class's degradation during the Reform era.

The representation of the *mingong* in Jia's films reflects the enormous social and economic changes China has been undergoing since Reform. For example, *Xiao Shan Going Home* follows the eponymous hero, a migrant worker in Beijing, and records his attempts to return home to his rural town for Spring Festival. *Xiao Wu* focuses on a peasant and his misadventures operating as a pickpocket in the small market town of Fenyang. Many of the characters in *The World* are a heterogeneous group of migrant workers from a variety of backgrounds who have come to Beijing not only for work but to improve their life chances. *Still Life* centers on two protagonists (one a nurse, the other a migrant worker) and their search for their lost spouses. The *mingong* appear in *A Touch of Sin* as factory workers, migrants, and even sex workers. Finally, one of the main characters in the first part of *Mountains May Depart* leaves his hometown to become a migrant miner. In an interview, Jia (2009) stated that they migrate to "become liberated individuals" and "escape" their families and work units.[37] Concerning this notion of liberation and escape, the films feature *mingong* characters that view migration as offering opportunity. These characters appear to be actively negotiating their socio-economic situation, and, although they struggle to adapt, some do succeed. These achievements, however, all come at a price, and this hopeful mood is ultimately met with sorrow and disillusionment. These different *mingong* juxtapose hopeful and hopeless migration; on the one hand, many of the characters are migrating for better opportunities, but on the other hand they also feature characters who migrate simply to survive. Similarly, both construct different structures of feelings for the era, ranging from Xiao Wu's hardscrabble yet hopeful existence as he repeatedly attempts to adapt to the changing economic climate of the Reform era, to Han's sense of resignation to his fate and his willingness to sacrifice himself for others in *Still Life*, to the *mingong* masses in the later films that appear to have no choice.

The difference between hopeful and hopeless migration is best highlighted by examining two of Jia's films that feature *mingong* protagonists – *Xiao Wu* and *Still Life*. These roles are played by two recurring actors: Han Sanming (韩三明, born 1971), who is Jia's cousin, and Wang Hongwei (王宏伟, born 1969), Jia's classmate from the Beijing Film Academy. Both of the actors have been praised for their average appearance. For example, as Jia declared in an interview, "One thing that initially attracted me to [Wang] was the plainness of his appearance, his face looks just like countless other Chinese people."[38] Similarly, Han Sanming

Figure 2.3 Wang Hongwei in *Xiao Wu* (screenshot)

has been described in the media as a peasant who "speaks simple words, wears simple clothes, and always smiles a simple smile."³⁹ However, they perform the "role" of the *mingong* very differently. Although he plays numerous roles in Jia's films, in *Xiao Wu* Wang represents the *mingong* who attempts to adapt, and is a dynamic character whose roles change through the films, while Han plays the role of sacrificial *mingong* who migrates to support his family, and neither his representation nor even his name changes from film to film. Thus, these films construct two different *mingong* figures who evoke different feelings – *Xiao Wu* offers the viewer an empathetic identification with the protagonist, but *Still Life* evokes a sympathetic reaction, because we are not positioned to identify with the protagonist, but rather feel sorry for him.

In *Xiao Wu*, Wang is a character that the viewer can feel with rather than for, as we witness and participate in his struggles and, ultimately, his failures. He is a pickpocket who steals from poor locals in an effort to gather enough money to give his childhood friend (from whom he is estranged) as a wedding gift. He does not identify as a thief, but rather tells people that he "works in business" (做点买卖) and that he is a "craftsman" who supports himself with his hands (凭手艺吃饭). However, it appears that pickpocketing is the only thing he knows how to do. Although he plays a petty criminal, his representation is not threatening, but endearing and comical – he wears huge thick-rimmed glasses, a Western-style suit that is too big for him, is abused by his friends and family, is unlucky in love, and the gang of pickpockets he leads is composed not of intimidating adults but of children who are also dressed in similar ill-fitting Western suits and are vainly attempting to grow adolescent mustaches. Even his name is diminutive, as Xiao Wu (小武) literally means "Little Wu" (his surname).

His attempt to adapt to the new era is symbolized by the Western suit he wears (Figure 2.3), which contrasts with the Mao suit worn by his elderly father and the peasants who have remained peasants, and the ideologies they once represented. Thus, Xiao Wu has taken on a new symbol of hope; while the Mao suit glorified the Socialist state, this suit valorizes the advent of the capitalist economy. Although popular amongst *mingong*, this choice of clothing is rather incongruous; outside of China it is usually reserved for business or formal occasions, but it has quickly become an integral component of migrant worker fashion. Prohibited during the Cultural Revolution, it has become a symbol of international modernity viewed as a "fast and easy way to modernize."⁴⁰ Jinhua Zhao argues that Western suits have become the "formal wear" of state officials, and are also popular with the rest of the population, but explains that, although "the Western suit . . . is supposed to be inherently modern and fashionable, when worn by migrant peasant workers [it] turns into something unfashionable and backwards."⁴¹ Similar to his adoption of the Western suit and various professions that obfuscate his true occupation as a thief, these surface changes ultimately do not alter Xiao Wu, and he remains a thief who is finally arrested for his crimes at the end of the film.

Comparatively, Han Sanming mostly appears as a minor character, but is one of the main protagonists in *Still Life*. In that role, however, he is passive and mostly silent, and lacks Wang's dynamism and agency. Instead, he is a sacrificial peasant, which is the same role that he plays in *Platform*, *Still Life*, *The World*, *Dong*, and *A Touch of Sin*. The empathetic feeling for the struggling protagonist played by Wang contrasts with the representation of the sympathetic sacrificial migrant characters Han Sanming portrays. The viewer feels sorry for him because he appears to not have a way out of his dire situations and he willingly offers to sacrifice himself for others. Unlike Wang whose roles change, Han's representation remains a consistent peasant trope that looks the same, acts the same, and even has the same name throughout Jia's oeuvre.

For example, Han is noble, self-sacrificial, docile, filial, and hardworking, but he is also illiterate and thus dependent upon his manual skills. In his roles, he remains very much a peasant migrant, and often appears wearing the blue Maoist jacket of the Socialist era. Throughout the films, he is consistently taciturn and silently suffers through the ordeals he faces: his sacrifice for his sister in *Platform*, in which he takes a job in a coal mine to support her educational goals, a decision which will probably lead to his death; his trip to Beijing to collect his cousin's corpse after he was killed on a construction site in *The World*; his search for his missing ex-wife in *Still Life*, and his eventual decision to return to the mines (and a likely death) so that he can "buy" her back, because she is being held as collateral for her family's debt; his brief appearance in *Dong* as one of the migrant workers whom Liu Xiaodong photographs, sketches, and paints; and in *A Touch of Sin* as a *mingong* who is leaving his village in Shanxi to visit his wife (who is presumably the same character as found in *Still Life*). He is emphatically non-threatening, and his representation evokes sympathy from the viewer. Thus, in this sacrificial representation, the films shift from a structure of feeling of empathy with the migrant, as found in *Xiao Wu*, to one of sympathy for the sacrificial *mingong*, as represented in Han's roles.

Han's representation relates to the characteristics traditionally attached to this class – "'hardworking' (*qinlao*), 'kind-hearted' (*shanliang*), 'honest' (*pushi*), [and] 'well-behaved' (*anfen*)."[42] For example, several segments in *Still Life* focus on his labor, his kindness to his fellow workers, his refusal to engage in criminal activity, and his deferential attitude towards his ex-wife's family. In addition to invoking the traditional Confucian representation of the peasant, this figure of the sacrificial *mingong* also references a larger contemporary valorization of the group in the media. As mentioned earlier, migrants are sometimes lauded in public newspapers as a group that "pay with their 'sweat and blood' (*fuchu xuehan*) and 'offer their youth respectfully' (*fengxian qingchun*)" for economic development.⁴³ Han is depicted as willing to "pay with (his) 'sweat and blood,'" and, ultimately, his life, as he risks his life for his sister in *Platform* and later his ex-wife in *Still Life*.

In the films, such self-sacrificial moments are often emphasized with a silent, pregnant pause, in which the narrative is slowed and time is stilled, offering a period of tensed time that underscores the gravity of his decision. The first example of this occurs when he chooses to sign a contract in *Platform* to work at a privately-owned mine. The contract states that his life and death are a matter of "fate," and his family will receive 500 Yuan reimbursement if he dies in the mine. When his cousin (played by Wang Hongwei) finishes reading the contract to Han, they both are silent and look away from one another. During this period of tensed time, both the characters and the viewers simultaneously realize that it is not only a work contract but is also likely a death contract. A further example is found when Han Sanming tells the migrant workers whom he lives and works with in *Still Life* that he is going back to Shanxi to work in the mines and that his pay will increase from 50 Yuan per day to 200 Yuan per day. They celebrate by drinking and become excited about the possibility of joining him in the mines. He cautions them, however, stating: "Mining is dangerous. Two guys were killed just before I left. Dozens are killed every year. Once you go down, who knows if you'll come back up. Be warned." A silence falls over the group, offering another pregnant pause. The camera, which had been focusing on Han during his monologue, slowly pans to the left, watching the assembled crowd of migrants smoking in contemplative silence.

Mingong agency is severely reduced in the later films, and the figure ceases to be the protagonist of the films, instead becoming a voiceless mass observed from a distance with slow pans and long takes. This remote distancing view has the opposite effect to the earlier empathetic view of the individual *mingong*. For example, in *Still Life*, migrants in the film work in demolition, and then migrate elsewhere, dragging their meager possessions with them in search of employment. In *24 City*, *mingong* pick amongst the ruins of the factory for items to salvage, as the remaining factory buildings collapse around them. In *Useless*, they appear as the new class of migrant factory workers laboring in a textile factory, and the film records their medical visits for work-related injuries. Finally, in *I Wish I Knew*, laborers that appear to be *mingong* manually load and unload cargo, barely managing the weight of the sacks. Each of these images emphasizes the labor of this group, but they do not depict the dynamic, energetic proletarian work as envisioned by the earlier propaganda poster with the peasant; rather, they are shown as menial workers who labor at the margins.

Although these migrants are obviously powerful, they are represented as unthreatening and silent, which is very similar to Feuerwerker's description of the hardworking and well-behaved peasant figures in Lu Xun's fiction.[44] In this depiction, the migrant workers in these films are not threatening to sanitation, culture, resources, or the urban residents. They are non-violent and in constant motion, and thus do not intimidate others by staying in one place. Such a passive representation is similar to those found in the Confucian and May Fourth periods as discussed above, which depict the *mingong* as hard working, non-menacing, and safe. Additionally, they are no longer half of the leading proletariat; unlike the representation of the powerful rural proletariat found in propaganda posters, in the films the *mingong* is more akin to a beast of burden, repeating a daily cycle of steady grunt work. Finally, the films' representation contrasts to the current state of affairs where members of such groups regularly participate in protests over money and labor rights.[45] Thus, these *mingong* are simply muscle-labor. Making no polemical demands to return to the earlier socialist era, they are unthreatening and therefore worthy of charity.

The sympathetic representation of the peasant/migrant in Jia's films is often lauded in Chinese-language scholarship, which uses terms such as "powerless/disadvantaged groups" (弱势群体), the "bottom level of society" (底层社会), and "grassroots" (草根) to describe them.[46] For instance, Lu Zhaoxu writes that Jia's films record the creation of an "emergent community" (新兴群体) of rural-to-urban migrant workers, one that is separate from the rest of society, and is furthermore described as weak and powerless (社会的弱势群体).[47] Similarly, Han Chen argues that Sixth Generation filmmakers have formed a social consciousness, a condition reflected in their humanitarian portrayals of the lowest levels of society.[48] As a result, these filmmakers have responded by developing a feeling of compassion towards those at the lowest level of society, one that, as Han argues, has been "internalized as part of their individual consciousness."[49] Finally, Ma Haoying argues that Jia gives a "voice" to the "voiceless," an altruistic position in which the films act as vehicles to remind the rest of society to treat these groups with compassion.[50] These descriptions laud the altruism of the films, without questioning how this positions the viewer to feel sorry for the *mingong* but also enhances their own feelings of superiority. As Alison Landsberg argues, "Sympathy implies condescension, for the sympathizer looks down at her object and in the process reaffirms her superiority."[51] This sympathetic view therefore allows the films to bemoan the negative effects of reform, but does not demand changing the system that causes them. Similar to the films' depictions of the worker class, the current pitiful situation of the workers and peasants in the films is something to be mourned, but neither these classes nor the politics of the Maoist era are to be restored to their past splendor. Thus, the films have shifted from an earlier focus on the dangers and trauma of reform, to an acceptance of them as something that is deplored but cannot be reversed.

In this third type of representation, the *mingong* mass is subaltern. Gayatri Spivak defines the subaltern as the "bottom layer of society," which ultimately lacks a subject position from which they can be heard.[52] She explains that the term was adopted by historians of South Asia "to mean persons and groups cut off from upward – and, in a sense, 'outward' – social mobility."[53] However, as Nikita Dhawan points out, "there is a fatal 'paradox' in the notion of 'migrant-as-subaltern,'" in that migration is an act of agency.[54] Although prevented from legally moving to urban areas due to *hukou* restrictions, the *mingong* are "mobile" physically as well as socially, in the sense that they have the potential to find work, training, and personal advancement. In this sense, they can be seen as trying to shed their subalternity through migration. In Jia's films, however, the individual *mingong* with individual agency, dreams, and ambitions is replaced by the *mingong* mass that moves from place to place in order to survive. This migration does not lead to social advancement, but provides the minimum to just sustain life. Even the dreams for advancement of the individualized *mingong* in the earlier films are rarely realized. For example, Xiao Wu is arrested at the end of the film, and Han Sanming in *Platform* and *Still Life* goes to work in the coal mines in order to support his family, a decision that will likely result in his death. Finally, the majority of deaths recorded in the films (before *A Touch of Sin*) are all of migrants who end up dying in pursuit of their dreams – Tao, Taisheng, and Little Sister in *The World*, Wang Qingsong in *Dong*, and Brother Mark in *Still Life*.

Cinematic Tropes: The POV Shot, Observation, Body, and the Gaze

This change from *mingong* as an individual agent to migrant as a sacrificial object, and the corresponding change in feeling from empathy to sympathy, is not only generated through their representation, but also by the cinematography. Specifically, there is a shift from the use of the point-of-view (POV) shot from the *mingong's* perspective to more observational shots of the *mingong*, as found in later films. I begin by briefly describing four of *Xiao Wu*'s POV scenes that I analyze. The first is Xiao Wu walking down an alley en route to see his childhood friend, a shot that is jittery and bounces as he walks along, and ends when he stops by a wall on which he and his friend had once inscribed their heights (Figure 2.4).[55]

Figure 2.4 First POV shot in *Xiao Wu* (screenshot).

In the second instance, he has gone to look for his romantic interest Mei Mei, but her roommate informs him that she has moved out and does not know where she now lives. He scans the room and, as he circles looking for clues as to where she might have gone, the shot becomes a POV of his anxious search, before ending when he stops and stares at a plastic bag and a newspaper left on her vacant bed (Figure 2.5). The third instance is after a fight with his parents in their rural village, when he runs to an intersection and tries to determine which way to go. Similar to his earlier search for Mei Mei, it becomes a POV shot of him looking around and attempting to figure out his next route (Figure 2.6). In the fourth and final example, he has been arrested for pickpocketing by the police and has been handcuffed to a pole, and a crowd gathers and stares at him, while he stares back (Figure 2.7).

The POV shot offers an insight into character perception, state of mind, and emotion. Murray Smith writes that it "plays a role in developing *multifaceted alignment* with a character . . . in which we have not only perceptual access (the POV shot shows us what we are to imagine a character sees), but a sense of what the character thinks and feels . . ."[56] Additionally, Marilyn Fabe argues that it

Figure 2.5 Second POV shot in *Xiao Wu* (screenshot)

Figure 2.6 Third POV shot in *Xiao Wu* (screenshot)

"can establish powerful identifications between the spectator and the characters on the screen," because "we merge with the on-screen characters, seeing the world as they do, from their point of view."[57] The use of the POV shot has an ideological angle in that it is positioning the viewer to identify not with the other characters in the film, but with the *mingong* figure who, as I have argued earlier, is non-threatening and more like a naughty child than a menace. In this way, like the moving portraits in *24 City*, the shot offers an empathetic connection with the viewer, an emotion that Allison Landsberg argues is "a feeling of cognitive, intellectual connection, an intellectual coming-to-terms with another person's circumstances."[58] Thus, we are asked to identify with – and embody – a specifically altruistic representation of a migrant who is a lovable scoundrel, and view his world from this empathic and compassionate viewpoint by "walking in his shoes."

Furthermore, the POV shots in the film sometimes occur during times of emotional crisis, and its positioning creates an embodied simulation in which the viewer feels Xiao Wu's confusion as well as his emotional and psychological distress. Examples of this are found in the second and third POV scenes, when Xiao Wu and the camera start to frantically turn in a circle. In the second instance, he has gone to his girlfriend's rented room and has been told that she has moved away. He turns around, scouring for clues, and his hunt becomes a fast-moving POV shot moving anti-clockwise around the room. This POV shot not only simulates his emotional state, but also stimulates it in the viewer. This is what Smith calls its "autonomic responses,"[59] effecting the same confusion (and motion sickness) in the viewer through its fast motion and spinning, a disorientation that not only represents Xiao Wu's confused state but also disorients the viewers and leaves them in the same state. Similarly, the third POV shot occurs after a fight with his parents. In this instance, Xiao Wu walks to the village's main road, and a slow pan of the surrounding area mimics his gaze. We hear a loudspeaker broadcasting a commercial for pork and an announcement about Hong Kong's impending return.[60] He looks past the brick walls and the dirt tracks, and appears stuck, as if searching for a way out of this village. As his gaze turns, he sees a man arrive in a horse-drawn cart, but his gaze does not stop until he sees a man riding his motorcycle out of the village, and longingly watches him as the motorcyclist escapes this rural backwater.

In addition to offering identification as well as its affective qualities, the POV shot allows the viewer to briefly "embody" Xiao Wu. This is a specifically corporeal view; unlike the observational shot, which I will analyze next, the POV shot is embodied, and thus the viewer is not only identified with the *mingong*, but also briefly embodied as the *mingong*. This signifies a conceptual shift; that is, a transformation from watching to being, and from the third person (the audience watches the subject act) to the first person (I watch myself act). For example, in the first POV shot, the viewer is seeing through the eyes of Xiao Wu as he walks down the alley. The shot is shaky and jittery, which emphasizes the corporeality of the shot, but it is also aesthetically jarring, because it is used rarely in the film. Furthermore, although filmmakers usually try to prevent this shakiness because it is sometimes seen as being "amateur," such a shot increases the veridicality of the scene because it appears "on the spot" and therefore "real."

However, this POV shot is not completely aligned with Xiao Wu's eyes. When we walk, no matter how rough the terrain, our vision does not quiver and shake but remains smooth, as our bodies absorb the shocks of movement. Thus, it is an affectation but one that is used to create a feeling of reality; as Bill Nichols argues, "the gritty realism of camcorder technology . . . impart[s] historical credibility to a fictional situation."[61] Furthermore, when Xiao Wu / the POV shot stops to look at the wall on which he and his best friend inscribed their names and heights during their childhood, the POV shot ends when he walks into the frame and touches the wall. This tactile response of stopping to touch the wall makes the shot even more embodied and haptic, because it breaks and rejects its embodiment at this instance – the POV shot is "shocked" by seeing these personal markings, and then emphasizes this embodiment/disembodiment further when Xiao Wu emerges from behind the camera to touch the wall. This sequence, therefore, allows the viewer to not only see through the eyes of Xiao Wu, but also see the body that they "inhabited" during this shot as Xiao Wu, making us further aware of our identification with this *mingong* figure.

Finally, the POV shot also positions the viewer as not only gazing out of the eyes of Xiao Wu, but also being looked at by others, as Xiao Wu is. For example, in the final POV shot, Xiao Wu has been arrested and handcuffed to a pole by a police officer, awaiting his punishment. A crowd slowly gathers, their gazes curious but condemning. Xiao Wu crouches back down, first avoiding their stares, but then looks back at the crowd from a low angle, staring up at their bodies looming above him. The camera watches him; at first he is nervous, and looks around furtively, but finally he stands up, the camera approaches him, and as he crouches down again, the camera "possesses" him and the scene suddenly shifts to a POV shot from his perspective staring back at the crowd. In this instance, instead of avoiding their gazes (which he attempted to do at the beginning of the shot), he (as the camera) receives their gazes and stares back at them, scanning the crowd sometimes slowly, oftentimes quickly, receiving the crowd's gazes of curiosity and condemnation as they look down at him (Figure 2.7).

The Peasant and the *Mingong* 67

Figure 2.7 The final POV shot – the crowd stares back in *Xiao Wu* (screenshot)

This POV shot concludes the film, and has been an object of much analysis. In regards to this shot, Jia stated "I felt that in some way, this crowd could serve as a kind of bridge with the audience. Like the audience, the crowd is also spectators, but there is a shift in perspective."[62] In his analysis of it, Michael Berry argues that it "emphasises Xiao Wu's identity in relation to society (the crowd), who are here cut off from him . . . It is society that creates and destroys Xiao Wu."[63] Similarly, Jason McGrath argues that this last scene "stages a direct confrontation between the perspective of the film's isolated protagonist and the gaze of the anonymous public for whom he is objectified and estranged by the mass media."[64] Kevin Lee describes it as a "cinematically rich moment of 'nakedness'," which turns the camera and Xiao Wu into public spectacles, but also brings to mind the various panoptic gazes operating in Chinese society, including those of the government and the community.[65] And finally, Shuqin Cui refers to it as Xiao Wu's "violation by public spectatorship in a public setting."[66] In these five statements, Jia, Berry, McGrath, Lee, and Cui all analyze the effects of the crowd's gaze – Jia's "bridge" with the audience, Berry's rejection, McGrath's confrontation, Lee's panopticon, and Cui's violation. A further point, however, can be made; namely, that these gazes affect the viewer. We, as the viewers, are receiving the crowd's condemning and curious gazes, and therefore, along with Xiao Wu, we too are being judged and found wanting, thus enhancing the viewer's empathetic identification with Xiao Wu through the effects of the crowd's gaze.

To return to my earlier analysis of the moving portraits in *24 City*, the crowd's gaze is similar to several of these moving portraits because they look back at the viewer. But it is also dissimilar, because the crowd in *Xiao Wu* is further away, its members appear to be staring at him/us and not a "camera," the camera often shifts position, and the people in the crowd come and go during the take. Being further away than *24 City's* moving portraits makes the gaze not as "direct" and challenging as the serious moving portraits, but the viewer is very much aware of their presence and of being the object of their gaze. Second, the subjects of the gaze in *Xiao Wu* do not appear to be concerned that they are being recorded, as they seem oblivious that they are looking at a camera and are not composing themselves for it. Third, unlike the moving portraits' motionless long takes, this POV shot is a shaky long take that moves, and is focused on a crowd that is always changing, as people casually come, stop, stare, and leave. The POV shot drags the viewer from gaze to gaze in the crowd, but these stares are always shifting, unlike *24 City's* prolonged and motionless gazes. This movement, similar to the spinning POV of the second and third gazes, communicates a feeling of disorientation and powerlessness, and lacks the contemplative stillness of the moving portrait. Referencing Chris Berry's notion of Jia's "on-the-spot" cinematic aesthetics that "simultaneously invoke the 'you are here' feeling of in-the-now,"[67] we can consider how this POV shot and the crowd's gaze positions the viewer *on* the spot, but also *in* the spot, in that the POV shot briefly places the viewer not only in the film, but also embodied in it as Xiao Wu, therefore sharing not only the time and space of the film as per the "on-the-spot" aesthetics, but the protagonist's corporeal form as well. Thus, in conclusion, there is no fourth wall to be broken because, with the POV gaze, we share the migrant's diegetic space and time, and are not being addressed by the film, per se, because we are Xiao Wu, and so we are in the film.

Now, I would like to compare the POV shots with the observational shots of the *mingong*, specifically of the *mingong* mass as found in the laboring bodies in *Still Life* and *Dong*. Here, the *mingong* increasingly become the subjects of the lens through the observational shot. These observational shots are composed of long shots, slow pans, and long takes that have become characteristic of Jia's oeuvre. The POV shot is coming from the body, a position that contrasts with the observational long takes that are of the body, which parallels a representational and narrative shift from the migrant as subject with agency to the migrant as sacrificial victim. Whereas the POV shot encourages viewer identification, which is an empathetic positioning that produces a feeling of equality with the viewer, I argue that the observational shot does not encourage viewer identification but rather elicits sympathy.

According to Jia, these long-take observational scenes can also be seen as veridical, in that they are objective, do not interfere with the events that are unfolding, and do not control the viewer's gaze but allow them "to maintain a distanced observation" as well as "their autonomy of observation."[68] The emphasis here is on the audience and their gaze, and the belief that the observational shots allow the viewers to retain their control and agency. Unlike the POV shot, this does not encourage spectatorial identification, but rather distances the viewers from the *mingong*. In this position, the audience witnesses the emotional state of the characters but, unlike the POV shot and its effects, does not share it, and thus we are invited to adopt not an empathetic view but a sympathetic one.

To examine these observational shots further, in *I Wish I Knew*, the camera observes dockworkers loading and unloading goods. During this scene, the intertitles state: "The Treaty of Nanjing between China and Britain, signed on August 29, 1842, made Shanghai a port open to foreign trade . . . The foreign concessions were established. So were the gangs." These intertitles narrate a historical past of exploitation, one that was supposedly ended by the Communist Revolution in 1949; after all, in Mao's 1926 analysis of class, coolies were a group that he described as "possessing nothing but their hands," and were thus seen by him as a potential revolutionary force.[69] The accompanying scene,

Figure 2.8   Dockworkers in *I Wish I Knew* (screenshot)

however, reads otherwise (Figure 2.8). If one looks carefully at these workers, one notices that they are not historical recreations of foreign imperialism or pre-Revolutionary Shanghai gangs. Rather, they are carrying goods in modern polyethylene sacks, and thus this action is happening in the contemporary present. In these observational shots, the camera records these modern-day coolies and their brute labor, and the viewer is left to realize the close similarities between the historical exploitation of these workers with their contemporary exploitation in the Reform era, and wonder if anything has really changed. Furthermore, what they haul or the purpose of their labor is never explained; rather, what is emphasized is the strain of the labor itself. The film features close-ups of the coolies' faces as they grimace under the strain, and is filmed in slow motion, thus emphasizing their excruciating labor. The dockworkers do not look into the lens, but cast their eyes downwards and away from the camera, concentrating on their task at hand. Although obviously strong and powerful, they are not threatening, but are filmed quietly laboring. Comparatively, if it was filmed in real time or sped-up, it could almost be heroic, evidence of the proletariat's industry and efficiency. However, this scene in slow motion is also accompanied by somber music, loud sounds of labored breathing (both human and animal), slow heavy footfall, and the sound of waves crashing in the background. Thus, the entire effect is to emphasize the brute labor of this group, while still representing them as unthreatening and pitiful.

Many of these observational shots found in the post-2004 films focus specifically on the migrant body, such as the (male) nudity in *Still Life*, and *Useless*, as well as the twinning of the commodified and disposable (male) *mingong* body and the (female) sex worker with the neoliberal motif of money in *Still Life* and *The World*. Along with the observational gaze, this display of the body is the third trope I want to examine in regard to the *mingong*. In these films, the *mingong* has been denuded, commodified, and placed as both an object to be sold and pitied. I argue that the films focus on the *mingong* body not only because the brute manual labor of their bodies pay for their existence (unlike the technical labor of the workers or mental labor of the intellectuals), but also because this focus associates this class primarily with its flesh and body, and thus its labor and not its mind. This emphasis echoes the past Mencian distinction of "those who used their minds (*laoxin*) ruled and those who used their muscles (*laoli*) were ruled."[70] Furthermore, this *mingong* body is often nude and "laid bare" to the viewer, unlike many of the other class figures under consideration here.

For example, in *Still Life* and *Dong*, the film devotes several scenes to recording the migrant workers using sledgehammers to manually tear down buildings

Figure 2.9 Workers in *Still Life* (screenshot)

in anticipation of the city's flooding during the construction of the Three Gorges Dam. These close-up long takes and slow pans examine the laboring and partially nude male migrant bodies, and study them in action from multiple angles, thus contemplating the strong, active, yet silent forms as they mutely perform their tasks (Figure 2.9). These long takes provide periods of extended observation of the *mingong* bodies, and they remain fixed on these figures, recording the sheen of the migrants' sweat, the concrete dust clinging to naked skin, and the ripple of muscle as their strong arms continuously swing the sledgehammers that are being used to pulverize the concrete, all to the sound of the hammers' rhythmic pulse.

In the films, the male migrant body is often denuded, stripped of its earlier Maoist suit with its symbolic and ideological connotations. For example, in *Xiao Wu*, the eponymous protagonist sings as he bathes naked; another scene in *Useless* studies miners showering and scrubbing the coal dust from their skin; and in *Dong*, the migrants Liu Xiaodong is painting wear nothing but their underwear. In these films, the male migrants have been literally "laid bare," almost completely exposed for the viewer, via the camera's emphasis on their near-naked bodies. But these bodies are neither sexualized nor threatening; rather, they are subdued, neutered, and exposed.

This state is particularly emphasized in *Dong*. During his visit to the family of the newly-deceased migrant worker Wang Qingsong, whom he had earlier painted, Liu gives Wang's widow and children photographs that he took of their father when he was preparing the painting, and in these photographs Wang is naked except for his underwear. Such a photographic representation is quite different than those that are usually taken for special occasions or for portraits in China, in which the subjects are composed – and, for lack of a better word, clothed. In the traditional Chinese socio-historical context, to have one's portrait taken was to have a conventional, formal photograph, not a partially nude one. Since public nudity was disapproved of, most nude visual representations were associated with pornography, not art.[71] As Rey Chow argues regarding the controversy surrounding Michelangelo Antonioni's *Chung Kuo* (1972), in which his film about daily life in modern China was banned by state authorities for supposedly emphasizing China's backwardness, "photography is about social space – in particular, how social space is, or should be, negotiated in relation to one's surroundings and fellow human beings, including in particular the photographer, who is armed."[72] In this light, the gift of the partially nude photograph of Wang is incongruous; it is highly intimate, and could have been cropped just to focus on his face, but instead it features his entire body. Thus, this focus on the *mingong's* partially nude body strips him of any possible modesty.

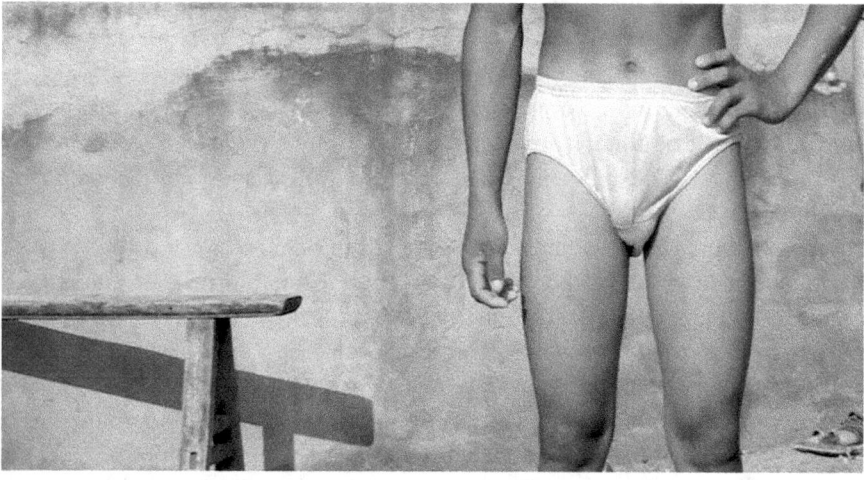

Figure 2.10   Still from *Dong* (screenshot)

This focus on the male migrant body is further emphasized in the film, when Liu talks about the penis of a young migrant, exclaiming: "Like that young fellow Xiao Zhu, when he strips off, his huge prick stands out. Fuck! How youthful and vigorous is he at 17! Despite growing up in a tough environment, nothing can cover up his beauty. The power of youth cannot be hidden." He also emphasizes and enhances the same migrant's erection in "Hotbed No. 1." In the film, there is a long-take close-up of Xiao Zhu's groin (Figure 2.10). He is headless and torso-less, and only exists as a crotch, thighs, and hands. Liu's focus on – and eroticization of – the migrant worker's penis as well as his art's focus on the partially nude male migrant body emphasizes the migrant workers as bodies, and also their very Otherness. As discussed earlier, the migrant workers have been conceived elsewhere as sexually dangerous, and as potential rapists of urban women. The migrant worker is the sexual Other, virile and uncontrollable – not only a body, but a sexualized body. Regarding racism and Othering towards those of African descent, Franz Fanon writes "one is no longer aware of the Negro but only of a penis; the Negro is eclipsed. He is turned into a penis. He *is* a penis."[73] If we take Fanon's concept of sexualized racial chauvinism and apply it to sexualized class chauvinism as expressed in these films, we see that this eroticization of the poor and powerless serves to further distance and Other the *mingong*. Thus, to paraphrase Fanon, the male migrant worker is turned into a penis. But, unlike Fanon and the examples in Chinese popular media that Wemheuer analyzes, it is not a threatening penis in Jia's films. Rather, Xiao's pose in the film is neither dynamic nor menacing, but is passive and still. His hand rests casually on his hip, a relaxed contrapposto stance that mimics the larger scene of leisure featuring men playing cards and reclining. Furthermore, his underwear is faded and stained, which further enhances the feeling of intimacy, almost embarrassingly so. In this light, the focus on the nude and partially-nude male migrant form can therefore be seen as a specific type of embodiment that positions the peasant/migrants as the Other, limited to their very physicality, yet still remaining unthreatening.

In addition to this cinematic emphasis on the nude peasant/migrant body, the body has also been commodified in the films, thus emphasizing the human cost of economic development during the Reform era. As Jia has stated in an interview, "Before, in Chinese society, being selfless was a way of becoming self . . . The idea that you were sacrificing yourself for the greater social good gave one a sense of meaning and purpose . . . Now, it's all about money."[74] Pairing money with the body is a reoccurring motif in the films: money appears as an object of longing, elusive, and out of grasp, yet the flesh remains, ready to be bought and spent. For example, in *Platform* and *Still Life*, in the pursuit of money, Han Sanming enters into dangerous work contracts with mining companies, which will probably cost his life; in *Still Life*, Han's ex-wife Missy Ma is used as collateral by her family for a loan and has thus become an indentured servant; in *The World*, a cash payment is received by an elderly peasant couple as compensation for their son's workplace death; and in *A Touch of Sin*, a migrant receptionist at a massage parlor/brothel is repeatedly beaten with a stack of cash for refusing to have sex with a client. Finally, most of the deaths that occur in Jia's films (before *A Touch of Sin*) are the deaths of *mingong*: Little Sister, Tao, and Taisheng in *The World* (Little Sister due to an accident on a construction site and Tao and Taisheng because of carbon monoxide poisoning); Brother Mark in *Still Life*, (killed in a gang-related attack); and Wang Qingsong in the documentary *Dong*, (a migrant laborer killed at work). In these films, migrant bodies are disposable – necessary for the nation's economic development, they are its fuel that can ultimately be expended. In this way, both the body's labor as well as the body itself has become a commodity, the body's migration circulating like currency in the market economy. Additionally, money even becomes a synecdoche for the homes that the *mingong* have left. For instance, in a scene in *Still Life*, migrant workers discuss where each person has come from and, because most have never heard of these places, they use the images of these areas that illustrate Chinese banknotes to show each other their home regions. In this scene, money and home have been fused together, and the characters identify their homes via the most basic of capitalist tools – cash.

Previously, I wrote about how Han's decision to sacrifice himself was accompanied by a period of affective tensed time that emphasized his sacrifice. It also emphasizes the price of life. For example, in *Platform*, Han Sanming plays the cousin of Cui Mingliang (performed by Wang Hongwei), who is a performer in a traveling song and dance troupe. Han tells Cui that, in order to fund his sister's education, he has become a miner, a decision that will probably lead to his death due to the industry's high mortality rate. According to a 2006 news report by the BBC (when *Still Life* was released), more than 5,000 miners died annually in mines in China.[75] Because Han never went to school and is illiterate, he takes his work contract to Cui and asks him to read it to him: "Contract: 1: Life and death are questions of fate. I am willing to work in Gao's mine. Management accepts no blame for accidents. 2: In cases of death or accident, the mine offers 500 Yuan compensation to families. 3. Daily wage is 10 Yuan." After reading the dismal conditions and the meager pay, Cui stops and becomes quiet. He sits down and continues to scan through the rest of the contract while Han patiently waits. Cui turns to Han, gives him back the contract and says "get it?" He looks away, as if embarrassed by his powerlessness to stop the contract from being signed, and resigns himself to both the situation and Han's fate. This moment stresses the gravity of Han's decision, and provides a brief period of reflection for both the characters and the audience to fully comprehend what Han's decision ultimately means. Han nods and takes it back to the person doing the hiring to submit it, who barks at him, "We're not responsible for anything. It's clearly stated." As Han is illiterate, he concludes the transaction by "signing" the contract with his body – his fingerprint.

A similar duration of tensed time that emphasizes the commodification of the body is also found in *The World*, when Little Sister's parents and their nephew Han Sanming arrive in Beijing to collect the payout from the construction company for their son's workplace death on the construction site. After Han signs the receipt, he looks towards his aunt and uncle, and the camera shows them looking downwards, deep in grief. This period of tensed time captured by his silence and gaze towards them and their quiet sorrow, however, is suddenly interrupted by the sound of the money being counted in the background, the crackle of bills in this otherwise poignant scene thus emphasizing the cost of Little Sister's life – and that his life had a price.

In addition to the male migrant workers who travel throughout the country in search of employment and sell the labor of their bodies, another group has returned in the Reform era – female sex workers. Many are also *mingong*. In the films, they mostly appear as secondary characters: in *Xiao Shan Going Home*, the eponymous protagonist meets one of his friends from his village who has become a sex worker in Beijing; in *Xiao Wu*, the protagonist falls in love with a sex worker from the countryside, who leaves as soon as she finds a wealthy client; in *Unknown Pleasures*, one of the protagonists is a dancer who also works in the sex trade; in *Still Life*, one of the characters is a sex worker in Beijing, sending money back to support her family in Russia; in *The World*, male migrant workers sell manual labor while female migrants sell sex; and in *A Touch of Sin*, sex workers appear working in massage parlors and performing erotic dances to punters in a brothel catering to the wealthy. Some of the sex workers in the films have successfully adapted to the new economic climate, and are portrayed as self-sufficient "business" women. For example, Mei Mei in *Xiao Wu* becomes a rich businessman's mistress and leaves Fenyang, while Anna in *The World* is able to earn enough money to realize her dream of visiting her sister in Ulaanbaatar. But, there are contrary representations as well. In some of the films, sex work appears as being the only way to survive. In one poignant scene in *Still Life*, sex workers appear to live in the ruins from which they ply their trade, and in *A Touch of Sin*, one sex worker states that it is the only occupation that allows her to support her three-year-old daughter. In these representations, like the male *mingong*, the sex workers are also dependent upon their bodies for survival, and appear to have no other choice.

In this way, the body is a vehicle for the migrant's advancement, but although this commodification has given it agency, it has also made it disposable. Although migration offers hope and personal progression, this hope slowly wanes in the films and the characters ultimately become disillusioned. These feelings are generated by labor conditions theorized today as "precarity." According to Paolo Virno, "Precarity refers to the relationship between temporary and flexible labour arrangements and an existence without predictability and security."[76] On one hand, this flexibility allows the migrants a certain level of agency that they did not have before Reform, as they are no longer tied to their work units but are free to find other career options. But, on the other hand, they have lost this previous social bedrock and are now rootless and at the whims of the market economy. As stated by Jia in an interview "People tend to think that moving will bring them greater happiness and prosperity, but then they usually find themselves trapped anew."[77]

Precarity has become a way of life for the indigent migrant workers. Regarding his motivation for his role, in an interview Han, who was born to a poor family in Fenyang in Shanxi and became a coal miner after graduating from middle school, stated: "I want to show the audiences what kind of lives poor people lead. The group of people who belongs to the lowest class of society must work hard every day and night in order to make a living."[78] In the later films, migration becomes a necessity, what Anita Chan in her analysis of migrants would call being "trapped in a 'culture of survival.'"[79] This is poignantly expressed in *A Touch of Sin*. Xiaohui, a young migrant who travels around working in various factories and later ends up working as an attendant in a brothel, receives a call from his mother asking him to send money. He has just checked his balance at the bank, and tells her that he is broke. The camera observes his one-sided conversation on his cell phone, but we never hear what his mother says, just his responses to her. He keeps repeating that he does not have the money, until he finally just holds the phone away from his ear and cries, as her muffled, demanding voice continues in the background. This scene is the last straw for this character. When first introduced, he was rather cavalier in his approach to migration and work, and would quickly drop one job to take up another and start and end relationships at will. But this insouciance withers during this scene, which is later followed by his suicide – his only way out from this entrapped culture of survival.

Simon During argues that the term precariat "connotes a much more widely felt mood and condition of unease and groundlessness, characteristic of modernity as such."[80] Such a feeling of groundlessness pervades the films, as the *mingong* are represented as in a permanent "rootless" state of never "belonging" to a place or having a sense of permanency; thus, not only has the *mingong* body been commodified, it has also been uprooted and turned increasingly transitory and ephemeral, and is emphasized in these films with scenes of eternal wandering, eternal migration, eternal movement, and eternal non-belonging. In the past, spatial mobility was limited. As Feuerwerker writes, the peasantry "remained geographically demarcated, accorded a clearly defined place by intellectuals in their discourses about the 'countryside.'"[81] The idea of a traditional "rooted" peasantry, therefore, had the effect of conceptually "tying" them to the places where they were born. In the films, however, the *mingong* have been uprooted.

Earlier, I referred to Jia's previous quote about rural-to-urban migrants who "escape" to the cities and "become liberated individuals."[82] This migration, however, is not a complete liberation. For example, Michael Berry argues that *Xiao Shan Going Home* is a *"longing* for home," one that connects to a deeper Chinese belief in the importance of home, asserting that the hometown has been "indelibly etched on the Chinese psyche," and was "a source of consolation."[83] Although they have left their rural homelands, they still do not have the legal right to remain in the urban centers and therefore are no longer "rooted" in any place. In *The Need for Roots*, Simone Weil writes about the 20th century European condition of uprootedness, caused not only from war but also from capitalism, referring to it as "the most dangerous malady to which human societies are exposed," and arguing that it has reduced the French proletariat "to a state of apathetic stupor."[84] Pun Ngai and Lu Huilin describe a sense of "spiritual disorientation" among the second generation of the peasant migrants, explaining:

> If transience was a dominant characteristic of the first generation of migrant workers, rupture characterizes the second generation, who now spend much more of their lives in urban areas. Transience suggests transitions, and so encourages hopes and dreams of transformation. Rupture, however, creates closure: there is no hope of either transforming oneself into an urban worker or of returning to the rural community to take up life as a peasant.[85]

This connects to Ben Anderson's assertion "what defines the affective quality of precarity is not only that the present is saturated with a sort of restlessness, but also that the future is made uncertain and becomes difficult or impossible to predict."[86] Jia's characters have been deracinated and his films capture and evoke this structure of feeling as concretized around the *mingong* figure, emphasizing their helplessness, powerlessness, and restlessness.

In addition to being structures of feeling that evoke the felt experience of the *mingong*, they are also psychogeographic reactions to this environmental condition. As written in Chapter 1, Guy Debord defines psychogeography as "the study of the precise laws and specific effects of the geographical environment, whether consciously organized or not, on the emotions and behavior of individuals."[87] The emotional attachment *to* place and the emotional alienation from place that migration brings is poignantly expressed in a scene in *Still Life* when Han Sanming hires a motorcycle taxi driver to take him to his estranged wife's last known address. He is driven to where her home once was, but it has now been completely submerged by the river due to the construction of the Three Gorges Dam. When Han complains, the driver responds that he has not deceived him, because that is where the address was and still "is," informing Han that his own home lies underneath the boat in the distance. The driver still remembers his personal, human geography of place even after the buildings and the physical landscape have disappeared. Similar to the workers who have been alienated from their previous environments – their factories – because they have been reduced to ruin, so too have the *mingong* been alienated from their ancestral homelands by their economic inability to remain in these places.[88]

The persistent images of boats and water in the films evoke the structures of feeling of precariousness and rootlessness as well as serve as metaphors for movement, travel, and motion. Such movement can have a purpose, or it can be simply drifting from place to place at the whims of the ocean's currents. As mentioned earlier, two of the dysphemisms for the migrants include *liudong* (流动, "flowing from place to place"), and *mangliu* (盲流, those who "blindly float"), emphasizing the fluidity of this group through the use of the word *liu* (流), which means "to flow," and "moving from place to place." Zygmunt Bauman writes of the increasing fluidity of modernity through deregulation, modernization, and flexible labor, and argues that modernity's "melting powers" have "melted" state and social institutions, and thus have not only changed the economy but also the human condition.[89] He writes of feelings of insecurity, which he calls "the mood of precariousness," and as "the combined experience of insecurity (of position, entitlements and livelihood), of uncertainty (as to their continuation and future stability) and of unsafety (of one's body, one's self and their extensions: possessions, neighbourhood, community)."[90] This "mood of precariousness" and the structure of feeling it produces is explored in the opening scene in *Still Life*, in which the title credits run on a black background while we hear a ship's whistle and the crash of waves. The Shanxi opera song "Lin Chong Flees into the Night" (林冲夜奔) begins, and the darkness starts to fade. The visuals that emerge are at first blurry, but then slowly focus to reveal a group of passengers on a boat, all of whom appear to be *mingong*. The camera moves among them and pans through the crowd, dipping in and out of focus, as it slowly observes the migrants' activities during the voyage. The atmosphere is jovial and hopeful; some smoke, play cards, or arm wrestle, while others talk, laugh, and check cell phones. The camera finally stops when it arrives at one of the film's main protagonists, a migrant worker played by Han Sanming, who is sitting at the boat's prow and is staring out at the Yangtze's shoreline as it moves past. Finally, the scene ends and the passengers disembark, carrying their possessions in cheap canvas and polyethylene bags, seemingly ready and hopeful to find work where they have landed. But the film also ends with a similar scene, and it is neither as joyful nor as hopeful as when it began; rather, the migrants appear to have exhausted their employment prospects, and have become economic refugees who must move on and find a new place to work. In this scene, Han asks a female migrant whom he has befriended where she is going, and she replies Guangdong, stating that she "has no choice," and needs to migrate in search of work. At the end of the film, we see Han and the other migrants walking through the ruins that they have been hired to create, carrying their worldly possessions in the same cheap polyethylene bags they arrived with. We hear the sound of sledgehammers and waves crashing, as well as the same opera song; thus, like Lin Chong, these migrants are also "fleeing" to their next destination.

I began this chapter by arguing that the peasants in the films were represented as elderly and soon to expire, while the depiction of the individual *mingong* shifted from an empathetic engagement and identification with the *mingong* to sympathy for and objectification of them. Then, I examined the *mingong* mass further, showing how they became a subaltern group, thus transitioning from subjects with agency to an objectified mass. I argued that this was an increasingly sympathetic view because, although it depicted the *mingong* as non-threatening and safe, it patronized them; thus, similar to sympathy, it positioned the viewer as superior to the humble and unthreatening *mingong*. To conclude, however, I want to add that even though the migrants have been turned into a wretched mass, they do not just remain as objects of the lens, but sometimes look back. This is not a wretched or pitiful look, or one that is threatening, and thus does not invoke either pity or fear; rather, its presence demands that we acknowledge this group and their continued existence. These direct gazes break the fourth wall, and are a form of agency, insofar as they block our patronizing sympathy by reflecting our gaze back, thus creating a feeling and an awareness of the vastly different power dynamics between what the class once was and now what it is.

This direct *mingong* gaze is first introduced in *The World*. The film begins with a motionless long take of Beijing World Park's Eiffel Tower as seen from a distance. A man walks into the frame from the left, carrying a bag on his back filled with plastic bottles and wearing a straw hat. He appears to be a *mingong* who is also a member of the new *lumpenproletariat*,[91] not only in a Marxist or Maoist theoretical sense as the unorganized and lowest level of society, but also literally, in that *"Lumpen"* means "rag," and the word *Lumpensammler* describes a person dependent upon scavenging to eek out survival,[92] as his bag of scrap indicates. In this long take, he turns towards the camera and stops, looking directly at it, thus breaking the fourth wall. Yingjin Zhang refers to this gaze as a "disruptive moment," in that the figure "represents the unspeakable poverty and misery glossed over by the sheer spectacle of globalization," as celebrated in the park.[93] Although the brim of his hat blocks his view and he is too far away from the camera for us to see his gaze, the look is still felt, and we are made aware of his presence, as he seemingly becomes aware of ours. After a moment of tensed time in which the viewer feels his silent gaze, he turns away from the camera and continues on his journey, walking to the right and out of the frame. This gaze introduces the film, and from this point onwards, the presence of this *mingong lumpenproletariat* figure lingers.

Earlier in my analysis of the moving portraits in *24 City*, I argued that the serious direct gaze confronted the viewers, while the friendly gaze "greeted" the audience and treated them like intimates, and, as gaze meets gaze, the viewers also acknowledged the presence of this figure. To examine this further, I would

Figure 2.11 *Mingong* in *24 City* (screenshot)

like to consider another gaze from *24 City* – generated by the moving portrait of a group of *mingong* – and analyze their direct gaze (Figure 2.11). Unlike the other moving portraits in the film that are mostly single, double, or family portraits of members of the worker class, this is a large group portrait composed of ten people who are *mingong*. In this moving portrait, these migrants are not recorded working or relaxing, but have been assembled to have their photograph taken. Some of the migrants look away from the camera, while others watch it warily, and seem uncomfortable. They wear regular clothing that lacks the authority or collective identity of a uniform, or the symbolic potency of the proletarian Mao suit. They hold rebar in their hands like walking sticks, not like weapons, and their poses are slouched and humble, not dynamic and threatening. Their faces are roughly in the horizontal center of the frame and are lower than the other moving portraits in the film, therefore positioning the viewer as if looking slightly downwards at them. If the angle was lower and we were looking up, their postures and the rebar that they are holding might evoke the heroic shots of the proletariat during the Maoist period, such as found in the inspirational "future perfect" gazes analyzed earlier, but this downwards angle combined with their humble posture evaporates any such dynamism.

The direct gaze, however, confronts the viewer by returning the viewer's gaze. Furthermore, although they are a wretched group, this gaze is neither shameful nor confrontational, but is rather a presence that remains and refuses to disappear. The subject looks back, and challenges the viewer, not aggressively or reproachfully, but simply by its mere presence, thus demanding the viewer to notice. In this light, we can consider how these peasants, who once composed half of the leading proletariat during the Maoist period, have now become *mingong*. No longer half of the leading proletariat, they have been excluded

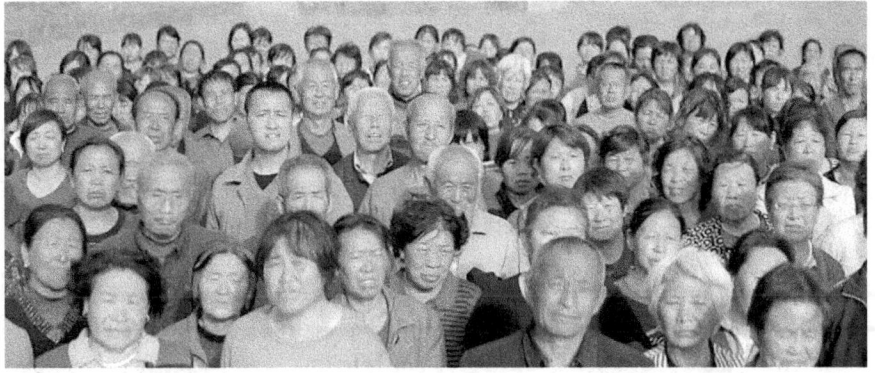

Figure 2.12   Final gaze in *A Touch of Sin* (screenshot)

from both society and the benefits of reform, yet still remain staring back, and we are required to acknowledge them.

A similar gaze is found in *A Touch of Sin*. In this final scene, the opera "The Faithful Courtesan" is being performed to an assembled outdoor crowd that appears to be composed of regular townspeople, and Xiaoyu, the main protagonist of the film's third narrative, who had earlier killed a man that had attempted to rape her, stops to watch. This tale is about a concubine named Su San who has been falsely incriminated for her master's murder by his wife, who later bribes officials to find Su San guilty so that she will be imprisoned. One of the performers sings "The magistrate changes his mind . . . Su San, a murderer! I am forced to confess . . ." When the magistrate replies, the camera cuts to a close-up of Xiaoyu, and he intones "Do you understand your crime?" (你可知罪?, which is subtitled in English "Do you understand your sin?") She looks down, as if in thought, and the scene quickly cuts to the crowd looking back at the viewer (Figure 2.12). This gaze ends the film – the gaze of the crowd looking back at the viewer, and the final line "Do you understand your sin?" hanging in the air.

This gaze in *A Touch of Sin* is similar to the crowd's gaze that ended *Xiao Wu*. In my earlier analysis of this gaze, I wrote that Jia referred to the crowd's gaze as a "bridge" with the audience, while others described it as severing him from society and objectifying him. I, however, argued that through the gaze and the POV shot, we the audience were positioned as a *mingong* and were receiving the curious and condemning stares. By returning our look, the direct *mingong* gaze puts us on the spot in more ways than simply putting us in the moment; rather, it also puts us "on the spot" in the sense that we are called to judgment and are prompted to respond. But, to whom is this question, "Do you understand your sin?," addressed? At the most basic level, it is asked of the actor who is playing Su San by the actor who is the magistrate. But Xiaoyu also reacts to it by looking down and frowning as if in distress, and we wonder if she herself escaped punishment after killing her rapist. Or the question could also be asked of the townspeople who refused to support Dahai, a character in the film's first story line who stood up to local government corruption in his village (and who will be analyzed in Chapter 3). But the question can also be asked of the audience – do you understand your sin? – with the gaze of the crowd staring back. When asked about this final line in an interview, Jia replied "It's about how we tolerate injustice, the gap between the rich and the poor. More than anything I think silence is a sin."[94] This "silence is a sin" suggests that the viewer is complicit in the injustice that we have witnessed during the film, in that we are forced to consider if we too have tolerated injustice and have not spoken up against it.

In this gaze, we are being "held" for our (possible) crimes, either as Su San on the stage (in a POV shot) or as a member of the audience who has been complacent and uncomplaining about the *mingong*'s wretched situation. But another interpretation connects with the message that is being declared. This rhetorical effect works in so far as the *mingong* direct gaze is addressing the audience as an audience, and therefore breaking the fourth wall – the "bridge" between the film's virtual people and the audience, briefly sharing the same moment and time. Bill Nichols writes about "forms of alliance" between the filmmaker, subjects, and the audience, which he semantically describes as "*I speak about them to you*," arguing "the third person pronoun implies a separation between speaker and subject. The I who speaks is not identical with those of whom it speaks."[95] The direct gaze initiates an awareness of this power dynamic, and it marks the transition from "*I* look at *them*" (the observational shot), to "*They* look back at *me*" (breaking the fourth wall). This is a shift from us observing the *mingong* to them looking back at us, and it is an affective moment in which the audience becomes keenly aware of the vastly different levels of power, and our positions, roles, and agencies. During this moment of tensed time, we receive their gazes at the same time as we hear this message, and we are put "on the spot" in a whole new way.

Chapter 3

The Soldier: From Degraded Reproduction to Avenging Hero

Introduction

This chapter analyzes the final figure of the Maoist triumvirate, the People's Liberation Army (PLA) soldier (兵). This figure is not a main figure in the films, but its presence is still symbolized, referenced, and felt. For example, in *Xiao Wu*, the presence of authority and the state is symbolized by the soldier's cognate, the figure of the police chief, who repeatedly tries to convince the film's eponymous protagonist to give up his life of petty crime, but who ends up later charging him with theft. In *Unknown Pleasures*, one of the main characters is instructed by his mother to leave and become a soldier, but a diagnosis of hepatitis prevents him both from enlisting and further separates him from society, because it is an illness that complicates his future intimate relationships. In *The World*, the soldier is alluded to in the form of security guards who wear military-style uniforms, but their authority has been weakened because they are represented as little more than errand-boys carrying water cooler bottles between venues, and one is even discovered to be a thief. In *Still Life*, the husband of one of the protagonists was a former soldier who left the military to work in a factory, and then became the business partner and lover of a corrupt entrepreneur who allegedly bankrupted the same factory. In *24 City*, one interviewee talks about a photograph of a young soldier, who supposedly died due to a poorly-assembled component from their factory, which had been shown to the workers as a warning, to remind them of the importance of production quality. In *I Wish I Knew*, soldiers are later revealed to actually be film extras in uniform who are performing on a movie set outside of Shanghai, and the inclusion of a movie clip from *The Shanghai Battle* (Wang Bing, 1959) represents the figure appearing as theatrical and fantastical. *A Touch of Sin* produces a heroic soldier-like character named Dahai who is fighting corruption in his village, while also juxtaposing this hero with sex workers that dress up as soldiers to entice their clients. Finally, a retired and elderly soldier who is the father of one of the film's main characters passes away while visiting a friend.

After discussing the soldier's socio-historical contexts and aesthetic representations, I outline how the figure is referenced in Jia's films as debased reproductions, a yearned-for memory, and a concretized legendary hero. I examine the positive Maoist structure of feelings of honor and bravery that have been associated around this figure, which emphasized the army's spirit of "serving the people" and the benevolent protection of the state, and contrast this with the feelings for this figure and its ersatz replica found in the films. First, I analyze the representations of the naïve or corrupt soldier-like figures consisting of the police officers, security guards, actors, and sex workers who dress up in PLA costumes in *Xiao Wu*, *The World*, *Still Life*, and *A Touch of Sin*. I argue that these are poor substitutes that have replaced the defender of the people and state, and are causing more harm than good, and outline how their representation and behavior contradicts the Maoist structures of feeling associated with the soldier. Then, I analyze the memory of the deceased air force pilot in *24 City*, and examine how it is an "absent presence," in that his "presence" is actually enhanced by its lack. I posit that this absence evokes the disappearance of the structures of feeling that the figure once induced, such as protection for the people, hope for social advancement for the poor, and the state's guardianship in everyday life. I argue that the mourning for the figure in this film is a synecdoche for the loss of this noble figure. Finally, I conclude by examining the reification of the soldier/martial-arts hero Dahai in *A Touch of Sin*, arguing that the concretization of this heroic and vengeful figure represents the yearning for this figure of salvation and a structure of feeling for the Maoist past. I analyze the *wuxia* (martial arts) cinematographic elements in this film, and argue that they emphasize the return of the legendary hero who, although forced to resort to violence, is a very human character battling corruption and evil to protect and avenge the downtrodden common people. In addition to this shift in genres, Dahai also signifies a change in Jia's cinematic aesthetics, and also an ideological shift from mourning the negative effects of the Reform era towards demanding redress. I conclude by examining how the yearning for this figure embodies a structure of feeling of nostalgia for the Maoist past and, most importantly, the noble structure of feelings associated with that era and their absence in the present day.

History of the Class

In China, soldiers had historically been conscripted "from the dregs of the population," and were often feared as criminals,[1] a concern that was reflected in the popular idiom "Good iron is not made into nails, a good man does not become a soldier" (好铁不打钉，好汉不当兵).[2] During the Communist Revolution, however, the PLA soldiers, unlike their antecedents, did not pillage the communities in which they were stationed, but worked with them to increase food production and develop local industry, and thus became benevolent figures to the common people.[3] For instance, during the Communist Revolution, Red Army troops were required to follow "The Main Rules of Discipline and Eight Points of Attention," which included rules that the soldiers be honest, pay for anything they have damaged, and not maltreat the people, but rather "help them whenever possible."[4]

During the Maoist era, the soldier defended and protected the people and the nation, and the profession offered social advancement, particularly for the rural poor. Recruitment into the military became a means of economic, social, and political advancement, and provided skills, training, and status that particularly benefited soldiers from rural and poor backgrounds.[5] The career provided training, and after being demobilized, men were often able to leverage their experience to obtain technical employment or even become cadres. Thus, demobilized veterans became "a privileged group," not just because of their training and status, but also because they contributed a range of "political, social, cultural and economic" assets to the communities to which they were demobilized.[6] Previous military leaders were appointed to local and central governments to such an extent that former military officers held approximately half of civilian central leadership posts and 60 to 70 per cent of provincial leadership positions.[7] The relationship between the soldiers and the common people was described as "Double Support" (双拥), since they shared a mutually-reciprocal relationship in which the people supported both the current PLA soldiers as well as helped those that were demobilized to integrate back into society, while the PLA "served the people" through youth training programs, environmental protection initiatives, providing medical assistance to impoverished areas and during disaster relief, and acting as domestic security.[8] Furthermore, after the Cultural Revolution, in which the PLA was used to suppress the Red Guards, they were lauded for bringing "domestic tranquility" to the nation, and their numbers were increased.[9] This role, representation, and relationship therefore constructed a structure of feeling around this figure, which evoked the ennobled Maoist feelings of public service, protection of the common people, and social harmony.

Representation

Propaganda was viewed as a crucial component of the PLA's activities.[10] In propaganda posters, members of the military, air force, and navy were represented as strong and powerful defenders. These images emphasized their defense capabilities against external forces, and they were commonly described as the group that "defends the nation's borders."[11] Therefore, this figure was not depicted as violent or aggressive, but staunch and protective, safeguarding the nation. Conversely, I discern four patterns of representation that refer to the soldier without representing them directly in Jia's films. First, various weaker or even corrupt solider-like figures appear, as a debased representation of the soldier in the present. Second, in *24 City*, the absence of the soldier is made present and palpable in the film as a commemorative evocation of a past Maoist era structure of feeling. Third, in *Mountains May Depart*, the metaphorical soldier contracts cancer and the elderly soldier dies. And finally, in *A Touch of Sin*, a soldier-like character reappears as a figure of righteous vengeance, marking a new turn in Jia's filmmaking.

To focus on the debased figures that simulate or invoke the soldier first, these appear in different forms in a number of films. *Xiao Wu* features police officers engaged in a local government campaign to fight crime, and during the film, information about the campaign is broadcast on loudspeakers throughout the city. Their authoritative and protective roles are later questioned, however, when they are revealed to be completely naïve about the endemic corruption surrounding them. To illustrate this, in the beginning of the film, Xiao Wu meets with his gang of child pickpockets in a restaurant, and they divide the day's spoils. Later, they walk down the street while an announcement about the police crackdown on crime and changes to the penal system is being broadcast on the public loudspeakers. A television news reporter suddenly stops a member of Xiao Wu's gang and asks him if he knows what is going on, but he looks at her blankly, perhaps fearing that he will be found out. His silence causes her to leave, and she later goes to the information table about the crackdown that the police officers have assembled. One of the officers informs her that they have initiated this program to raise awareness among the public about recent changes in the criminal and penal codes, which probably refers to the extensive changes to the criminal code that the state made in 1997. These included changes to the *laogai* (劳改, short for 劳动改造), meaning reform through labor, otherwise known as prison labor camps, and *laojiao* (劳教, short for 劳动教养), meaning re-education through labor, including political education, which were claimed to "not only improve the Chinese criminal justice system, but also help China bring the country under [the] Rule of Law."[12] Therefore, this is not only a campaign about criminality, but also more importantly a media campaign to emphasize the police officers' honesty, reliability, and effectiveness.

In this film, the police officers serve as a synecdoche for the soldier figure. This substitution appears to be part of a larger shift in Chinese visual culture that began in the 1980s. Stefan Landsberger writes that, during this decade, images of the police began to mimic the soldiers' earlier "martial posturing" in order to invoke the symbolic authority of the Maoist trinity.[13] He argues this was "an attempt to put the people's minds at rest by showing that the government was taking steps against the increase in criminal activities."[14] In the film, however, this rhetoric is undermined when the police chief Hao Youliang meets Xiao Wu. He asks him if he has heard the public announcements, and quickly tells him "Listen, you be a good boy now. All your buddies from the old days are good boys now." Hao is a stern, fatherly figure who holds a position of authority in the film. Yet, although his attempts to persuade *Xiao Wu* away from his life of crime are honorable, he is ultimately clueless about the greater thievery and corruption that is happening under his nose. For example, it is later revealed that the "good boys" he is referring to include Xiao Wu's ex-best friend, Xiao Yong, whose success is dependent upon cigarette smuggling and prostitution. Finally, at the end of the film, Xiao Wu is arrested after a botched pickpocketing attempt, and is taken into custody. Thus, while the police are busy cracking down on the minor thieves, the more established and powerful criminals like Xiao Yong remain unscathed.

As explained above, the soldier is briefly advanced as a possible career for Bin Bin, one of the protagonists in *Unknown Pleasures*, but this career is never realized in the film. His mother urges him to become a *Beijing* soldier, obviously a prestigious post of authority to her, not only as one of the lauded Maoist figures, but one stationed in the nation's capital. She convinces him to enlist, and he is filmed going through his medical checkup in preparation for joining up. Becoming a soldier will not only provide employment for this unemployed youth, but it will also offer a way out of Datong, which is represented as in decline. Furthermore, it also might even allow him to continue his relationship with his girlfriend, who has been admitted to a university in Beijing. His dreams are dashed, however, when his results come back and he learns that he will never be accepted in the military due to the discovery that he has Hepatitis B. Therefore, the soldier becomes a figure of unrealized promise.

Soldiers briefly materialize in *I Wish I Knew*, but they are quickly revealed to be actors on a movie set called the Chedun Film Base, which is a recreation of the historic Nanjing Road in Shanghai. The camera follows the troupe from behind as they march, apparently recreating the PLA's liberation of Shanghai in

1949, and is quickly followed by a clip from Wang Bing's propaganda film *Shanghai Battle* (1959) reenacting this event. The civilian crowd in this clip shouts "Long Live Chairman Mao!" and welcomes the Communist soldiers to the city, while a military leader narrates "The Liberation of Shanghai marks the thorough destruction of imperialist forces in China, as well as the complete independence and liberation of the Chinese people!" In this light, the soldier is a figure of the heroic past, but not of the present, and its environment is virtual, not concrete. Furthermore, the melodrama of the scene and its theatrical qualities, such as the soldier's makeup that alludes to that worn by opera performers and his dramatic demeanor, make the event feel overacted and fabricated. In this way, the figure is "performed," but never realized, and remains a pale shadow of its former self and a figure of theater and fantasy.

In *The World*, security guards in the film's eponymous amusement park are dressed in army-inspired uniforms, and wear red armbands similar to those worn by policemen and soldiers, and on which is written "on duty" (值勤). However, they lack the power and authority of the soldiers they imitate, and just patrol the grounds and carry water cooler bottles for the park's other employees. Furthermore, one of the security guards is later revealed to be corrupt. In one scene, the camera follows him on his patrol, watching him as he goes from dressing room to dressing room and from purse to purse, pilfering the entertainers' money, thus revealing him to be a thief. He is later charged with theft, and is forced to leave the park – not in his uniform, but in the common clothes he arrived in. He is just another *mingong* moving on to his next job.

In *Still Life*, a demobilized ex-soldier appears in the figure of Guo Bin, who is the husband of Shen Hong, one of the film's protagonists. She has not seen him in years, and has traveled to the Three Gorges area to find him and serve him with divorce papers. As the film progresses, it is revealed that after he was discharged from the army, he went to work at a factory in the area. During her search, she visits this factory, and learns that it has gone bankrupt and is in the process of being scrapped for salvage. In Chapter 1, I wrote about Shen Hong's visit to the factory and how one of the few remaining employees helps her find his work locker, which is located in a long-abandoned workshop, but she is unable to open it because the lock has rusted. Shen, however, picks up a discarded tool and smashes it open, revealing the tea, gloves, and ID cards that he has left behind. The presence of the rusted lock is very significant. In the previous scene, we have just learnt of his military background, and this linkage of Guo's former status as a soldier to the rusted lock evokes the much-lauded soldier-hero named Lei Feng, who was valorized in state propaganda as a "rustless screw." Lei Feng was an apocryphal peasant-turned PLA soldier who became a famous model proletarian for his acts of altruism and patriotism, and these Maoist structures of feeling still cling to this figure. In his diary, which was published after his accidental death in 1963, he wrote "I will be a screw that never rusts and will glitter anywhere I am placed."[15] Not only was Lei Feng used as a model during the Cultural Revolution, he was also advanced as a model in the early years of Reform, after Tiananmen in 1989,[16] and is currently invoked as a figure advocating for "social harmony."[17] But, unlike Lei Feng's "rustless screw" that is self-*less*, Guo Bin is particularly self-*ish*. Not only did he abandon his post at the state-owned factory, he also abandoned his wife. Furthermore, he is currently working for the entrepreneur who has allegedly conspired to bankrupt the factory for her personal financial gain. He is therefore complicit in her corruption, and he is even rumored to be having an adulterous affair with her.

A female version of the corrupted soldier figure is also found in *A Touch of Sin*. The film's final segment is partially set in a brothel in which the female sex workers dress up in seductive costumes in order to entice clients. In these varying roles, they become "sexy" anime characters, "sexy" Peking opera actors (incongruously dressed in bathing suits with opera makeup and headdresses), and then finally "sexy" nurses and "sexy" blue-uniformed train attendants, who entertain their clients in a mock train carriage for Party cadres. In one scene, they also appear as "sexy" soldiers. A group of about 30 to 40 sex workers parade into a brothel's lounge where wealthy punters await them, accompanied by a recording of patriotic brass band music. The camera pans around and through them as they march, and finally stops to record them saluting their future clients. They wear identical PLA and Red Guard-inspired costumes, which are army-green mini-dresses with a shoulder-cape that is designed to look like a military dress shirt, but cut in a way that exposes their cleavage and appears to be constructed for quick removal (Figure 3.1). They also wear caps with a single red star and thigh-high leather boots. These costumes are not based on the current uniform worn by the PLA (which changed in 1988 to caps with visors and western-style jackets with neckties),[18] but are "retro" costumes from the Maoist period that have been redesigned and eroticized. Thus, they are "sexy" soldiers whose "uniforms" are designed to enhance their legs and breasts. Furthermore, their shoulder sleeve insignia is not a declaration of rank, but is later revealed to be their personal work numbers, so that punters can more easily select them afterwards for their sexual services. After their performance, they are filmed chatting amongst themselves and checking their cell phones as the clients walk around to inspect them further. In this representation, the once powerful soldier figures have been degraded into being a costume for sexual titillation.

The Soldier 91

Figure 3.1 Sex workers dressed as PLA soldiers in *A Touch of Sin* (screenshot)

In summary, similar to the representations of the worker and peasant figures in Jia's films, the soldier figure is no longer what it once was. The group has disappeared during the Reform era, and now exists only as a corrupt facsimile. In this way, these lauded Maoist figures have been permanently changed: the workers are vanishing, and are a group to be commemorated and mourned; the peasants are elderly and their children have turned into a new class of wandering rootless *mingong* who lead a precarious existence; and the soldiers have vanished and been replaced by naïve, corrupt, harmful, or degraded simulations.

However, compared to the depiction of the worker class in decline and the peasants in a precarious and pitiful state, the corrupted depiction of the soldier is not wretched but obscene. This group was once the paragon of the Maoist class figures, and held pseudo-religious importance; therefore, their corruption into thieves and sex workers is almost sacrilegious, and is debasing the noble structures of feeling that are formed around this group. This corruption may echo the figure's post-Tiananmen situation, a division that separated the people from the PLA for the first time since their "bonding" during Chinese civil war, because they were the ones who, following government orders, quelled the demonstration and were responsible for killing an unknown number of protesters, therefore badly damaging their previous sterling representation.[19] Thus, these corrupted soldier reproductions are fundamentally flawed, evacuating the past Maoist values, morals, and emotions attached to this figure.

As analyzed previously in Chapter 1, *24 City* is based on the memories surrounding Factory 420, a military airplane-manufacturing facility in the process of being destroyed and redeveloped into a luxury residential, shopping, and entertainment complex. Factory 420 is representative of a regular occurrence during the Reform era, in which the PLA became responsible for funding its own development, by converting its industries for civilian use;[20] hence, the factory in *24 City* is being sold to fund the PLA's aeronautic development and production at another location. In this film, no substitute figure for the soldier appears. Rather, a second pattern emerges in this film where the very absence of the soldier is itself represented to constitute what Peggy Phelan describes as a "continuing 'presence,' despite the absence."[21]

To explore this context further, during the Four Modernizations campaign, which was adopted at the Third Plenum of the CCP's Eleventh Central Committee in December 1978, the Party introduced economic reforms while, at the same time, cutting funds to the PLA.[22] The military's budget cuts in the mid-1980s therefore went hand-in-hand with economic growth, because the money saved from cuts was instead used for the nation's "modernization drive."[23] Furthermore, shrinking the soldier population through demobilization also helped to provide the necessary increase in labor power to develop the nation.[24] But, at the same time that the state cut the military budget, it also placed the onus on the PLA to finance its own development and modernization via commercial activities, agriculture, and light industry,[25] thus resulting in a situation that Landsberger describes as "almost plunging the PLA from its position of pre-eminence to one of supplicant."[26] However, this was not met with meek acceptance. There were protests from demobilized soldiers who had realized that they not only lost their former entitlements and status, but had also lost the benefits that they had been promised.[27]

The current situation contrasts with the Maoist era, when the soldier was a lauded figure who represented the protector of the state and symbolized the "Great Iron Wall defending the mother country and the revolution."[28] During this time, military careers often led to political careers, as witnessed by the number of political leaders with a military background, such as Mao Zedong, Deng Xiaoping, and Lin Biao. This situation reflected positively on the PLA and therefore "contributed to the formation of a mystique of the army as a disciplined, politically conscious force that was closely engaged with the task of rebuilding the nation."[29] After Reform, however, the soldier figure began to disappear from visual propaganda, because joining the army became less of a career opportunity and was instead replaced by employment in private enterprise.[30] Furthermore,

Figure 3.2 Factory 420's stage in *24 City* (screenshot)

because PLA recruiters also started to favor university graduates, it has gradually ceased being a vehicle for advancement for the rural unskilled.[31]

This disappearance from the public stage resonates with the absence of the soldier figure throughout Jia's films. In the case of *24 City*, although Factory 420 was an airplane manufacturing facility for the Chinese military, the soldier figure is not actually physically represented but only alluded to in the film. Perversely, this absence makes the figure conceptually very present. In one of the film's first interviews, the former Head of Security explains that the factory and the workers were originally moved from Shenyang in northeast China's Liaoning province to Chengdu in southwest China's Sichuan province as part of the state's "Third Line" strategy of moving militarily sensitive industry away from the coast and the industrial northeast where it could be more easily attacked. The interview is held in an auditorium that has a stage with a backdrop that features an image of the Great Wall, fighter jets, tanks, missiles, and mountains (Figure 3.2). This alludes not only to the military's strength and its weaponry, but also to its symbolic role as the aforementioned "Great Iron Wall," which physically and metaphorically protected the nation. These images are robust and powerful; for instance, much of the real Great Wall is in ruin, but this section portrayed has been renovated. Furthermore, it continues into the distance, as if inexhaustible, as are the row of tanks. Missiles thrust upwards from the left, and fighter jets launch from the right. This dramatic backdrop features a national symbol surrounded by virile weaponry, but the soldiers are absent. Instead, a long take that records two men strangely playing badminton on the stage in front of this backdrop subverts this patriotic stage.

During the interview with Gu Minhua (performed by Joan Chen), she recalls a photograph of a young man posted on her workshop's notice board. As there was no accompanying text, the workers speculated amongst themselves as to his identity, some suggesting that he was a Communist Youth League representative. After someone said that Gu and the mystery man would make an attractive couple, Gu started to fall in love with him, and began to hope that he would visit the factory. However, this dream was shattered when the factory's Party Secretary told them it was that of a young pilot whose plane had crashed due to a defective part that the factory had made. He had placed the photo on the noticeboard as a warning to the workers and to stress the point that the Party had invested 200,000 Yuan and eight years in training the pilot. The Party Secretary declared "amongst all of you, there's someone who was responsible for this tragedy," and instructed them to reflect (反省) on their mistakes, a word used to mean "to engage in introspection, self-examination or soul-searching."[32] When she narrates this point about being told to reflect, the segment fades to black, thus emphasizing the loss of this heroic figure who sacrificed his life, and also creating a period of tensed time in which the viewer, like Gu, can reflect on what has just been said. Additionally, this pause also emphasizes that he is a dead figure who remains only in memory and its retelling, as he is never seen physically or even represented through the photograph that she discusses during her

Figure 3.3 Zhao Gang and his father in *24 City* (screenshot)

interview. Thus, the memory of the photograph and the pilot parallels that of the soldier figure, in that neither appears in the film and both are spoken of only in memory, and felt through the figure's past structure of feeling.

The photograph was not only a warning, but also became a memorial to the dead pilot, resonating with the commemorative elements of the film that I examined previously in Chapter 1. Additionally, several scenes that follow depict the factory's monuments of military airplanes and helicopters, which serve as memorials to the past industry of this military factory, as well as the history of the Chinese air force. In one of the moving portraits, Zhao Gang and his father pose in front of a helicopter as if having their snapshot taken (Figure 3.3). They are smiling into the lens, and the photograph is composed so that they share the frame equally with the helicopter, as both are important. This "photograph" not only memorializes this moment of Zhao Gang with his father, but also the site. It is unknown if these monuments will remain after the factory has been redeveloped, and so the photograph commemorates the space and the military monuments before they, like the pilot, disappear.

In Chapter 1, I referenced Pierre Nora's concept of "sites of memory," which are created when the environments that once existed have been destroyed.[33] They are created out of a fear of being forgotten and, in this way, the film not only captures the memories of these workers before they disappear into oblivion, but also the factory and its monuments, producing them as a "site of memory" to the Maoist past and its noble figures. Furthermore, this desire to remember as well as the memory of the air force pilot in this film is what Peggy Phelan describes as a "presence" that is emphasized by its very absence, a term that she uses in her analysis of Sophie Calle's installation titled "Last Seen" at the Isabella Stewart Gardner Museum in 1991. For this installation, Calle interviewed people about their memories of paintings that were stolen from the museum during an infamous robbery in 1990, and then placed the transcriptions of these interviews besides photographs of the missing works. Phelan argues that this installation "suggests that the descriptions and memories of the paintings constitute their continuing 'presence,' despite the absence of the paintings themselves."[34] In this way, similar to the stolen paintings, the pilot is an "absent presence" in the film, in that he exists only in memory. Much as how Calle's installation invoked the "presence" of the stolen art, so too does the memory of the pilot narrated during Gu's interview invoke his "presence" in the film, at the same time as it emphasizes his disappearance and mourns his loss. As Phelan later argues about the transcripts of the memories of the paintings, "[they] remind us how loss acquires meaning and generates recovery – not only of and for the object, but for the one who remembers . . . it rehearses and repeats the disappearance of the subject who longs always to be remembered."[35]

To probe the concept of "how loss acquires meaning" further, the lost pilot evokes many of the past heroic Maoist structures of feeling. These include dedication to the Party, because he risked his life to save the plane that was so important to the state; a willingness to sacrifice himself for the greater good of the nation; and a sworn oath to protect the people. In her examination of Czech theatre, Lisa Peschel writes about the use of "residual" structures of feeling from the past, explaining: "By performing plays that included residual elements from a period when communism had been a hopeful and idealistic project, artists created an alternative to the stagnation of the present and articulated the emergence of an alternative structure of feeling."[36] These past structures of feeling are a reminder of what has been lost; as she argues, "By staging residual elements of that earlier social formation, members of the survivors' generation reached back toward an unrealized promise from their past and brought it into their lived experience of the present."[37] The narrative about the pilot evokes the residual Maoist structure of feeling, and how these noble feelings have been lost – another "unrealized promise from the past." Thus, the film not only commemorates the factory, but also mourns the loss of these figures and the structures of feeling that they evoked.

In this way, the memory of the pilot and the structure of feelings that formed around this figure haunts Gu's interview, a haunting that makes its absent presence felt. This haunted presence connects with Chris Berry and Mary Farquhar's notion of "haunted time," in which "the present is not haunted by the past, but by the better future the characters have been cheated out of."[38] Similar to nostalgia, both concepts of "haunted time" and "absent presence" emphasize that something is wrong, and that the people have been cheated out of the projected utopian future. Thus, what is being mourned is a potential future that never came to pass. Furthermore, Phelan also describes the Catholic Mass as a ritual that functions in order "to learn not the meaning but the value of what cannot be reproduced or seen (again)."[39] Just as the Mass mourns and remembers a loss that can never be rectified, so too does the memory of the soldier mourn and remember the loss of this figure and invokes what it once represented, thus making it very present in the film. The vacuum created by its disappearance therefore emphasizes that these noble figures have instead vanished and the masses have been left to defend and fend for themselves.

In *Mountains May Depart*, this loss is alluded to, and also seen. One of the main figures, nicknamed Liangzi, has the full name of Liang Jianjun (梁建军) – Liang is his surname but Jianjun means "build up the PLA." He becomes a *mingong* mine laborer, and later is shown as gravely ill after contracting cancer, presumably as a result of his work in mining. Also in the film, one of the protagonist's aged father takes a train to visit his old army buddy (战友), who is celebrating his birthday. This retired, elderly soldier never makes it to the party, however; instead, he dies in the small rural train station, apparently while taking a nap.

Finally, in *A Touch of Sin*, the yearning for this lost figure is concretized in Dahai, a miner who is represented as the incarnation of a heroic fantasy warrior figure, and his storyline records his struggle against corrupt officials and the owner of the town's mine. At first, Dahai tries to fight against the mine's owner, Boss Jiao, by planning a trip to Beijing to file a petition against him and the village government. He attempts to enlist his fellow villagers' support, but their fear of Boss Jiao leaves Dahai to confront him by himself, which results in Dahai being beaten by Boss Jiao's henchmen. Finally, Dahai retrieves his gun and kills the henchmen, corrupt officials, and finally Boss Jiao, thus purging the village of corruption through mass murder.

Although Dahai is a miner, he invokes both the figure of the legendary warrior as well as that of the heroic Maoist soldier in the film. For example, he wears a PLA jacket, and is told by a character in the film in reference to his righteous battle against corruption, "It's a shame you were not born, for example, before the war. Surely you would have made the rank of General." Throughout his story line, he also strikes heroic poses similar to those of the soldier figure as found

Figure 3.4 "Charge the Enemy to the Last Breath" (生命不息，冲锋不止). Fine Arts Section of the Chinese Revolutionary Army Museum (中国人民革命军事博物馆美术组). Shanghai: Renmin Meishu Chubanshe, 1970. *ChinesePosters.Net*. Accessed February 20, 2014. Available: http://chineseposters.net/posters/e13-564.php

Figure 3.5 Dahai in *A Touch of Sin* (screenshot)

in propaganda posters, with the same stern gaze, extended rifle, and look of authority, determination, and intensity (see Figures 3.4 and 3.5).

Dahai's representation as a soldier is also associated with the *kunqu* opera performance "Lin Chong Flees in the Night" that appears throughout the film. This performance is from the historical drama "Forced up Mount Liang" that was based on the Ming dynasty classical novel *Water Margin*. In this tale, the protagonist Lin Chong is being chased by his enemies because he has been unjustly framed for attempted assassination, and is trying to escape to Mt. Liang in order to join the assembled rebels. During his flight, he expresses concern for his family and recollects his past role as a military commander, thus transitioning from an ex-commander of a large army to becoming a noble outlaw hero who is described as "a sad and frightened martial man who remains loyal to his emperor, filial towards his old mother, and devoted to his young wife."[40] "Lin Chong Flees in the Night" not only has metaphorical meaning in the film in that both narratives are about fighting against oppression, but it also has ideological and political significance, because it was invoked twice by Mao Zedong, who was a fan of *Water Margin*.[41] For instance, after viewing it as a drama in 1944, Mao praised it "for 'restoring history's true face',," and for "making positive characters not out of 'lords and ladies' . . . but of rebels and the masses."[42] Thirteen years later in his "Speech at Conference of Members and Cadres of Provincial-Level Organizations of CPC in Shandong" on 18 March 1957, Mao again invoked the play during his lecture about the need to rectify internal problems and government corruption in order "to resolve contradictions between the Party and the people."[43] He was specifically concerned about the issues of corruption, the decline in class struggle, and "the decrease in the spirit of serving the people wholeheartedly."[44] During his criticism of the increasing selfishness of comrades, who he claimed "fight over fame, over status, [and] compare salaries, clothes, luxuries," he referred to a line in the opera which states: "A man's tears are not lightly shed; but only because he had not yet come to the moment of heart breaking."[45] He emphasizes that this "heart breaking point" should be "the moment when the survival of the working class and the peasant class is threatened," and not for personal desires.[46] Thus, the play that once was valorized for representing the people as rising up against feudal oppression was again invoked in order to inspire the people to fight against corruption and self-interest in the CCP's cadre class. The play's use in the film can therefore be seen as echoing the need for this rectification in the corrupt present.

The figure of Lin Chong echoes the depiction of Dahai, as both are middle-aged, noble, and vengeful heroes. Lin Chong is a typical example of "the mature and heroic man," and is a popular model character that represents "*wu* heroism" (the martial hero), "determination to revenge," and "the resilient and feeling man," who appears in "all kinds of performing arts, ranging from traditional *kunqu* to experimental theater to populist movies and TV serials."[47] Similar to Lei Feng, Lin Chong has also concretized various noble structures of feeling, and thus Dahai is the film's materialization of this heroic character. Like Lin Chong, he too is a mature, moral, and avenging hero who, although persecuted, remains loyal to the state and the people while also fighting against corruption. But his loyalty is to the Maoist state and its socialist values, not the current state's "capitalism with Chinese characteristics." Similar to Lin Chong, by choosing to attack Boss Jiao and his gang, Dahai also becomes an outlaw hero. Furthermore, like Mao's valorization of the play because it emphasized the need for class struggle in order to ensure the survival of the common people, Dahai also draws attention to the importance of ensuring that leaders do not become corrupt and abuse the masses. For example, in one scene in the film he argues that, because the village mine was once state property before the village chief illegally sold it, the luxury vehicle that Boss Jiao bought using the mine's profits belongs to the village and is actually collective property. Finally, this struggle against corruption is also symbolically expressed, as he wraps his shotgun in a blanket decorated with an image of a tiger, before setting out on his killing spree. The tiger is a metaphor for senior officials,[48] and "hunting tigers" is a euphemism for eradicating corruption and exposing corrupt officials.[49] However, although Dahai is a heroic figure, he is not a super-hero, but remains very human. This is made evident when he is filmed being beaten unconscious by Boss Jiao's thugs, crying over his lost love, and administering his insulin injection for his diabetes, all of which constructs him as a believable and "normal" person who has been forced to take up arms against his oppressors – a quotidian man-turned-hero.

Cinematic Tropes: *Wuxia* and the Close-up

A Touch of Sin, although based on real-life events, is a marked departure from Jia's previous "art house" aesthetics, but is also derived from a different genre – the action-adventure, specifically the popular Chinese genre known as *wuxia*. The word *wuxia* (武俠) combines "marital arts" (武) and "chivalry/knight" (俠), and the heroic figure associated with it is sometimes referred to as a "knight errant," who is in search of adventure, and is associated with the qualities of "altruism, justice, individual freedom, personal loyalty, courage, truthfulness and mutual faith, honor and fame, and generosity and contempt for wealth."[50] Although *A Touch of Sin* does not include martial arts scenes and Dahai is not literally a wandering knight, he is very much a "knight-errant" figure struggling against evil. In an interview in 2013, Jia referred to the film's four main characters as *"wuxia* warriors," explaining:

> When I was in university, I was writing about how all the *wuxia* films I had seen were indeed political allegories. They portray individuals suffering the pressures and injustices of society, and that brings about a tragic destiny where they have to resort to violence. I see this in direct connection to the state of things now in contemporary China, the social injustices felt by ordinary people who have no means of expressing their state, who must resort to violence to treat violence.[51]

This statement contrasts with his earlier views. For instance, in 2006, Jia stated that his films "reveal the impact of the state's indoctrination through the individual's *fan-kang* (resistance) instead of *fan-pan* (rebellion). [The individual] challenges but does not overthrow power."[52] But this film is specifically about "rebellion"; during another interview, he explained that he felt that society had undergone an "ideological shift" in which "money and violence were becoming interchangeable."[53] Finally, as Jia summarized in another interview about *A Touch of Sin*, "It is true this film is extremely violent compared to my old works, but in my old films the characters also lived under certain kinds of pressures but they . . . tolerated the pressure."[54] In this way, the film marks both an ideological and an aesthetic shift into the action adventure *wuxia* genre and away from feelings of empathy and sympathy towards the demand for redress.

In addition to Dahai's representation as a *wuxia* hero, the camera plays close attention to his acts of violence – the redress. This attention includes both the effects that the violence has on his victims as well as its effects on him. It is achieved through the use of the close-up, which first focuses on Dahai's face and records his initial struggles to kill, then the blood he spills, and finally his reaction to his own violence. In these revenge scenes, the camera often uses medium close-ups to record Dahai confronting his soon-to-be victims, with the camera gliding back and forth between them as they interact before he kills them. For instance, the first murder he commits is of Liu, who is Boss Jiao's accountant. Dahai goes to Liu's house and sits down at the table where Liu is eating his lunch. In one long take, the camera focuses on Dahai, then pans right to Liu, and slowly pans left back to Dahai as they quarrel over Dahai's demand that Liu sign a document confessing his crimes. Liu is not remorseful for what he has done, and when he refuses, Dahai reveals his rifle and points it at him. The camera travels rightwards down the length of the rifle to record Liu's frightened expression before sliding back to Dahai who repeatedly commands him to sign the confession. At this point, Dahai's facial expressions appear very conflicted; he appears stunned, and blinks repeatedly, looking down, seemingly doubting what he is doing. The sound of a siren is heard in the background, and it appears that the police may be on their way to arrest Dahai. He begins to put down his rifle, and Liu calls him a coward as the camera focuses on Dahai's downcast face. Suddenly, Dahai raises it and pulls the trigger, and the take abruptly cuts to record Liu being shot in the head and the blood and brain matter splattering against the window and wall. The camera then cuts again to record Dahai's stunned expression, seemingly surprised by his own actions (Figure 3.6). Liu's wife enters the room and screams, and Dahai quickly stands up and shoots her. The scene then cuts to her crashing through the window, due to the force of the blast, and landing on the pavement outside. The camera records the blood gushing from her wounds, and then cuts again to a long take close-up of Dahai breathing heavily and his face splattered with blood, capturing his shocked reaction to what he has done (Figure 3.7).

Figure 3.6 Close-ups of Dahai's first murder sequence of Liu – from struggle, to action, to effect, and to his stunned realization of what he has done in *A Touch of Sin* (screenshot)

Figure 3.7 Dahai's stunned expression after his second murder in *A Touch of Sin* (screenshot)

To examine the cinematography further, Dahai's first murder focuses on his internal struggle over whether or not to kill the unrepentant Liu, while his second murder is caused by his startled response to Liu's wife's scream. During his argument with Liu, he appears very conflicted over what he should do, as evidenced by the close-ups focusing on his stunned expression and repeated blinking as he reacts to Liu's refusal to sign the confession. As Liu and Dahai never appear together in the same frame during this altercation, close-ups are used to isolate each figure, thus emphasizing their reactions to one another during their debate by stressing what is said by one character and how the other reacts. Furthermore, it is all recorded in one long take; it is not segmented by cuts to close-ups of each characters' face, but rather slides between them as they argue, thus recording an unabridged block of time to capture the scene, which only ends when he abruptly shoots Liu.

Similar to the concept of "tensed time" that I discussed in the previous chapters, this block of "real" time makes us keenly aware as to the event unfolding and how the drama is quickly escalating. This is a time not of anticipation, but of tension, in that we feel something will happen but do not know what – will the police arrest Dahai? Will he flee? Will he kill Liu? Furthermore, unlike so many of Jia's earlier films, the event is not unfolding at a distance. Rather, with these close-ups, we see how the heroic Dahai is struggling with his threat to kill Liu, and also witness how Liu's initial fear quickly turns to disgust. Finally, after both of the murders, the camera focuses on Dahai's shocked reaction to what he has just done, again using a duration of tensed time that stresses his initial personal dismay over his actions. This emphasizes that these murders were not performed for amusement or because he was a psychotic serial killer (unlike another character in the film), but because of revenge (in the first instance) and surprise (in the second).

After his first and second murders, the film then cuts to him in what appears to be a local government building, and the camera follows him with a medium close-up as he moves through the empty corridors looking for his next victims. He finds one of Boss Jiao's henchmen, and after a brief argument, Dahai shoots

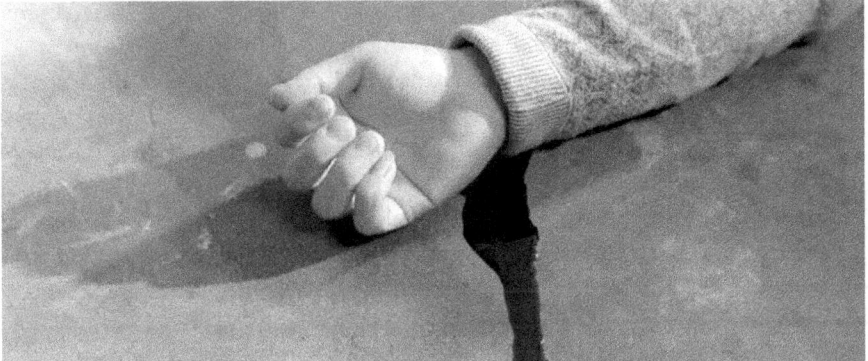

Figure 3.8 Close-up of the blood in *A Touch of Sin* (screenshot)

him. This murder is recorded in a rapid series of close-ups and cuts. First, there is a close-up of Dahai pointing his gun at the henchman, which then cuts to a close-up of him being shot in the chest, which rapidly cuts to a close-up of the white wall behind him being sprayed with blood, and then cuts again to the henchman's corpse falling over from the strength of the blast. This rapid-fire action is contrasted with a subsequent long-take close-up that examines the corpse, first focusing on the blood streaming from the wounds, and then following it as it pools on the floor (Figure 3.8). This is death up close, which has not been seen in Jia's other films. Previously, when death has occurred, it has remained hidden, such as the pile of rubble and later the blanket that covers Brother Mark's corpse in *Still Life*. Or, in other cases, the deaths have been nonviolent, such as the monoxide poisoning that supposedly killed Tao and Taisheng in *The World*, which left their corpses looking as if they were sleeping. But in four of Dahai's murders, the camera records bullets ripping through heads and bodies, and captures the resulting blood and gore, therefore emphasizing his violence and its effects.

Furthermore, the close-ups of the bodily damage and Dahai's reaction shots seem to pause time and the narrative, injecting durations of tensed time, in which we become keenly aware of what has transpired and its effects on Dahai and his victims, particularly when it is juxtaposed by fast-action violence. In this way, it creates a space for awareness and reflection, an element that is often lacking in "action films." For instance, Stephen Prince argues that violence in film is often presented as a spectacle, and is seldom "treated in a serious and provocative way that invites reflection and contemplation."[55] The close-ups of the blood and bullet holes and Dahai's reaction shot invite this reflection, however, while also emphasizing that this is not senseless violence, but virtuous revenge; in this segment of tensed time, we know the reason, we see Dahai's action, and we witness the effects of this via the corpses and Dahai's reactions to what he has done.

As the film progresses, the killings become increasingly easy for Dahai. In his fourth murder, he kills the Village Chief who had conspired with Boss Jiao. In this vengeance scene, the camera also pans back and forth between them as the village chief tries to negotiate with Dahai, before a close-up records him getting shot in the chest. In this instance, however, there is no reaction shot of Dahai's face. Rather, after shooting him, the scene then cuts to a long shot long take of Dahai holding the rifle and his victim lying prone on the ground, recording his triumph. Likewise, in the fifth murder, he shoots a man who is whipping a horse, and a long shot records the victim's fall and Dahai shouting "idiot" at the corpse before continuing his hunt for Boss Jiao. Again, there is no reaction shot, thus emphasizing Dahai's diminishing reactions to his own violence.

The Soldier 105

Not only are these killings increasingly facile, but also violence appears to have become the solution for revenge, be it corruption or animal abuse. For instance, in the sixth and final murder scene, Dahai locates Boss Jiao's car, and sits in the backseat awaiting his next victim. He has therefore transitioned from a figure who "accidentally" began a killing spree to one who is now stalking his victims and has become inured to violence. He no longer argues with his victims or asks them to confess; rather, he simply exterminates them. When Boss Jiao gets in the driver's seat, there is a close-up of Dahai putting the muzzle of his rifle on the back of Boss Jiao's head. As Boss Jiao tries to convince Dahai not to kill him, the camera cuts to a close-up of Dahai's face, still splattered with the blood of his previous victims, then turns to follow Dahai's rifle back to Boss Jiao's head. Unlike the previous murders, Dahai is quiet; they do not argue, and there are no back-and-forth close-ups between the characters. Boss Jiao asks him "How can we take care of it? Let's just talk . . ." but Dahai remains silent. A close-up of his face shows him breathing heavily, and then the camera moves down the length of his rifle. He abruptly shoots Boss Jiao. When he pulls the trigger, there are three rapid cuts; the first cuts to the driver's side window being shattered by the blast, the second cuts to a close-up of the blood and gore as it sprays onto the dirt, and the third cuts to a long shot of the car. Next, it cuts to a close-up long take of Dahai covered in blood in the backseat. He is breathing heavily but then breaks into a grin, and it is this blood-splattered triumphant look that ends the film's first chapter (Figure 3.9).

In the first two murders, there is a reaction shot of Dahai's stunned expression, as if he does not believe what he has done, but there is no such shot after the third murder; rather, it cuts to him walking through town. Similarly, the fourth

Figure 3.9 Dahai after the final murder in *A Touch of Sin* (screenshot)

and fifth murders do not have reaction shots, but instead have long shots that record Dahai, his outstretched rifle, and the victims on the ground. The reaction shot returns in the sixth and final murder. However, it is no longer a stupefied look, as found in the first and second murders, but a blood-splattered grin. As Jia stated in an interview, "Violence is increasing. It's clear that resorting to violence is the quickest and most direct way that the weak can try to restore their lost dignity."[56] In this light, during his murder spree, Jia's distinctive and changing *wuxia* action cinematography communicates how Dahai has shifted from being a noble hero who struggles with taking others' lives, to becoming a killing machine, albeit one with a purpose. In this final scene, his look has gone from shock to satisfaction, as his just revenge has been realized.

Among the various different representations of the soldier-like figure, only Dahai in *A Touch of Sin* is rendered through the cinematic tropes of the *wuxia* action genre. However, all the different representations, including Dahai's, carry the affect of nostalgia, and not just for a PLA soldier, but also specifically for the Maoist era PLA soldier, because that is the figure that these various substitutions are being juxtaposed against. As I have already demonstrated, the Maoist pilot is an "absent presence" who is mourned in *24 City*. Similarly, Dahai also evokes these Maoist structures of feeling, such as communal solidarity, the importance of protecting the people, and fighting oppression and corruption. However, the nostalgia for this figure is even echoed by Lian Rong, one of the "sexy" soldiers in the film's final chapter, when she reveals that her QQ instant messaging username is "fish seeks water," which is strikingly similar to the phrase formerly used to describe the relationship between the PLA and the people: "the soldiers are fish and the people water."[57] Thus, the suggestion that she is a fish who does not have water implies nostalgia for this now lost relationship, and the current lack of the former Maoist structures of feeling.

This nostalgia for the Maoist figure is different from the retro fetish of the punters at the brothel, who enjoy the erotic performance by the "sexy" soldiers, in that these soldier figures have been evacuated of deeper meaning and have literally become a fetish costume. For instance, although the performance and the costumes reference elements of the past, it is rather a pastiche of Mao-esque objects and styles, not a sincere recreation of the Maoist past and the values and ideology associated with it. Furthermore, it is doubtful that such a brothel would have existed during the Maoist era, as it would not have been considered ideologically correct, but the contemporary period does not share these morals; instead, the brothel in the film eroticizes elements of the past and brings them into the present for sexual gratification, but keeps the divide between the past and the present firm.

This type of retro nostalgia connects with "red culture" nostalgia that was re-kindled by the 60th anniversary of the Communist Revolution (2009) and the 90th anniversary of the founding of the CCP (2011), in which the state held commemoration ceremonies to mark these events, and promoted "red culture" to remind the people what the CCP had done for them.[58] This nostalgic turn was seen by some as "justifying" CCP rule, and also as addressing a contemporary "ideological vacuum" created during Reform,[59] but was viewed by others as incongruous, because although the CCP's legitimacy derived from the Communist Revolution, their legitimacy had been systematically dismantled by the chaos of the Cultural Revolution and the corruption of the Reform era, which "shook China's faith in socialism . . . and undermined the people's trust in government leaders."[60]

The films' nostalgia for the Maoist soldier figure emphasizes the Maoist past, suggesting that the nation, like the soldier figure, has become corrupted during the Reform era and shifted from noble to harmful. Unlike the PLA-themed brothel performance, Dahai's depiction is not an example of red culture nostalgia, because it critiques it. Furthermore, the film makes several veiled critiques of "red culture"; for example, Dahai is first introduced at the scene of a vehicle accident on the highway, in which a truck has overturned and its load of tomatoes has spilled over the road. The tomato is symbolic, because it refers to the Bo Xilai scandal of 2013, in which the Communist Party Secretary in Chongqing was found guilty of corruption, his chief of police Wang Lijun sought sanctuary in the American embassy, and Bo's wife Gu Kailai was found guilty of the murder of their British family friend and financial consultant, Neil Heywood.[61] Bo Xilai was one of the main proponents of red culture, and led several programs to promote it. It was an integral part of the social and economic model he advanced, called the "Chongqing Model," which involved a crackdown on crime, the public singing of patriotic songs, and state investment in public infrastructure,[62] all elements that were seen as his attempt to earn a seat on the National Political Bureau Standing Committee.[63] Discussing the scandal on Chinese microblogs and the internet was censored, however, so people began to reference Bo and the scandal as "西红柿," the Chinese word for "tomato," because the word sounded similar to the phrase "western red city" (西红市), which was a meme for Bo Xilai's name. This word was chosen because Bo had been the Communist Party chief in Chongqing, which is in the west (西), he was famous for campaigning for a return to "red" Maoist beliefs (红), and finally because he was the mayor of a city (市), which is a homophone for 柿.[64] Thus, similar to the depiction of the tiger on Dahai's blanket that symbolized fighting state corruption, the spilled tomatoes also satirize the red culture movement.

The films emphasize the loss of the noble Mao-era PLA soldier by representing its replacement as corrupt, by commemorating the loss of it through memory, its retirement and death onscreen, and by briefly concretizing it through the heroic figure of Dahai. This is nostalgia not only for the figure itself, but also for the structures of feeling associated with the Maoist era. As Barmé writes, "Despite all its horrors, for many people, the Mao era was a time of deeply stirred passions and beliefs firmly held."[65] To repeat Phelan's earlier quote on how the absent presence "repeats the disappearance of the subject who longs always to be remembered,"[66] similar wording is found in one of the Chinese terms for nostalgia – "怀旧," meaning the longing (怀) for the past (旧). In the films, this is not nostalgia for Maoist politics, but for Maoist structure of feelings associated with that era, a longing for this past state of communal solidarity, protection, and righteousness. In the next two chapters, I examine the final two figures – the intellectual and the entrepreneur – and consider how they are the models that advance into the future, but also how they still evoke these past Maoist sentiments.

Chapter 4
The Intellectual: Power and the Voice

Introduction

This chapter examines the figure of the intellectual (士), as represented by the artist Liu Xiaodong (the subject of *Dong*), the designer Ma Ke (the main focus of *Useless*), as well as the director Jia Zhangke, who is the artist/intellectual responsible for creating these films. I examine this humanitarian figure and the structures of feeling that are associated with it, which include patriotism, altruism, and the desire to "save" the nation and its people. In Jia's films, the intellectuals are distinguished by their agency and their "voice," which is a continuation of the scholarly tradition of viewing themselves as the "voice of the people." This is not only a declaration of agency that enforces their position, but also an act of agency, and is a cultural role that gives them a degree of power. Therefore, in this chapter, I pay particular attention to the voice; who commands it, what it says, how it is filmed, and what it does.

During their interviews, several similar feelings arise: a mission to serve society and speak for the masses; national patriotism; and nostalgia for the distant Chinese past. As controllers of the voice, they possess a superior position – literally and figuratively – as they appear to be both the subjects and the authorities of their respective documentaries, and are filmed as having authority through this voice. This is not only concretized via their interviews, but is also expressed in their numerous voice-overs as well as scenes that show them creating their respective art works. This activity emphasizes their status as the class of creators who design works that, in turn, also "speak." Furthermore, both Liu and Ma are filmed with reoccurring artist tropes that further position them as members of the successful artist/intellectual class, and that emphasize the power and agency of the class. For example, Liu is recorded painting, conducting business, traveling, and other activities associated with the role of the artist, while Ma is interviewed in her pastoral atelier, and is filmed designing, touring her workshops, and exhibiting her show in Paris.

The agency of the voice, what the voice says, and how it is recorded emphasizes this group's power. In doing so, other groups are positioned as powerless – specifically the peasants and the *mingong*. I examine how the power of the voice granted to this figure creates a structure of feeling of humanistic anxiety for the masses, and analyze how this figure in Jia's films connects to a larger contemporary middle class Chinese structure of feeling that emphasizes anxiety and sympathy for the lower classes. I conclude by analyzing how the observatory lens and the exploratory lens used in Jia's films are from the point of view of an intellectual, and how their focus on the peasantry produces feelings of sympathy for the peasants. I argue, however, that these structures of feeling of sympathy Other the lower classes while empowering the intellectuals, thus underlining the intellectuals' superiority and alterity from the masses.

History of the Class

The modern intellectual's antecedents are the Confucian scholar gentry (士). This group was composed of educated civil servants and bureaucrats, who had served in state administration for over 2,000 years, from the Han to the Qing dynasties (202 BCE–1912 CE). Yi-tsi Mei Feuerwerker argues that a binary was constructed between the *shi* (士, scholar) and the *min* (民, people) that was based on Mencius's fourth-century BCE notion that those who used their muscles were ruled by those who used their minds, which placed the peasantry at the bottom of the social hierarchy, and the scholar near the top.[1] According to Mencius, although the "masses" were to be ruled, "the mandate to rule was deserved only if the people's economic and moral welfare were properly attended to," and thus the masses "were always 'there,' both as objects of paternalistic concern and as a yardstick for evaluating governmental success."[2] Feuerwerker describes the traditional Confucian role of the intellectual as being responsible for "enlightening" the peasants, a notion developed from the Confucian concept "of those above nurturing those down below."[3] This attitude was invoked by intellectuals during the May Fourth Movement (1915–21), who claimed that they had the mission of speaking for the people, particularly the oppressed peasantry, therefore developing a "sense of anguish and moral culpability" towards this group.[4] They also based their "power, authority, and legitimacy . . . on their fulfilling the obligation to nurture and look after the welfare of the ruled; it was in that sense that 'people' were the foundation of the entire system."[5]

After the Communist Revolution, intellectuals were reclassified as cadres in the 1950s, and their mandate changed from speaking for the masses to serving them. As Mao declared in his 12 March 1957 speech at the "Chinese Communist Party's National Conference on Propaganda Work":

> Without intellectuals our work cannot be done well, and we should therefore do a good job of uniting with them. Socialist society mainly comprises three sections of people, the workers, the peasants and the intellectuals. Intellectuals are mental workers. Their work is in the service of the people, that is, in the service of the workers and the peasants.[6]

During the Maoist period, intellectuals were required to "transform" their consciousness and identify with the workers, peasants, soldiers, and the Party.[7] However, at the same time, they were expected to recognize their inferiority to these lauded Maoist class figures,[8] and were also "urged to 'become one with the thoughts and emotions of the great masses of workers, peasants, and soldiers'" and serve them.[9] During the Cultural Revolution, however, the intellectuals came to be ranked among the lowest social orders, and were called the "stinking ninths" (臭老九),[10] who were often struggled against and sent-down to the countryside for re-education. But after Reform began in 1979, they were re-classified as "working class,"[11] thus joining the worker-peasant-soldiers, and began to be placed in visual propaganda along with them.[12] Their recategorization and admittance into the worker-peasant-soldier trinity indicated a positive shift in the political climate for them, as it portrayed them "as the trailblazers of the modernization effort," who were contributing to the nation's development because they "were seen as the linchpin around which the whole process of modernization revolved."[13]

Representation

The early Reform era's emphasis on economic modernization changed visual propaganda, due to the emphasis on technological development. Thus, intellectuals (often depicted wearing lab coats and glasses) began to appear, and the group was also promoted "to improve their country and its international position" through learning and technology.[14] Another responsibility attached to the intellectuals was that of "building a socialist spiritual civilization." This program ran from 1980 to 2000, and was based on Deng Xiaoping's "Four Basic Principles" of March 1979, which included: "We must keep to the socialist road; we must uphold the dictatorship of the proletariat; we must uphold the leadership of the Communist Party; we must uphold Marxism-Leninism-Mao Zedong Thought."[15] This was implemented to minimize the negative effects of Reform.

As Stefan Landsberger explains, it was "a framework for a new social structure that reflects the 'New Age' that started with the reforms," an age that would precipitate "raising the people's political consciousness and morality, and by fostering revolutionary ideals, morality and discipline, all with communist ideology at its core."[16]

The intellectuals found in Jia's films are usually minor characters who appear only briefly, such as college and university students (*Platform* and *Unknown Pleasures*) and disaffected intellectuals-turned-Yuppies (*Cry Me a River*). The intellectual is the main character in *Dong* and *Useless*, and thus this chapter focuses on these two films. These are the first two of Jia's "Trilogy of Artists" series that he has made so far, and are dedicated to this figure, as represented by the artist Liu Xiaodong in *Dong* and the fashion designer Ma Ke in *Useless*. Regarding his motivation for making the series, Jia explained that he felt that Chinese intellectuals had been "marginalized" after Tiananmen in 1989, and that "the general public lost interest in what intellectuals were thinking and saying . . . Their insights are obviously interesting, and I've long wanted to make films to introduce them and their ideas about society to a larger audience."[17] Thus, he decided to make documentaries in order "to help audiences appreciate and understand the work and thought of these intellectuals."[18] *Dong* grew out of Jia's desire to film a documentary about Liu, who suggested the Three Gorges as a setting, and in 2005 they traveled to Fengjie to create the film. (While shooting *Dong*, Jia decided to also create *Still Life* and shot the two films consecutively, sharing similar locations and many of the same extras). Jia chose to create *Useless* because it "made me reflect on China's social realities, not to mention history, memory, consumerism, interpersonal relationships and the rise and fall of industrial production."[19] He added that, in the film, he wanted to use clothing "as a medium for looking at society," to examine the "wide range of social levels" that were involved in garment manufacturing in China.[20]

Before analyzing this representation further, I briefly outline the biographies of Liu, Ma, and Jia, to better understand the typical characteristics of this class group. Born in 1963 in Jinzhou, Liaoning Province, Liu Xiaodong graduated from the Central Academy of Fine Arts (CAFA) in Beijing in 1993 with a degree in oil painting. Following his graduation, he and his wife, the artist Yu Hong, went to study in the US. Afterwards, Liu earned an MA from CAFA and the Facultad de Bellas Artes, Universidad Complutense in Madrid, where he also taught. He has been Professor of Oil Painting at CAFA since 1996. Liu's work has been exhibited internationally, and his paintings have sold for millions; for example, his "Hotbed No. 1" (2005) sold for $8.2 million

USD in 2007.²¹ In addition to being the eponymous subject of *Dong*, Liu was a production designer for Zhang Yuan's *Beijing Bastards* (1993),²² a producer for Jiang Wen's *Devils on the Doorstep* (2000),²³ briefly appeared as an extra in Jia's *The World* (2006), and was the Artistic Consultant for *Mountains May Depart* (2015). Both he and his wife acted as the main protagonists in Wang Xiaoshuai's film *The Days* (1993), and Liu's return to his hometown is the subject of the documentary *Hometown Boy* (2012), directed by Yao Hung-I and produced by Hou Hsiao-Hsien.

Ma Ke was born in 1971 in Changchun, Jilin Province, to parents who were both college teachers.²⁴ She studied design and fashion modeling, and earned her Associate Bachelor's in Fashion Design and Fashion Model Performance from the Suzhou Institute of Silk Textile Technology (now Suzhou University). After working as a designer and design director, she founded her first label "Exception de Mixmind" in 1996, followed by her second label "Useless" (无用) in 2006. Named one of China's "Top Ten Chinese Fashion Designers" in 1995,²⁵ her preparation for Paris Fashion Week 2007 is the subject of *Useless*, which won "Best Documentary" at the Venice Film Festival in 2007.²⁶

Jia was born in 1970 in Fenyang, Shanxi province, the son of a local teacher and a sales clerk in a state-run store. While studying painting at Shanxi University, he was inspired to study directing and applied to the Beijing Film Academy (BFA) twice, but was rejected. On his third attempt in 1993, he was admitted to the department of Film Literature (film theory). In addition to his work in film, he has shot commercials, worked as a fashion photographer, ghostwritten a TV serial, published a novel, and has also had his poetry and fiction published in literary magazines. He is also a co-founder of the production company XStream Pictures (along with Yu Likwai and Chow Keung) that was established in 2003 with the goal "to explore and to promote talented Chinese directors,"²⁷ and is also the founder of the art cinema production company Fabula Entertainment, which has signed distribution deals with French film distributor MK2.²⁸ Additionally, he established the film investment company Yihui Media in 2012,²⁹ founded Ke Premiere (柯首映, JiaScreen.com), an online platform for short films,³⁰ and co-created the Pingyao International Film Festival (2017).³¹ Jia, however, identifies as a peasant, and stated in an interview that he worked in the fields during the summer harvest and feels that he has experienced prejudice as a result of his peasant background.³² Furthermore, he describes himself as "a people's director from the grassroots of China."³³ Although he identifies with the peasantry and hails from a rural area, his background is not strictly proletarian, however. His grandfather was a doctor and his family was punished for this by being "sent down" to the countryside during the Cultural Revolution,³⁴ and his father was not allowed to go to university due to his "bad" background.[35] Similar to Liu and Ma, Jia is also an intellectual who has become successful in the new economy; he is a graduate of the renowned and exclusive BFA, a published literary author, and is a recipient of numerous national and international awards, including the Venice Film Festival's Golden Lion (2006), France's Legion of Honor (2009), and the Best Screenplay Award at Cannes (2013), which has made him a member of China's cultural elite.

In their respective documentaries and interviews, Liu and Ma share several similar themes that represent them as intellectuals, and evoke the structures of feeling associated with this class figure during the Reform era. For instance, both declare a desire to "serve" society and be of "use" to the masses, proclaim nationalistic sentiments, and nostalgically look to the past for inspiration as well as solutions to current problems. These feelings position contemporary intellectuals as integral to society, thus reaffirming the class's power and agency in the post-Reform era via this social and moral role as the people's voice. Ma, Liu, and Jia continue the traditional role of the intellectual of caring for the peasantry by acting as their "voice," speaking for and representing the masses who are believed to be unable to represent themselves. This voice is patriotic and benevolent, and supports the people. However, it is ultimately sympathetic and patronizing, not empowering. Nor is it politically threatening, because it is tempered with nationalistic platitudes and the nostalgia for the distant past when the nation was powerful.

First, in both of their respective documentaries, Liu and Ma emphasize their responsibility to critique, enlighten, and improve society. For instance, Ma Ke exclaims that *Wuyong*'s "benefit to society is my biggest satisfaction,"[36] and declares in the film that it is her "duty" to show that the Chinese people are able to not only manufacture clothing but also create fashion. In *Dong*, Liu claims that it is his responsibility to "witness and testify" as to the incredible changes that have happened during the Reform period and its effects on the poor,[37] expresses his desire to "be useful to society,"[38] and states his wish to help the sex workers and migrant workers whom he paints in the film, proclaiming "I wish I could give them something through my art." This sentiment is also expressed by Jia, who declared that he had a moral imperative to focus on the disenfranchised (in this case, the laid off workers in *24 City*), stating: "If this group is marginalized . . . then their faces, their language, their food, their living conditions, their homes, their expressions – all of that – is erased from the screen, to zero. Anything I can do to hold on to them and make people see them onscreen is the most important thing I can do! Otherwise, they're silenced!"[39] Finally, due to this sense of social responsibility, Jia has been referred to as a "citizen intellectual,"[40] and the Chinese students and intellectuals who are fans of his films have been described as people "whose idea of cinema and its role extends beyond entertainment to include this idea of public service."[41]

Although altruistic and laudatory, this mission to serve society is a common intellectual and artistic trope that positions the intellectuals as integral to society and reaffirms their authority through this self-given moral mandate. An important element of "serving" society is giving the masses a "voice" through aesthetic representation. For instance, Yi-tsi Mei Feuerwerker states that, during the May Fourth Movement (1915–21), many writers, such as Lu Xun, focused on the oppressed peasant, therefore developing a "sense of anguish and moral culpability" towards this group, and felt that it was their duty "To speak about and speak for these hitherto marginalized, silent, and invisible 'others'."[42] She writes about the intellectuals' concept of themselves as "crucially positioned within the moral and political order of society," as well as viewing themselves as "moral exemplar[s]."[43]

This belief in serving society continues into the current day. For instance, Sheng Hao declares "An artist has the responsibility to use his critical powers to observe and reflect on society . . . to cut through social issues from an objective and dispassionate standpoint,"[44] while Francesca Dal Lago argues that the role of the Chinese artist is "to enlighten the viewer about the problems of contemporary society," as well as have a "sense of mission" in which "a true intellectual was meant to use his culture and knowledge to serve the greater good of his society."[45] Similar sentiments are also found in the post-Tiananmen New Documentary Movement, which these two documentaries can be considered part of. This cinematic movement wanted to help people by "connecting to" rather than "lecturing to" society (as was done previously in Chinese documentary film), and was motivated by a "sense of urgency and social responsibility"[46] as its goal was to create a "dialogue" by investigating social problems, expressing them publicly, and therefore "solving" them.[47]

This mission to serve society is not only a humanitarian mandate but also has political implications. Although in the interviews they declare their "commitment to social issues" – Liu the poor, Ma the environment, and Jia the marginalized – they are not threatening to the state, as they refrain from blaming the negative effects of reform on the political system that instigated the neoliberal economy. This is a mode of criticism referred to as "patriotic worrying." As Gloria Davies explains, patriotic worrying about China is a common trope in Chinese intellectual discourse, which "carries the moral obligation of first identifying and then solving perceived Chinese problems (Zhongguo wenti), whether social, political, cultural, historical, or economic, in relation to the unified public cause of achieving China's national perfection."[48] This worrying, however, is not politically threatening, but supports the Party-state. As she argues, "the rhetoric of 'loving the nation' (*aiguo*) remains integral to Sinophone critical discourse and serves as its implicit raison d'être."[49] This is part of a larger cultural trend and a larger structure of feeling that is associated with this group. As Kin-Yan Szeto argues, *Still Life* was a film that "satisfied the government by continuing a trend on state-run channels, such as China Central Television (CCTV), of social-problem documentaries about ordinary people in China ... [that] serve the government's interests by appearing sympathetic and responsive to the public while actually avoiding serious challenges to the regime's goals or methods."[50] In this light, their humanitarian concern for the poor, the environment, and the marginalized actually reflects a structure of feeling that supports the state through their patriotic worrying and their sympathy for the people.

Furthermore, both Liu and Ma express strong nationalist sentiments not to demand political change but to support the state. For example, both emphasize their desire to create a specifically *Chinese* art, a "Chineseness" that is not only conceptual but is also "rooted" in the earth of the nation. For instance, Liu declares: "China adopted this thing called oil painting, planted it in this soil and let it take root. It will naturally grow into something different."[51] He also expresses his desire "to paint what was familiar to me, an art that would grow from this soil, not the art of another country ... I wanted to be like a plant, growing from the ground of this country."[52] In these two statements, Liu defends the "Chineseness" of his art – not only the style, but the very medium as well, as if its materiality would somehow make it Chinese or un-Chinese.

Comparable sentiments are echoed by Ma. After winning a design award, she was offered the opportunity to study in Italy but refused the offer because she "believed that the place where one was born and where one lived provided design inspiration."[53] Similar to Liu's desires to grow from the soil, in *Useless* Ma is filmed burying her fashions in the earth, stating her belief that this process will imbue them with time, history, and memory. Additionally, on her website, Ma writes that her travels to remote areas have developed her attraction to "Chinese traditional craftsmanship," writing that the peasants in these areas "live their lives the way our ancestors did," with an "intimacy and harmony" with nature.[54] In these statements, Ma credits the genesis of her artistic ability to the nation – not only a conceptual nation, but a geographical entity as well, one whose soil would imbue her clothing line with not only a sense of history, but actual Chinese ancestral memory.

This nationalism is not only physical and ideological, but is also "biological," and is portrayed by Liu as genetic. He declares in *Dong*, "damn it, can't we live our lives with the blood of our race coursing through our hearts?" This frustration is reflected by Ma, whose desire to develop a new clothing line was in order "to prove that Chinese could be creative in these areas as well."[55] Additionally, in *Useless* she declares that it was really "shameful" (可悲的事情) that China did not have its own brands and that the products the country produced were considered cheap and low quality, explaining that she felt it was her "duty to do something about it." Such a sentiment is also expressed by her in the *Useless* press kit, where she states: "Even if there's little that we can accomplish as individuals, we have a responsibility to try to discover some Chinese originality."[56] This is a desire to not only discover and connect with a deeper Chinese artistic creativity, but an implied moral obligation to do this.

Through the lineage of this rhetoric, not only are both Liu and Ma declaring their patriotism, but they are also resuming their traditional class power and role. They are projecting themselves as literati (文人) who are scholar-officials "versed in Confucian classics and talented in literature and arts."[57] This stance echoes an earlier filmic representation of the intellectual class of the 1920s and 30s as possessing "the wisdom of the Confucian patriarch."[58] This tendency is part of a larger trend followed by contemporary Chinese intellectuals. Wang Hui writes that intellectuals have responded to the post-Reform and post-Tiananmen period by turning to traditional values and promoting altruism, which "appealed to a sense of the intellectuals' mission."[59] Furthermore, Wu Guanjun explains that there are two different definitions for intellectuals: The first describes them as a group that includes all educated professionals, while the second connects to the Confucian ideal of the scholar class, and its role as being personally responsible "for all under Heaven," which is seen by post-Maoist intellectuals as the "ideal model."[60] Wu argues that there has been a "radical break" between the Maoist era's intellectuals (1949–78) and the post-Maoist intellectuals (1978–present), writing that in the Reform era, the intellectuals view themselves as Confucian moral and intellectual leaders and as a "social elite" who "now guide the production of Chinese social and political thought," and see the country's metamorphosis "as their *personal* mission."[61]

Liu, Ma, and Jia's comments are also tinted with anxiety about the perceived threats that "modernity" brings, which is part of a larger structure of feeling associated with this class. Liu tries to find the "silver lining," and states in *Dong* "Even in a deeply tragic environment, or a condition of utter despair, you discover that life itself is truly moving. Like a tree, it grows freely, full of luxuriance." But this anxiety is best expressed by Ma, who declares: "So what are the values of all the new developments? I think mankind is in a bad place: what we are pursuing today brings us pain and despair."[62] She expands on this further on her website, arguing that globalization has destroyed "cultural variety and regional diversity," and that traditional craftsmanship "can now only be found in museum exhibits."[63] She states: "Through these tremendous social changes, my country is undergoing a heart-breaking loss of tradition for the sake of an irresponsible pursuit of the future."[64]

Jia also believes that the economic changes have not all been beneficial, saying: "Today, the so-called modernization of China is a campaign-style modernization; we have come to own the material things of modernization within a short period, but modernization itself is far from being material things in themselves."[65] He has stated that the socio-economic changes have caused the people "to lose our confidence in Chinese culture. In fact, we lost our *faith* in Chinese culture. This cultural crisis is still continuing today."[66]

These descriptions of a present-day "tragic environment," "pain and despair," and "the loss of faith in Chinese culture" are not only a type of patriotic worrying, but also express a structure of feeling of anxiety for the present. In Chapter 1, I wrote that, like the ruin, nostalgia "indicates a rupture with the past, and both are symptoms that something has irrevocably changed for the worse." This nostalgia of "looking back" is, to use Boym's terms, not a restorative nostalgia to recreate the past, but is rather reflective, taking comfort in an idea of the past but with no intention of reconstructing it in the present.[67] Additionally, it connects to Glenn Albrecht's concept of "solastalgia," which he describes as not exactly nostalgia or the desire to return home, but rather is "a desire to be connected with a positively perceived period in the past . . . a longing for a cultural setting in the past in which a person felt more 'at home' than the present."[68] Similar to the "Ostalgie" of the older members of the working class, Liu and Ma also look towards a past when their group was celebrated – in this case, the "traditional" pre-Modern past, when they were positioned as the epitome of the social order, as sage-like scholar-officials. But, unlike the "Ostalgie" of these workers who long for the not-so-distant Maoist past that they have actually lived through, and which had positioned them as leaders of the people, Liu and Ma are not nostalgic for the Maoist era but the ancient past that they have never experienced. In this ancient past, Liu and Ma search for an original cultural essence, an idealized past that they describe in glowing and patriotic terms, and a past in which they most likely would have had a high-class position.

This fear of the present and the future is entwined in the aspiration to produce "Chineseness" by drawing from the past. For Liu, it is expressed as the past of the Northern Wei dynasty that ruled China over 1,500 years ago, while for Ma it is an undetermined era deep in history. For example, she claims

The Intellectual 119

to have "philosophically returned" to a more traditional state,[69] and speaks at length about her Taoist beliefs that she says were "created by our ancestors" and are "full of wisdom."[70] Gloria Davies argues that this contemporary desire of Chinese intellectuals "to return to tradition . . . and to establish Sino-centered norms that adhere to international academic standards," mimics the earlier rhetoric and "moral purpose" of the intellectuals of the May Fourth era.[71] This discourse, therefore, is part of an older intellectual ideology that believes that the salvation to the nation's problems can be found in the past – specifically, the *Chinese* past.

Cinematic Tropes: Pseudomonologues and Observation

In *Dong* and *Useless*, the interviews with Liu and Ma are conducted by someone behind the camera, and the interviewees primarily look in the direction of this person who remains off-screen and is never heard (Figures 4.1 and 4.2). Bill Nichols refers to this style of interview as a "pseudomonologue," because it combines "[t]he visible presence of the social actor as evidentiary witness and the visible absence of the filmmaker (the filmmaker's presence as absence)."[72] He argues that these pseudomonologues seem "to deliver the thoughts, impressions, feelings, and memories of the individual witness directly to the viewer," which "sutures" viewer and subject.[73] Even though the structure of the interview

Figure 4.1 Liu Xiaodong interviewed in *Dong* (screenshot)

Figure 4.2 Ma Ke interviewed in *Useless* (screenshot)

remains obvious because the interviewees address the camera or look towards the interviewer, he stresses that this "oral history" style of documentary positions the viewer as a "witness" to the interviewee's "historical world," creating a "sense of being addressed by others who are themselves historically situated or implanted and who speak directly to us."[74] This interview format therefore has the potential to move the viewer. It not only positions the viewer and the interviewee in relation to one another (Nichol's "suturing effect") by removing the presence of the interviewer, it also positions the viewer as "witness" to the interviewee's personal recollections as if they are "speak[ing] directly to us." Therefore, this technique heightens the "bond" between the interviewee and the viewer.

The pseudomonologue is also used in Jia's other interview-based documentaries, such as *24 City* and *I Wish I Knew*. Similar to these other interview subjects, Liu and Ma are usually filmed in locations associated with their lives, which imbue these segments with a sense of veridicality. For example, Ma is filmed in her pastoral atelier, driving her SUV, and during her trip to Paris fashion week. Liu is recorded creating his artwork in situ, first in the Three Gorges area and then in Bangkok. However, the intellectuals have long monologues in which they expound on their personal philosophies, whereas the others are responding to interview questions. Anna Grimshaw and Amanda Ravetz argue that the documentary interview "raises questions about whether the camera obliges – or simply stimulates – people to speak."[75] In Jia's documentaries, the intellectuals appear stimulated whilst the workers and peasants seem obligated to speak. Unlike the workers being interviewed, both Liu and Ma in *Dong* and *Useless* "command" the interview process and speak at length about their work and personal philosophies. Liu and Ma therefore have the power of the "voice" in their interviews and appear to control the interview, and are "partners" in the films rather than simply being its objects – the films are, after all, largely about them and their work, and it is they who have the power to use these interviews to expound on their work and beliefs.

In Chapter 1, I wrote that the interviews with members of the worker class projected an intimacy with the viewer, because they were presenting a moment *of* time and *in* time, and were constructing themselves not as "talking heads" but as real people with memories and emotions, which combined memory, emotion, and time to "reconstruct" the class. But unlike the interviews with the workers, Liu and Ma do not speak of their personal and intimate memories and their feelings for the past, but rather speak about their philosophies and opinions. This is not as emotional and is more instructive, and less vulnerable in that intellectuals are not "sharing" intimate memories and thus emotions with the viewer, but are expounding on their views. Furthermore, the interviews with Liu and Ma are longer than the interviews with the workers, as Liu and Ma are the primary subjects of their respective documentaries – approximately two-thirds of *Dong* (70 minutes) focuses on Liu and his art, and two-thirds of *Useless* (81 minutes) focuses on her and her designs. Therefore, we spend more time with these figures learning about their philosophies.

While expounding on their thoughts and beliefs, the intellectuals even have the power of the voice-over to narrate certain scenes. In these voice-overs, the voice is disembodied. Unlike the monologues that precede and follow it, the viewer does not see Liu and Ma speak during these segments. In this way, during the voice-over the voice becomes omniscient, not only speaking for itself but also for the film. Thus, not only do Ma and Liu become the subjects of the films, but briefly, they also become the voice of the films. Mladen Dolar describes the voice as "a sound which appears to be endowed in itself with the will to 'say something,' with an inner intentionality."[76] It is this "will to say something" that is projected in these interviews, and Liu and Ma command their interviews through the agency of the voice. This contrasts with the interviews with the workers in *24 City*, who also have a voice, but who appear reticent before the camera and are very much responding to questions asked by the unnamed interviewer. Furthermore, it also contrasts with the observational shots of the silent peasantry and *mingong* that I analyzed in the previous chapter on the peasants,

122 Moving Figures

who are the objects – not the subjects – of the lens. These objects are mostly seen and not heard, and when finally interviewed (such as found in *Useless*), they are shy and hesitantly respond to the questions that they are asked.

To illustrate this, throughout the film, Ma discusses her thoughts on art, culture, and society. She does not appear to be questioned by the interviewer, but rather lengthily expounds on her philosophies. She appears in control of the interview, and looks earnestly at whoever is interviewing her, and is not reticent or ashamed (Figure 4.2). Conversely, the tailor-turned-miner family is interrogated. We first meet the wife (who is nameless) as she goes to a tailor's shop to pick up the trousers she left for repair. Up until this point, the camera had been silently observing life unfolding in this small town, but suddenly the man behind the camera (perhaps Jia himself) addresses her. She is a stranger to him, but he calls her "Big Sister" (大姐), which is a term of casual address, and we instantly realize that she does not have the same authority as Ma and is in a deferential position. He asks her a series of direct, non-open-ended questions: Can you sew your own clothes? What does your husband do now? Where do you work? She answers briefly and shyly, as if afraid to speak. She is being interrogated by someone with a higher level of power than her, and who therefore feels entitled to ask such questions. This interview style continues as the film cuts to her at home with her husband and son. Unlike Ma's romantic pastoral atelier, theirs is a rundown hut with mud walls and paper over the windows. The interviewer asks: Where did you buy the clothes you're wearing? What do you like to see her wear? Why did you choose them? Would you go back to working as a tailor? Although the miner talks more than this wife, he still is hesitant and looks uncomfortable during the interrogation, while his wife looks sheepishly towards the viewer (Figure 4.3). They do not respond like the workers and intellectuals; rather, they are shy and apprehensive before the camera, and embarrassedly reply to the interviewer's questions. These two groups are therefore filmed differently according to the people's class, in that the intellectuals have more authority and power in the interviews, while the lower classes lack this agency. Thus, these interviews emphasize and reinforce who is the subject (and controls the voice) during the interview, and who must respond to it.

As Bill Nichols points out, "Interviews are a distinct form of social encounter. They differ from ordinary conversation and the more coercive process of interrogation by dint of the institutional framework in which they occur and the specific protocols of guidelines that structure them."[77] The interview with the miners is a very different type of "social encounter"; they lack the authority that Ma expressed in her interviews in the film, and are very much obliged to

Figure 4.3 The miners in *Useless* (screenshot)

respond, even to questions that are highly personal, such as how they like to see each other dressed. Shy, seemingly unaccustomed to such attention, the woman answers the questions nervously, and when her husband begins his interview, he is also awkward before the lens. Unlike Ma, they are hesitant to meet the gaze of the interviewer behind the camera or the camera itself, and when they do, they grin embarrassedly and look away. Furthermore, such intimate questions are not asked of Ma (or Liu for that matter); she is not questioned as to her romantic relationships and what she likes to see her spouse or lover wear, but is rather asked her opinions on larger social issues, and one gets the feeling that such an intimate yet inane question would not be asked of this philosophical and serious artist/intellectual, nor would it be tolerated by her. Regarding the peasantry, however, anything is fair game – any question, no matter how intimate, can be asked, and they embarrassedly comply. This power differential is stressed further when the viewer realizes that, as the end credits roll, Ma is listed as the "main character" in English (and "人物" in Chinese), yet this couple's names are not mentioned – rather, they remain nameless.

Although many of the interviews in these films are "word-led" because they focus on the narration of memory and thought, they also contain observational scenes that show un-narrated, phenomenological "lived experience." In this way, they combine "showing" and "telling," as the camera observes and "shows" while the interview and voice-over "tells."[78] During their interviews, both Liu and Ma elaborate at length about their work and their thoughts on contemporary society, and these scenes are followed or preceded by observational long takes of them interacting with their employees, conducting business, exercising, and playing, thus providing an insight into their daily lives. For example, Ma is interviewed in her atelier. She directs her speech towards someone behind and to the left of the camera, and talks about her design process and her philosophies to the interviewer. Sometimes, her voiceover is heard as the camera records her walking through her atelier, playing with her dogs, draping clothes on models, and supervising the women who are weaving her textiles. In one example, a long take slow pan records her walking through the weaving room. She carefully watches the weavers as they work on traditional wooden looms, and the only sound is that of the movement of the treadles, levers, and shuttles. As she watches them work, her voice over is heard declaring "Objects made by hand convey emotions . . . making things by hand is a long, laborious process, so handmade objects contain emotional elements quite different from mass-produced objects." This statement is thus supported by her practice – namely, the use of artisanal hand-woven textiles in her garments as recorded in this segment.

Scenes of observing from a distance sometimes switch to moving close-ups that engage more intimately with the characters. These scenes complement and support their narratives, but also introduce an extra "protagonist" to the narrative – the camera – and introduce its "voice." Thus, not only is there a juxtaposition of who speaks and who is silent, or who commands the interview and who responds to questions asked, there is also an added level of "speech" provided by the film, which is controlled by another intellectual – the director Jia Zhangke himself – and the camera serves as the "voice" of this intellectual.

Sometimes this camera observes motionless from a distance, while at other times it explores the scenes through movement and close-ups. In order to differentiate these two approaches, I term the first a distanced "observatory lens," and the second a close-up "exploratory lens." Building on my earlier comparison of the empathetic POV lens with the sympathetic yet distancing observatory lens in Chapter 2, in what follows I examine how the observatory and exploratory lenses can be seen as the voice of the camera, and therefore the director, and how they create structures of feeling for the subjects and objects of the lens. I analyze how the camera switches roles from being a passive recorder of the interview to becoming a mobile and engaged observer, shifting from watching motionless at a distance to appearing to have its own agency through its movement. In this role, it also becomes an agent that abandons its focus on Liu and Ma and leaves their orbit in order to examine other people and environments, thus giving the films more "depth" by showing that there is something else besides their main protagonists.

To better understand this use of the camera as the director's voice, I turn to Bill Nichols's notion of "observational cinema" and Anna Grimshaw and Amanda Ravetz's comparison between "word-led" and "observational" documentaries. First, Nichols offers the term "observational cinema" as an alternative for direct cinema and cinema verité, writing that it stresses "an empathetic, nonjudgmental, participatory mode of observation," and refers to it as "an affective form of learning" which "affords the viewer an opportunity to look in on and overhear something of the lived experience of others, to gain some sense of the distinct rhythms of everyday life."[79] For example, in both *Dong* and *Useless*, the camera turns away from the main protagonists and breaks their orbits to explore the scene as well as follow alternative narratives, and these observatory scenes compose a significant percentage of the films. In *Useless*, the first 47 minutes centers on Ma Ke. Afterwards, the camera follows other story lines, such as exploring life in a small town, and stopping to interview a miner's family in the film's last 30 minutes. In *Dong*, the camera spends more than half of the film primarily focused on Liu, recording his interview and following him as he paints, travels, and conducts business. But later, it changes when the camera accompanies him on his visit to the family of Wang Qingsong, a migrant worker and an extra in *Dong* and "Hotbed No. 1" who was killed in a workplace accident (a scene I will analyze further shortly), and leaves his orbit a second time to follow one of the sex workers whom he paints.

Second, Anna Grimshaw and Amanda Ravetz describe "observational" filmmaking as "a mode of inquiry that sticks close to lived experience and that seeks to render the finely grained texture of lived experience," and acts "as an extension of human consciousness, an almost objective correlative of what the filmmaker sees, hears, and feels," which they contrast with "word-led" documentaries (such as interviews).[80] I would like to take this concept and consider how Grimshaw and Ravetz's "observational filmmaking" is "an extension of human consciousness." Specifically, I view it as a "prosthetic" for the filmmaker, what Celia Lury would define as perceptual and mechanical devices that "extend" the self.[81] This observational lens, however, only grants the other characters a "voice" through representation. They only appear and do not speak, and so remain the objects of Jia's lens.

For example, a segment in *Dong* records Liu's visit to the village of the deceased migrant worker, Wang Qingsong. The camera follows Liu walking up a mud road in the rain to Wang's house, and him meeting Wang's widow and daughter outside. The scene begins with a close-up of the widow's torso, depicting her without a head, and is accompanied by the sound of someone, presumably her, expelling mucus. Liu shows her the photographs of her husband that he took for his painting, and she begins to examine them thoroughly, and they then go inside where a larger crowd has gathered. During the visit, the camera remains focused on Liu, but then begins to slowly drift away from him and focus on the crowd and becomes an exploratory lens. In a series of long takes, Dong greets the family and sits with them. He presents gifts to Wang's children, and the assembled crowd laughs at the comedic plush toys he gives them. Previously in the film, Liu spoke directly towards the interviewer, seemingly controlling the interview process, apparently taking on the role of the narrator but, in this scene, although Liu continues to speak (and most of what he says continues to appear in the film's subtitles), the camera leaves him to instead observe the crowd, thus shifting from its previous expository format. People in the crowd start talking in their dialect (which is unsubtitled), and laugh about the toys, but then the camera cuts to a long take of a group of older men sitting and smoking, and then cuts to a long take close-up of Wang's father sitting quietly and crying (Figure 4.4). After silently recording his grief, it cuts to another close-up long take of another elderly man, presumably a relative, looking on. He is also blinking in order to fight back his tears, but still they fall.

In this light, we can reconsider Nichols's notion of the "forms of alliance" – "*I* speak about *them* to *you*" – and consider the "*them*." During these scenes, the

Figure 4.4 Wang's father in *Dong* (screenshot)

camera does not just watch from a distance, but changes its depth, from far to near and back again, exploring the mise-en-scène. It begins by focusing mainly on Liu's interactions with the people, but then stops and examines characters or narratives that at first appear in the background. In this fashion, it does not simply follow the narrative, but has its own agency; it breaks its orbit around Liu, and becomes an active, mobile "eye," an exploratory lens that studies the people, examines their reaction to Liu and the photographs, and watches as they mourn the deceased. Liu's voice is heard in the distance and it is subtitled when he explains the photographs and the gifts, but soon it just becomes background noise. We hear members of the crowd speak in their local dialects, but the majority of the speech is not subtitled, and is only subtitled when one of the peasants speaks directly to Liu, presumably because what they say is not important unless it provides context for what Liu is saying. The camera returns to focus on Liu and watches as he cries, while Wang's father looks on numbly, and Wang's young daughter watches curiously.

Although these shots are sympathetic, they emphasize the powerlessness of these peasants compared to Liu. During his visit, Liu cries over Wang's death, but his grief is different from that of the gathered peasants, because their situation is so very dissimilar to Liu's. While the peasant family remains in poverty, Liu can return to his urban life as a wealthy and famous artist, leaving the peasants in this remote location to eke out their existence. These scenes are affective and provide the aforementioned "texture of lived experience" and "extension of human consciousness,"[82] thus producing a sympathetic structure of feeling associated with this group. However, extended focus on the mute objects, particularly in regards to Liu's scenes with the peasants as described above, makes the peasants, in their tears and misery, people to be pitied. Although they are given a "voice" through depiction, unlike Liu they are not really given an actual voice and thus lack the cinematic agency of the intellectuals.

In addition to lingering on their tears and grief, the camera also depicts the peasantry as uncouth. For instance, the camera records the widow pinching the bridge of her nose so that she can blow her nose without the aid of a tissue, thus capturing the sights and sounds of the snot being expelled. Furthermore, like the miner couple in *Useless*, the peasants in *Dong* are also uncomfortable being filmed. Some are nervous and others try to avoid the lens; one man looks at it warily, another with confused apprehension, a woman tries to hide behind her hands, and another looks away. The camera is an invasive presence that, like the long take close-ups of Wang's father and the other old man crying, is capitalizing on their grief. Throughout Liu's visit, Wang's widow looks anxious, angry, and worried. She is obviously uncomfortable in front of the

Figure 4.5 The upset widow in *Dong* (screenshot)

camera, as it often focuses on her and follows her – she is, after all, the widow of the man who has just died, but must also act the role of hostess for the mourners who have gathered as well as this visiting artist and his film crew. Although she tries to avoid looking into the lens, during one brief scene while she is nervously fretting, she glares into it and purses her lips, as if in extreme annoyance (Figure 4.5). But then she looks away, breaking her angry gaze. She is powerless to stop the recording.

Regarding the peasantry in Lu Xun's literature, Feuerwerker writes: "The peasant does not appear so much as a subject in his or her own right, but rather as someone who is encountered by an intellectual."[83] In this concept, the intellectual is the one with agency; s/he is the subject of the action, while the peasant remains the object, its agency-less recipients who are "encountered." During his visit to Wang Qingsong's village, Liu encounters these peasants, and they are encountered by him. In this visit, we do not learn much about the deceased Wang Qingsong, the man they grieve. Rather, the overall effect is that of taking advantage of their misery, as if these peasants and their sorrow over Wang's death are simply a vehicle for Liu (and, by extension the film) to promote his sympathy towards his fellow man. This observation therefore supports Liu in performing his role of an intellectual, caring for and speaking for the pitiful masses while they perform their role of simply being pitiful. As Yingjin Zhang writes about independent Chinese documentaries, although they appear to challenge the mainstream media by focusing on the marginalized, this focus does not benefit the subject, per se, but rather the filmmaker, because the filmmaker "extracts information from the informant" and thus "secures public recognition," but the subjects do not benefit from this encounter; rather, they "fade into a shadowy background, if not into utter oblivion."[84] Finally, similar to the treatment of the miner family in *Useless*'s credits, the peasants are not even listed in the film's credits, and thus they also remain nameless.

After the camera explores the peasantry at Wang's house, it resumes its focus on Liu and follows him to Bangkok, where he goes to paint the female Thai sex workers. It remains focused on him during most of this segment, watching as he paints one of the women reclining on a mattress. Liu tells her to take a break, and then he exits the camera's frame. But the camera remains focused on her. Similar to the earlier example of his visit to the village, in this segment the viewer hears Liu's voice in the distance, which is often subtitled as he discusses his art process and the subjects that he is painting. But the camera maintains its focus on the unnamed and voiceless sex worker. It cuts to her standing up and stretching near the canvas that he has been working on. She then walks away, but the camera hurries to catch up with her – it is not gliding on a track, but is shaky and the camera operator is obviously struggling to keep up, thus breaking free from Liu's orbit by following her. In this exploratory lens segment, it trails her as she goes into an office and sits down on a couch, but stays at the doorframe voyeuristically watching her. It observes as she retrieves her phone and starts checking her messages, as we hear Liu's voice from a distance. He is talking about his art process, and it is subtitled. The scene then cuts to a medium close-up of her still checking her phone. We hear Liu's voice saying "They all move this way . . . the body language of tropical people," but it continues to watch her as she intently goes through her messages. She makes a call, but does not say anything. It then cuts to a long take of her undressing, shot from behind. It cuts again to her dressing, then again to her checking her phone for messages. She remains silent.

The next scene cuts to a busy street in daylight. The camera pans past parked motorbikes, and we see the model/sex worker walking down the sidewalk. This begins the film's first segment without Liu. She does not speak, but she is the focus of this new narrative, which observes her and the surrounding crowd, her trip on the public bus, and the traffic, in several unnarrated long takes. It then cuts to her watching a television news report about a flood, again checking her phone, and then cuts to her walking to the train station at night while talking briefly on her phone. Because her voice is muffled and is not subtitled for those who do not understand Thai during the brief moment that we hear her voice, the viewer cannot rely on speech to understand what is going on. Rather, we must piece the narrative together via these observatory scenes that involve the report of a flood and telephone conversations failed and realized. This effort in trying to understand the plot has the effect of engrossing the viewer in this mystery via this largely silent observation. This absorbed state echoes the sense of anticipation that the moving portraits generate in *24 City*, which increased the portraits' connection with the viewer as we became more and more engrossed in watching the moving portrait transform. Similarly, here we ask ourselves why she is constantly checking her phone, to whom she is waiting to talk, and wonder how it relates to the scenes of flooding that are shown on TV. This drama is made even more poignant in its voicelessness. The anticipation heightens the emotional tension of the scene, and introduces a quality of tensed time, which stresses the importance of the mystery unfolding, and the viewer is engulfed by and reacts to this tension. But, although the exploratory lens has offered this figure agency through depiction, like the crowd of peasants the camera explores in Liu's visit to Wang's village, she still remains largely voiceless and thus is denied the agency of the voice.

In addition to commanding their interviews in their respective films, Liu and Ma are also recorded in another act of agency – the act of artistic creation – which further emphasizes their power. Unlike the migrant workers whom Liu positions and configures for his tableaus, or the workers in the textile factory, Liu and Ma create – they "bring into existence" and "produce through imaginative skill,"[85] whilst the masses make – "the labor, task, or duty that is one's accustomed means of labor."[86] This distinction is found in the labor

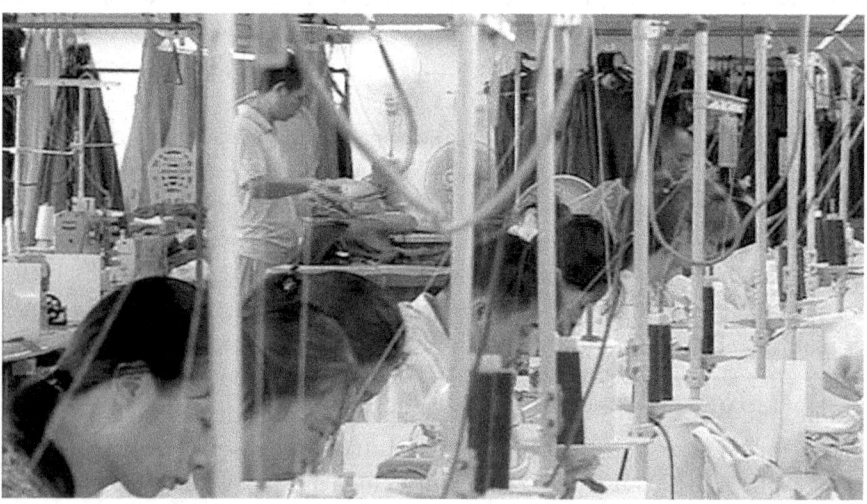

Figure 4.6   Factory employees in *Useless* (screenshot)

Figure 4.7 Ma Ke's atelier in *Useless* (screenshot)

conditions in *Useless* where employees are hunched over their sewing machines (Figure 4.6), which contrasts with bucolic natural splendor of Ma's art studio (Figure 4.7). For example, *Useless* follows each stage of the fashion process, from design, to the weaving of the fabric, to cutting and sewing, to factory production and, finally, to exhibition. The film begins with a close-up long pan of the factory workers ironing the garments, and then the camera scrolls to the right, almost as if on a conveyer belt, going from person to person as they complete each stage in the production process. It then zooms out but continues the same long pan, observing the workers from outside the factory windows as they work. The create-versus-make dichotomy is further emphasized in a scene that follows that features a doctor's visit to the workers in a textile factory. They complain of coughs, tiredness, sore throats, and inflamed eyes, which is later juxtaposed with the positive rewards that Ma earns for her creative design in the film.

A further example is found in *Dong*, which records Liu arranging the subjects of his paintings, photographing them, and then sketching and painting them. The paintings are left in a state that at first appears unfinished. The underdrawing is exposed, alterations are only partially erased, and some sections appear untouched, stressing the materiality of the works and the gestures that created them. The film records the slow progression of his paintings, and dwells on the act of painting and its creation more so than the final product. Wu Hung describes Liu's work as "an action painting and a site-specific performance in itself ... the painting's significance lies in revealing the artist's existence."[87] We can therefore consider how both films are about the act of being artists, revealing not only their creation and existence, but also their agency as artists. Similar to Dolar's earlier concept of the voice as "the will," these scenes of creativity underscore the agency of this class group; they are creators, and by recording them in the act of creation, these scenes emphasize this creative act and how it enhances their authority.

In Chapter 2, I examined how the intellectuals have traditionally Othered the peasantry, and how this act "defined" the intellectuals and, in effect, was necessary for forming their identity. In this section, I consider the power of doing the Othering, and how it underscores the return of the intellectuals' agency during the Reform era, in that it "emphasiz[es] the perceived weaknesses of marginalized groups as a way of stressing the alleged strength of those in positions of power."[88] Although the observational shots can be seen as representing the masses, those "masses" do not have the power over their own representation, and the focus of the documentaries still remains on the primary "voiced" protagonists, Liu and Ma. Finally, although it is a sympathetic view of this group, as argued in Chapter 2, sympathy is also disempowering.

For example, although Liu, Ma, and Jia all express a moral imperative to be the voice for the masses, is it not the masses' voice but that of the intellectuals, in that they claim to represent them; furthermore, the intellectuals do not appear to be self-reflective considering their authority to make this claim. As Jason McGrath points out:

> Though [*Dong*] is not unsympathetic to Liu Xiaodong, it does implicitly meditate upon the inevitable distance between the painter and the subjects he seeks to represent. As an intellectual and a successful artist based in Beijing, how indeed can Liu – or Jia Zhangke himself for that matter – be completely comfortable in his capacity to speak for postsocialist modernity's dispossessed?[89]

Such a question, however, is not discussed by Liu, Ma, or even Jia himself. They do not acknowledge that speaking for the silent masses does not give those masses agency; rather, the sympathy they express reinforces the intellectual's previous "moral authority" and thus reaffirms the intellectuals' power, because this sympathy is the only result from their actions.

This humanitarian mandate, bestowed upon the intellectual class by the intellectuals themselves and the structure of feeling that has become associated with this class, is a role that positions them not only as subjects with agency and the masses as their agent-less objects, but also positions them as having a patronizing view of these groups, in that they care for and speak for these people. Such a humanitarian mandate does several different things. First, it reinforces the intellectuals' importance and, through this altruistic mission, underscores their right to have this power via this "moral yardstick." Second, it allows the intellectual to be magnanimous and exercise their power by showing that they have it, reinforcing the fact that they are no longer the victims of the Maoist period but the leaders of the current age. Finally, this humanitarianism requires a pitiful object who is in need of assistance; it is not humanitarian if it is for yourself, but rather is a sympathy for a decidedly inferior group, which reaffirms the intellectual's superiority. This humanitarianism stems from the intellectual's historical sense of mission; not only a desire to speak for the masses, but rather a mandate, an expectation of speaking for the masses. As Liu declares in the film about the *mingong* and sex workers he paints, "I wish I could give them something through my art." This is not empathy with these people, but is rather sympathy for them. This sympathy reaffirms the intellectual's moral authority and superiority, and thus is ultimately an act of Othering in that, unlike empathy, it is not a "feeling for" someone who is an equal, but a feeling of pity for someone who is an inferior other. As Alison Landsberg argues, "Sympathy implies condescension, for the sympathizer looks down at her object and in the process reaffirms her superiority."[90] This humanitarianism actually supports the state narrative by providing a "safe" way to criticize society, using its abject and harmless peasant masses as, once again, the "yardstick," and thus focusing on the Other not only reflects their self-given mandate of speaking for this class, but also emphasizes their superiority to those they sympathize for.

Furthermore, it is ultimately self-gratifying, in that it allows the intellectuals to position themselves as the heroes of the new era because they are the protectors of the masses who cannot protect themselves, thus giving them a reason for having the power of the voice. Like sympathy, Othering also allows the intellectuals to adopt a "charity view" of the masses in that they are helping those poorer and less powerful than they are, which also enhances their status; as Laura Augustín argues about the idea of victimhood, "supporters position [people] as victims in order to claim rights for them, but this move also turns them into victims, and victims need help, need saving – which gives a primary role to supporters."[91] Thus, this primary role allows the intellectuals to re-assert their domination and superiority over the masses, a power that they lost during the Cultural Revolution when they became the despised "Stinking Ninths" and were persecuted.

Edward Said began his treatise *Orientalism*, about Western Othering of the East, by quoting "The Eighteenth Brumaire of Louis Bonaparte," a pamphlet Karl Marx wrote regarding the class struggle in France during the turn of the 19th century, in which he states that the peasantry "cannot represent themselves, they must be represented."[92] This snippet of text was from a longer statement, the original reading:

> They cannot represent themselves, they must be represented. Their representative must at the same time appear as their master, as an authority over them, an unlimited governmental power which protects them from the other classes and sends them rain and sunshine from above.[93]

This is strikingly similar to how Feuerwerker describes the scholar-peasant dichotomy in traditional China, where she writes that the peasantry were traditionally visualized as being intimately connected to nature, like the "flowers and birds,"[94] and were seen as voiceless and unable to represent themselves. Both statements describe the peasantry as a natural phenomenon, one that is like the non-threatening floral and fauna, harmless and in need of protection by those with the agency to do it – the intellectuals – and emphasizes the difference in these two classes by contrasting the conflicting structures of feeling associated with each. The peasants are not being protected by fellow equals, however, but by their biological, intellectual, and moral "superiors."

Finally, this Othering through their representation and the structures of feeling they generate does not only separate them socially but also temporally. Earlier I wrote how Ma declared that her artistic inspiration came from her travels to remote areas, places where the peasants "live their lives the way our ancestors did," and who had an "intimacy and harmony" with nature.[95] In *Useless*, she also talks about distant rural areas, and how their inhabitants are "very different, maybe even utterly different," and that "when you go to such places and see how the people live, it seems to me a bit like recovering a lost memory . . . [and] you gradually start to remember things you once felt." While praising this return to memory, the peasant ancestral Other has been imbued with a genetic memory, and tied to the land and the distant past. Although meant as a claim of "authenticity," it also places the rural in a primordial, utopian past of "ancestors," and separates them from the modern "present." In his analysis of the European peasantry, Teodor Shanin refers to them as "remainders of the past."[96] Thus, to borrow this concept, we can consider that the intellectual's self-given responsibility to "testify" for the peasantry and give them a "voice" has the effect of conceptualizing the peasantry as not being *in* the present, but *of* and *in* the past, the eternal Other in that the two classes will never conceptually exist in the same chronotope; rather, the peasants stay in the past, while the intellectuals advance into the future. Modernity is therefore denied to this group; they will conceptually remain in the past, the traditional Other, valorized for these qualities yet will never be seen as equals in this class patronization.

I would like to finish this chapter by re-considering Feuerwerker's description of the intellectuals as seeing themselves as "exemplars."[97] Taking this concept, I argue that Liu and Ma are these exemplars in their respective films, not only in what they say but also in that they also represent a new model figure – the entrepreneur – thus introducing another class figure that has become the new emulatory figure for Reform-era China. Both Liu and Ma are financially successful, and these films glorify the entrepreneurial aspect of these artists' activities. For example, both are filmed as they travel abroad to exhibit their work – Liu in Bangkok, and Ma in Paris. Furthermore, they are also represented as financially successful in the mass media. As mentioned earlier, Liu's paintings have sold for millions of dollars, and as of 2013, Ma's "Exception" label had an annual revenue of over 900,000,000 Yuan (approximately $144,800,000 USD).[98] Therefore, they have become famous not only for their creations but also for the money they have earned through their talent, and they are filmed enjoying this success by traveling abroad, conducting business, and winning prizes. On the surface level, Liu and Ma are lauded for being artists in these films, but they are also serving as a synecdoche for the success of the market economy. Unlike the Maoist archetypes of the peasant and worker who are represented as in decline in Jia's earlier films, the artist/entrepreneur/intellectual has become successful in the Reform era. They speak for the masses, but do not share their problems. Although they bemoan the symptoms of the market economy, such as the growing gap between the rich and the poor and environmental consequences of development, they do not challenge it. This represents a shift in Jia's films towards valorizing entrepreneurs, which I will analyze in the next and final chapter.

Chapter 5

The Entrepreneur: From Crook to "New Reform Model"

Introduction

In Chapter 1, I wrote that, in Maoist rhetoric, ruins were seen as signs of development, Mao himself proclaiming "there is no construction without destruction ... Put destruction first, and in the process you have construction."¹ In Jia's films, the Maoist worker, peasant, and soldier figures are in ruins, while the entrepreneur has risen from their destruction. Thus, just as the worker class was created by the socialist state to industrialize the nation and help build the planned economy, now a class of entrepreneurs has been created during the Reform era to develop the market economy. In this chapter, I conclude by analyzing the figure of the entrepreneur and compare its two representations and structures of feeling. The first is that of a sinister criminal figure who is found primarily in the earlier films (1997–2006), but reappears (2013–2015), and the second is a benevolent *rushang* (儒商) – an intellectual turned businessperson, or a businessperson who has an intellectual's character – which appears in the films 2007–2012.² In this chapter, I posit that the figure of the threatening entrepreneur in the films concretizes the anxiety surrounding the Reform era, and that its presence evokes initial feelings of insecurity, reflecting confusion, economic abuses, and fear of change, while the *rushang* is a figure of hope and one that represents the benefits of Reform and is proffered as a possible solution to some of these problems. These contradictory representations evoke the varying feelings around social changes that have occurred during the past 35 years of economic reforms, and thus create their own different structures of feeling. As written earlier, Raymond Williams argues that structures of feeling emerge from a particular time, space, and generation, and capture the "feeling" of the age. In this chapter, I use this concept to examine how the different entrepreneur figures in the films capture the changing feelings around Reform, including Reform as threatening and Reform as opportunity. Furthermore, according to Williams, structures of feeling differ between generations, are connected to social changes, and are responses to the rise, fracture, or change of a class. Although class norms are broken during the transition, the class' previous affiliations are still retained but "articulated in radically new semantic figures."[3] In this chapter, I examine both kinds of entrepreneur figures in Jia's films, who are these "radically new semantic figures" that have arisen from the ruins of Maoist society.

History of the Class

In Chinese, the formal words for "entrepreneur" are 企业家 "enterprise/business person," and 事业家 "career person."[4] Their premodern antecedent was the merchant/trader (商), "the bottommost and least respected" of the class figures,[5] because business was historically seen "as a byproduct of random luck, rather than a virtue."[6] Although their wealth could buy them status,[7] "business success, though admired, did not elicit respect because businesspeople served themselves (and their families), while the Confucian literati served society."[8] After the Communist Revolution, business owners were classified as "capitalists" (资本家, 资产阶级), with subcategories for commercial, industrial, and compradore capitalists.[9] Carolyn Hsu explains that in order to redesign society during the Maoist era, the Party lowered the status of entrepreneurs and decreased the importance of economic capital, while simultaneously raising the status of workers and cadres and increasing the importance of their political capital.[10] Thus, a "new morality" was developed that advanced the notion that political capital was more valuable – and moral – than economic capital, placing the cadres at the top of the social order and the capitalists at the bottom.[11] To promote this new order, the state created moral narratives in which status was based on contributions to "the collective good," and advocated for state-led industrialization as "China's road to wealth and power" while denouncing capitalists for being "exploitative, selfish, and immoral."[12]

This negative representation of the entrepreneur continued into the early Reform period. Business was initially seen as "uncultured" and looked down upon, because it was believed that it was practiced by "rascals"[13] who became rich through corruption.[14] During this time, the self-employed or those with small businesses, known as the *getihu* (个体户), became negative stock characters in popular narratives, and were portrayed as having "low status, little education, and weak morals."[15] This negative representation continued into the mid-1990s, and those who left their work units and went "outside" (also called "jumping into the sea" (下海)) to find employment were often viewed in the same light.[16] Another negative term was the *xin furen* (新富人), the "nouveau riche" who were alleged to make their money from "questionable business practices and collaboration with corrupt officials."[17] By the late 1990s, however, the terms "businessperson" (商人) and "entrepreneur" (企业家) were seen favorably,[18] and such people were viewed as "the key driver[s] of growth."[19] This was followed by the Party's conceptual "rehabilitation" of this growing group. In 2001, it began to describe them as "private entrepreneurs" and not "capitalists," because they claimed that the new generation of entrepreneurs "were originally members of the working class, and work under a political system opposed to exploitation."[20] In this discursive shift, private entrepreneurs became China's new models in the new millennium, thus transitioning from embodying a structure of feeling of anxiety over the early Reform era to one evoking hope and inspiration for the later Reform period.

Representation

In 2000, Jiang Zemin advanced his theory of "Three Represents" (三个代表), which stipulated that the Party represented "the most advanced forces of production, the most developed culture, and the interests of the broadest masses," and was enacted to "legitimate" the Party's decisions during the Reform era and "revamp the theory and credibility of socialism."[21] For instance, the first "represent" focused on advancing Chinese science and technology, and was "seen as a theoretical justification for co-opting successful managers, private entrepreneurs and intellectuals into the Party," by focusing on the interests of the middle class rather than the traditional proletariat.[22]

To return to the propaganda poster that I analyzed in the introduction, "Chinese Are Amazing" (Figure 5.1) features the Maoist worker-peasant-soldier figures in the foreground, and the "new heroes" of the athlete, intellectual, and manager in the background. Similar to the peasant who holds the shaft of wheat, the soldier who carries the gun, and the athlete who carries her trophy, the entrepreneur carries the symbol of his trade – the cell phone. This figure is the one who has made the most "progress" in visual propaganda, as what was once the most despised figure is now a "new hero" that is lauded for his skills in developing the nation's industry. Not only is the figure celebrated in this image, but it has also been elevated to the extent that Lei Feng, the apocryphal selfless soldier that I wrote about in Chapter 3, has been advanced as the "possible patron saint of the private entrepreneurs,"[23] in an attempt to mitigate "the crasser aspects of the worship of money" that was believed to be corrupting larger society.[24]

In Jia's pre-2007 films, the entrepreneurs are corrupt or destructive figures. The term "entrepreneur" is often used as a euphemism for "criminal,"

Figure 5.1 "Chinese Are Amazing!" (中国人了不起). Yin, Hong and Ke Da (尹洪, 大可). Hubei: Hubei Meishu Chubanshe, 1996. *ChinesePosters.Net*. (1996). Accessed February 10, 2011. http://chineseposters.net/gallery/e13-747.php

and this figure is represented as using business as a smokescreen to conceal criminal activity. Furthermore, this figure is rarely punished for such transgressions. For instance, in *Xiao Wu*, Xiao Wu's ex-best friend Xiao Yong is a former pickpocket-turned-entrepreneur, lauded by the other characters as a successful businessman. However, this success is later revealed to be based on black market trading, cigarette smuggling, and running a prostitution ring. During a scene in which Xiao Yong is being interviewed for the local TV news, the reporter refers to him firstly as an "entrepreneur" (企业家) and then as a "director" (经理). Later in the film, the police chief informs Xiao Wu that Xiao Yong has been nominated as a county-level "model worker" (劳模, short for 劳动模范) due to his business success. This references the state's decision in the late 1980s to add entrepreneurs and managers to the list of people who could be nominated for this honorific originally bestowed upon members of the proletariat, such as the textile worker Huang Baomei in *I Wish I Knew*.[25]

While Xiao Yong is a thief-turned-businessman whose crimes are not acknowledged, Xiao Wu is a thief who remains a thief. For instance, Xiao Wu is denied an invitation to Xiao Yong's wedding because the groom wants to avoid all association with his criminal past. When Xiao Wu challenges one of Xiao Yong's lackeys with his knowledge of Xiao Yong's current criminal activities, the lackey replies that they are not crimes but are rather just examples of "free trade" (贸易) and the "entertainment industry" (娱乐业). In this way, his involvement in the "black economy" is semantically transformed into legal entrepreneurial activity. By revealing the circumstances Xiao Yong tries to hide, the film blurs the lines between criminal and entrepreneur, thievery and business, and casts doubt on the quick ascent of this figure during this era.

Similar corrupt figures are found in the films that follow, such as the entrepreneur who owns the private coalmine in *Platform*, the "Mongolian King Liquor" entrepreneur who has a gang and works as a pimp, the small business entrepreneur who runs a fashion counterfeiting workshop in *The World*, and the entrepreneur in *Still Life* who allegedly bankrupted the state-owned factory for her own financial gain. To examine some of these representations further, in *Platform*, Han Sanming applies for a job as a miner in a private coalmine, and must sign an employment contract. In the Peasant chapter, I examined this scene and argued that it emphasized Han's position as a sacrificial figure, and now will examine further the contract itself. As written in the contract and narrated by Han Sanming's cousin Cui Mingliang, "1. Life and death are questions of fate. I am willing to work in Gao's mine. Management accepts no blame for accidents." (生死有命 富贵在天. 本人自愿在高家庄煤矿采煤如遇万一, 与煤矿无任何关系). This statement not only attempts to remove all potential liability from the employer and the state's employment laws, but also shifts the onus towards "fate," by combining the rhetoric of traditional Chinese philosophy with contemporary business-speak. The axiom "Life and death are questions of fate" (生死有命富贵在天) appears in Confucius' *Analects*, Book 12, Verse 5 (written ca. 400 BCE), which states "Death and life are the decree of Heaven; wealth and rank depend upon the will of Heaven.'"[26] In the film, this ancient axiom of resignation to fate is merged with another phrase – "management not responsible" (无任何关系) – but this phrase is from the Reform era, and thus creates a monstrous hybrid of Confucian philosophy with neoliberal corporate jargon to reject both the entrepreneur's legal and ethical responsibilities towards their employees.

In *Unknown Pleasures*, Qiao San is a threatening and powerful entrepreneur who is depicted with money, henchmen, and even a gun. He owns Mongolian King Liquor, an alcohol company that is advertised throughout the film, but it appears to also be a front for his criminal operations because, similar to Xiao Yong in *Xiao Wu*, he also appears to run a smuggling and prostitution ring. He is a powerful figure. During a scene at a dance club, he has his minions hold down and slap Xiao Ji, the film's protagonist who had flirted with Qiao San's girlfriend Qiao Qiao, as Qiao San looks on in amusement. He later goes back to dance with Qiao Qiao, and the camera zooms in on his gun that he places on the dance floor, while he and the other patrons dance around it. In his final appearance in the film, he tries to prevent Qiao Qiao from leaving the Mongolian King Liquor entertainment tour bus by blocking its exit and pushing her back into her seat every time she makes an attempt to depart. In this long take which films the futility of her resistance against his power, the camera records a medium close-up of her face and torso, and jerks to the right when she tries to leave and whips back left when she is pushed back down by Qiao San. She attempts to leave eleven times; the camera lurches back and forth recording each of her futile efforts, and, by her eighth try, she is crying, yet he still forces her back. Later in the film, a character reveals that Qiao San has died in a highway accident, and this *deus-ex-machina* event is greeted with shock and relief. But, this sinister entrepreneur has not died from his criminal activities but from a common highway accident, and therefore has not been "punished" for his crimes – rather, his death appears as a fluke accident rather than a just reward.

In *Still Life*, the entrepreneur does not appear directly in the film but her presence as a threatening unseen force is felt. During the film, it is revealed that she and the manager of a local state-owned factory have allegedly conspired to bankrupt the factory in order to reap their own personal profits, regardless of the workers they have laid off and left destitute. In this scene, which I also analyzed in Chapter 1, a man accuses the factory manager that he "sold the factory for almost nothing to that Xiamen business woman," thus forcing the workers to find employment elsewhere, which resulted in one man's loss of an arm in a workplace accident and the rest of the employees not being paid their wages. This fictional situation actually reflects a larger recurring problem in the early days of Reform in which "bureaucratic profiteering" (*guangdao*, 官倒) appeared, a situation in which those with political or bureaucratic power used

142 Moving Figures

their influence and connections to become wealthy by leasing land rights to select developers at cheaper rates, who then quickly sold these rights to other developers at inflated prices.[27] This became one of the common "exit" strategies for SOEs to transition into private enterprise,[28] and thus the privatization of state-owned assets produced enormous wealth for a few, but resulted in massive unemployment for SOE workers.

The argument between the manager and the workers occurs under the portraits of Marx, Engels, Lenin, Stalin, and Mao, who are not looking down and observing the scene but are instead gazing away (Figure 5.2). Earlier, in Chapter 1, I examined this scene and argued that these portraits and their three-quarter socialist realist gaze looked towards a promising future seemingly over the horizon, "into the mists of the future perfect,"[29] but argued that the portraits' position high on the wall made them appear disconnected from the present and as if they were looking not to the "future perfect" but to the past. Now, I would like to return to this image and consider that due to their placement high on the wall, the portraits' gazes could also be seen as looking away, as if in shame over the current state of this former SOE at the hands of the manager and the "Xiamen business woman." If the portraits were placed directly before the audience and the portraits' eyelines were at the same level or slightly higher than the viewer and shared the same center of vision, the gazes would be inspirational, but with this higher placement their socialist realist gaze is not over the horizon and "in the mists of the future perfect," but rather looks away as if in embarrassment.

Figure 5.2 Argument in the manager's office in *Still Life* (screenshot)

Although the films shift towards valorizing the *rushang* figure, as found in *Useless*, *24 City*, and *Words of a Journey* (which I analyze below), the threatening entrepreneur does not disappear completely but returns in *A Touch of Sin* and *Mountains May Depart*. This return emphasizes the need to address the corruptive influence of this figure while also stressing the need for the *rushang*. As in *Still Life*, the *guangdao* bureaucratic profiteering situation reappears in *A Touch of Sin*'s first chapter, when it is revealed that the village chief conspired with Boss Jiao, the manager of the village's coalmine who purchased the mine and promised to transfer 40% of its annual profit to the village, but has since reneged on his promise. Boss Jiao appears to control the town, and numerous scenes in the film emphasize his power, such as his personal jet that he takes on trips to Hong Kong, his wife who is clothed in expensive brands, and the thugs that he commands to ensure that his power is not challenged. In one scene, a bus travels through the village to recruit people to greet Boss Jiao at the airport for a photo op, and all volunteers are offered a bag of flour for their service. When they arrive at the airport, a band has been assembled to play music, and school children have been prepared to present flowers to Boss Jiao and his wife. During the ceremony, Boss Jiao unironically declares the Maoist maxim "Let's Progress Together" (共同进步) to the assembled crowd. This phrase appears to be connected to the contemporary rhetoric surrounding the "Chinese Dream," which has been advanced by the Party and advocates that everyone is benefiting from Reform. For example, as stated by Cai Mingzhao (2013), Minister of the State Council Information Office, "The Chinese Dream in essence means the dream of the people who live in our great country at this great time to have the opportunity to enjoy a successful life, the opportunity to realize one's dream, and the opportunity to grow and progress together with the country."[30] But Boss Jiao's declaration of this platitude to the assembled crowd is incongruous, since his progress has earned him a private jet whilst theirs amounts to nothing more than a humble bag of flour. After this declaration, Dahai wades through the crowd and loudly congratulates Boss Jiao before asking him to sponsor his trip to Beijing so that he can file charges of corruption against him with the Discipline Commission. Dahai appears to be the only person in this film's chapter who is willing to stand up for the rest of the villagers, who appear to be too scared or apathetic to do anything about the situation. In response, Boss Jiao has one of his henchmen attack Dahai after the crowd has departed, and he repeatedly hits Dahai on the head with a small shovel until he begins to bleed and is finally knocked unconscious. This henchman is performed by Li Zhubin, who played the sinister Mongolian King liquor entrepreneur in *Unknown Pleasures*, and Shen Hong's husband Guo Bin, the soldier-turned-corrupt businessman in *Still Life*, thus not only reinforcing this actor's recurring role, but also this reappearing sinister figure in Jia's films.

Another malevolent entrepreneur is found in the film's third chapter, as a man who is involved in a racketeering operation that demands toll fees on a public road. He is performed by Wang Hongwei, the actor who played Xiao Wu, and thus his thieving has reappeared in Jia's oeuvre. He and his business partner go to a massage parlor/brothel, and demand sex from the receptionist, who is played by Zhao Tao. When she refuses, he slaps her more than twenty times with a stack of money. Similar to the scenes in *Unknown Pleasures* when Zhao Tao's character Qiao Qiao is being repeatedly forced back into her seat every time she tries to leave the bus, and when Bin Bin is repeatedly slapped by Qiao San's goons, this recurring slap is a declaration of power upon the powerless, and its repetition emphasizes this figure's utter domination and the willingness to use it to shame and control those whom they have power over.

A Touch of Sin, however, complicates the representation of the entrepreneur further by offering two business managers who are neither sinister nor *rushang*. Rather, they are neutral characters, and are found in the film's last chapter, which involves the young migrant worker Xiaohui. When his segment begins, he is working in a clothing factory. While chatting with his co-worker who is cutting fabric, the colleague is distracted and accidentally cuts his own thumb. Xiaohui is then brought in front of the factory's manager to explain his role in the accident. His manager is very strict, but does not fire Xiaohui. Rather, he tells him that the factory will pay for the medical bills, but Xiaohui's wage will be paid to his colleague until he is able to return to work. Later, Xiaohui begins a job at an electronics assembly plant and meets his Taiwanese boss who is friendly and chats casually with him, telling him employees are rewarded with trips to Taiwan. Unlike Boss Jiao, these two managers are not evil, but rather serve to develop Xiaohui's character, in that the first punishes him while the second offers potential opportunity. In this way, their neutral representation in the last part of the film emphasizes the sinister entrepreneurs in the first part, but also acknowledges the disparate nature of this class.

Finally, *Mountains May Depart* features a main character named Jinsheng who starts as a *getihu* but becomes increasingly malevolent as the film develops. The film is divided into three time periods: 1999, 2014, and 2025. In 1999, Jinsheng owns a gas station and likes to show off his wealth – he brags about how much money he has made so far and drives a sporty imported German car – and thus his friends teasingly refer to him as "boss Zhang" (张总), and as an "elite"/"high-end personage" (高端人士). He and another man named Liangzi are competing for the affections of a woman named Tao. In an attempt to neutralize his rival, Jinsheng buys the mine that Liangzi works in, and offers him a job managing it. When Jiangzi refuses, Jinsheng fires him, and Liangzi is forced to pack his bag and leave the workplace dormitory. Jinsheng's vendetta does not end there; frustrated that Liangzi is still pursuing Tao, Jinsheng asks his assistant to procure a gun, but the assistant apologizes that he cannot. Later, we discover that Jinsheng took dynamite from the mine and planned to blow up Liangzi, but his plan is thwarted by Tao's discovery of the cache. It is only when Jinsheng and Tao become engaged that the rivalry ends, and Liangzi leaves town and becomes a *mingong*. Later, Tao and Jinsheng marry and have a son, whom Jinsheng names Dollar after the US currency (transliteration of 到乐), because Jinsheng promises "to give my baby many American dollars!" In the film's next temporal chapter, which begins in 2014, we learn that Jinsheng has moved to Shanghai to work in venture capital, and has become, in the words of an ex-employee, a "capitalist" (资本家). Not only is he much more wealthy and powerful, he has divorced Tao and has sole custody of their son, who is estranged from his mother. In the film's final temporal chapter, which begins in 2025, we learn that Jinsheng has changed his name to Peter, and he and Dollar now live in Australia. In one scene, a now-elderly Peter is reminiscing with a group of Chinese expats about the anticorruption movement of 2014, which refers to "Operation Fox Hunt," a state-led initiative that targeted corrupt officials that had fled China with their wealth to avoid prosecution.[31] They recall the scandal surrounding Mr. Xing, which probably refers to Xing Libin, the founder of the Shanxi-based coal-mining firm Liansheng Energy who had stayed in Hong Kong while his company was being investigated by the Chinese authorities, and was later arrested when he returned to Shanxi.[32] During the conversation, we learn that Peter has also been in hiding in Australia for ten years, and therefore appears to be another corrupt fugitive, but one that has never been caught. When another man asks him if he will go back, Peter noncommittally replies "maybe later." Later, we see that his coffee table at home is littered with guns and ammunition, and hear him complain "I now have a pile of guns, but no one to fire them at!" (Figure 5.3). Thus, Peter has transitioned from being a *getihu* to a corrupt and sinister figure who is unrepentant and threatening.

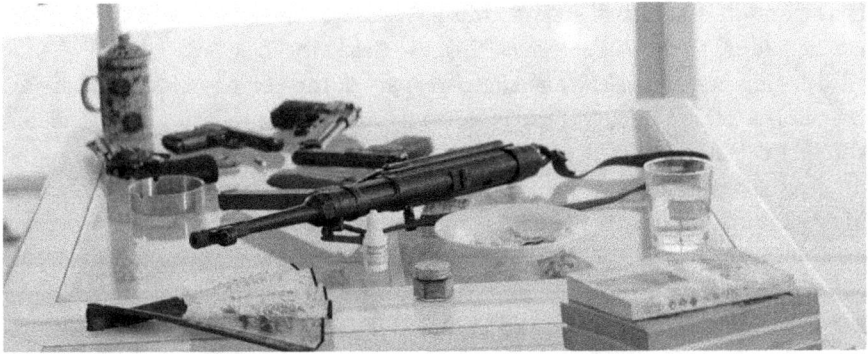

Figure 5.3 Coffee table with guns in *Moutains May Depart* (screenshot)

But, although he is a fearful character, he is also pitiful; he appears to be separated or divorced, lives alone with his son whom he cannot communicate with, except in short messages using Google Translate (since Dollar can speak only English and Peter can speak only Chinese), and it is apparent that his ambition and wealth have brought him only unhappiness.

Turning to the representation of the benevolent entrepreneur, as noted earlier, entrepreneurs were conceptually "rehabilitated" by the Party in the 1990s, and by 2001 were described positively as "private entrepreneurs."[33] Famous foreign entrepreneurs such as Bill Gates and Lee Iacocca became very popular in the 1990s in China, because they were valorized not just for their economic success but because they became successful in technological fields due to their education and knowledge; unlike the "crooked" *getihu* or "self-employed individuals" that exploit others, these entrepreneurs "serve society and the greater good."[34] Therefore, these foreign entrepreneurs were viewed as *rushang* because they used technology and knowledge to develop businesses, and become positive new role models that echoed the Confucian scholar/intellectuals who "were infused with morality and concern for serving society."[35] This shift was also found in politics. For example, entrepreneurs are now eligible for Party-appointed "model worker" awards. These awards were initiated in 1950 to celebrate primarily manual laborers, such as the textile worker Huang Baomei who appears in *I Wish I Knew*. During the Maoist era, their work ethic and contributions to the nation were envisaged "to inspire the masses and inculcate such virtues as hard work, modesty and patriotism,"[36] structures of feeling that defined the class and the era. After Reform began, however, the award started to honor entrepreneurs and managers, who thus became the era's "new" model workers. For example, more than 340 entrepreneurs and managers were elected in 1989, and 409 heads of enterprises were appointed in 1995.[37] Furthermore, in 2005, the model worker title was awarded to the billionaire Liu Yonghao, a chicken farmer turned agribusiness mogul who in 2013 was worth $3.3 billion USD,[38] and the basketball star Yao Ming,[39] who was the eighth wealthiest celebrity according to the 2012 Forbes "Chinese Celebrity" List.[40]

Turning first to *Useless*, although it is part of the "Trilogy of Artists" series, the subject of the film, Ma Ke, is not only an artist/intellectual but is also a successful fashion entrepreneur. Continuing the analysis that I began in the intellectual chapter, I now focus on the business and entrepreneurial aspects of Ma Ke's work. I argue that she is proffered as a *rushang* via her appearance, her environment, and her philosophies in *Useless*. For instance, she appears as an ascetic who wears neutral colors, fashions her hair in a simple braid, and does not wear makeup or jewelry, and is filmed in her idyllic rural atelier that she has retreated to live and work, in a manner reminiscent of the scholar gentry of yore. During her interviews, she projects her fashion design not as a product but as a philosophy, distinguishing herself from the negatively represented *getihu*. In this way, hers is the first representation in Jia's films of the entrepreneur as a benevolent, philosophical, and anti-materialist *rushang*, who embodies this positive structure of feeling for the entrepreneur figure.

Ma owns two labels: "Exception de Mixmind" and "Useless." Exception is the ready-to-wear line, and Useless is a collection of one-of-a-kind textile art pieces, which she created after being invited to present at Paris Fashion Week, Autumn/Winter 2007 (Haute Couture).[41] Ma's entrepreneurial skills and business acumen are lauded by Christine Tsui, who explains that Ma's "Exception" label has become an "icon" for Chinese designer brands, due to the fact that the label "was the first Chinese fashion brand featuring an obvious designer's temperament rather than having a typical 'Chinese' flavour," and also because of its high annual revenue of over 100 million Yuan in 2009, which Tsui refers to as "a level deemed the pinnacle in designer brands."[42] Because of its success, Ma Ke hired young designers to continue the label, and was therefore able to focus on her art and begin Useless as her "retirement project."[43] Her brand has also exponentially increased in value; as of 2013, Exception's worth has multiplied nine-fold and, as mentioned in Chapter 4, is now estimated at 900 million Yuan.[44] Finally, the label has received additional positive press because Peng Liyuan, the renowned People's Liberation Army singer and wife of CCP leader Xi Jinpeng, has also been photographed wearing it.[45]

In the film, Ma's brands are projected as philosophies, and thus the film reinforces the idea of her label as a synecdoche for these *rushang* ideals and structure of feeling. For example, Ma advances "Useless" not as a product, but rather as a vehicle for the "values of other times" and the "values for the future."[46] These sentiments are not only felt by Ma, but are also reported by Jia. For instance, in the press kit, he describes the brand as an "idea" that challenges "China's rapid development," as well as "the obliteration of memory, the over-exploitation of natural resources, and the speed at which all this is happening."[47] Furthermore, in the film, Ma describes Exception as a "protest" to the "vacuous" products produced in China that had been flooding the market, and on her website declares that "Useless" is a language and a media of communication, stating "I believe clothing could be a specific creative language, and has infinite possibilities for communicating ideas and transmitting thoughts, for inspiring you and shaping your behavior."[48] In the film, she also argues that her brand has a "spirit, soul and values . . . like an independent person," and believes that this quality is a result of its artisanal production. In these statements, Ma claims that objects have memories and a spirit, imbuing these hand-made objects with powers that are not extended to mass-produced objects. In this way, Ma as artist/intellectual/philosopher/entrepreneur is the perfect model for the *rushang* figure, who emphasizes the greater philosophical, emotional, and intellectual importance of her clothing line.

In order to stress the philosophical significance of her brand further, in the film, her interviews, and on her company's website (www.wuyonguseless.com), she also presents herself as a *rushang* who is concerned with the costs of China's fast-paced economic development. In this narrative, she is emphatically anti-materialistic and environmentally conscientious; for instance, she warns "after 200 years of industrial over-development we have to face a deepening environmental crisis caused by short-sightedness and a radicalization of human activity ... Our resources are running out, while our desires are proliferating."[49] These philosophies are best illustrated in the following segment in the film, which contrasts her idyllic rural atelier with a Louis Vuitton store in a high-end shopping district in urban Guangzhou, which is constructed of glass and chrome with fancy advertisements for Prada and Dior in the windows. One scene explores a group of young women dressed in luxurious branded clothing. They are members of the store's "Friends of Louis Vuitton Club," who are relaxing, socializing, and drinking cocktails in the store's lounge. An exploratory lens examines this group and records their conversation, but this shot rarely shows their heads; instead, its close-ups focuses on their torsos, feet and accessories, all conspicuously marked with the Louis Vuitton label. One woman demands in a petulant voice that the shop assistant bring her something "more refined," and he suggests Prada, stating that their designs are "very philosophical" (很有哲学概念的) The camera roams amongst the assembled group, studying their shoes and handbags (Figures 5.4 and 5.5), and again the male store assistant's voice is heard, declaring "Since the products sold in China are

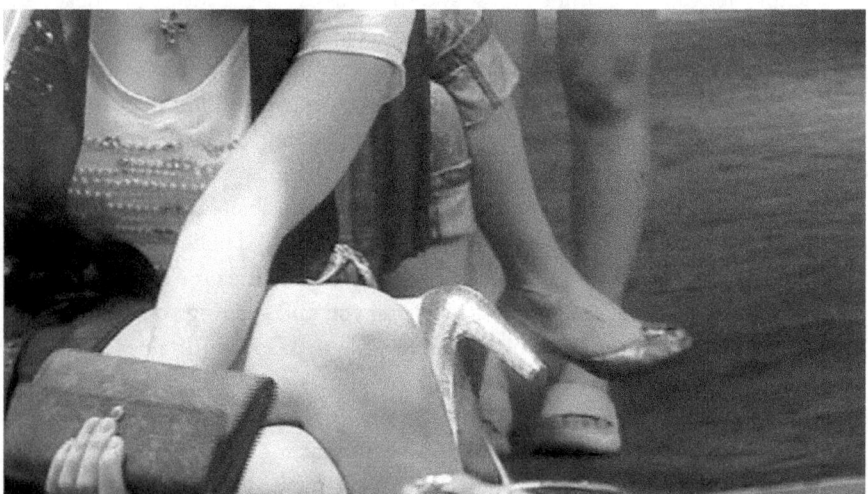

Figure 5.4 Shoppers at Louis Vuitton in *Useless* (screenshot)

Figure 5.5 Shoppers at Louis Vuitton in *Useless* (screenshot)

all mass-produced in China, they are quite low-quality. They don't feel right." The scene then cuts to a shot from outside and the reflection of the shoppers in the store window before cutting to a scene observing Ma walking with her dog in the forest surrounding her atelier.

This scene in the Louis Vuitton store is a direct critique of materialism and, less directly, non-patriotism. First, it focuses on the shallow materialism and conspicuous consumption of the wealthy as they shop for foreign luxury products. This focus is sharply juxtaposed with what the *rushang* Ma has been arguing against earlier in the film – namely, the destructiveness of consumption. Jia also reinforced her statements in favor of artisanal production and against materialism in an interview, stating:

> In recent years, "fashion" has become a buzz-word in China. The nouveau-riche class is wild about such brands as Louis Vuitton, Armani and Prada. But many people buy these brands because they're famous and expensive, not because they appreciate the designs. And many young people spend way beyond their means in buying these brands, which suggests that ostentatious wealth has become the most important – maybe the only – index of a person's social value.[50]

This anti-materialism also appears to be part of a larger discursive shift against materialism associated with artistic and intellectual circles in China. For example, the art curator Huang Du posits that the market economy's replacement of the socialist planned economy has increased "materialistic desire," which "is an indication of 'spiritual paleness,'"⁵¹ while Dai Jinhua argues that commercialism has replaced communist ideals and thus "material consumption has now become heaven on earth in China."⁵² This intellectual environment valorizes Ma's designs by stressing that they are philosophical, not materialistic; are Chinese, not foreign; and have "spirit, soul, and values," as opposed to being shallow and materialistic.

But, although Ma denounces materialism and commodity fetishism, at the same time she is the obvious beneficiary of it. Her philosophies and anti-materialism obfuscate the obviously materialistic nature of her work by positioning her production as "art," and spin her brand as a "philosophy," which is similar to the language employed by the shop assistant and the customer who describe Prada as "philosophical." Thus, this scene and its critique of the shoppers' pseudo-philosophical materialism also can be seen as questioning Ma's claims as well through its use of the exploratory lens. Furthermore, simply having and marketing a brand requires capitalism and commodity fetishism, but this is not addressed in the film or in her interviews. As Karl Marx argues, commodities are fetishized under capitalism when their use-value (the object's ability to perform a task – its utility) is replaced by its exchange-value (the value that the market places on an object – its price).⁵³ In this concept, a handbag has the use-value of holding its owner's possessions, but its exchange-value is based on the label. For example, a generic handbag sold in a Chinese market could cost a few Yuan, but one from Ma's "Exception" label sells for 2,500 Yuan ($400 USD) due to its label,⁵⁴ undermining her claims that her brand is "spiritual." However, she mounts a defense against attacks, arguing that her designs are not commodities but are rather art that transcends the commodity, stating: "the difference is the *reasons* why they are created – meaning their origination. Those created for faith and joy are art; for fame and benefits are commodity. I define success as *not* creating for selling and fame."⁵⁵

The paradoxes and contradictions of Ma's claims and practices also emphasize the discordant characteristics of the *rushang* entrepreneur figure, which combines contrasting qualities of the scholar/aesthete with the merchant/entrepreneur. For example, she has become wealthy and famous because of the value of her labels. Her company earns over 900 million Yuan per year, and its success has allowed her to follow her artistic pursuits.⁵⁶ It is precisely her wealth that has permitted this *rushang* figure to further separate herself from morally-debasing commerce, a position which also harkens back to an earlier Confucian disdain for money. Furthermore, Jia is not innocent either; rather, he has been described as "a savvy investor with a diverse portfolio that includes businesses in the entertainment industry, hotels, restaurants, spirits distilleries and even coal mines," but when asked if he was concerned at being referred to as a businessman, replied "in modern times we are all part of some form of commercial activity, unless we choose to retreat into a remote mountain forest."[57]

This representation of Ma as a *rushang* is not ironic. Not only is Ma's philosophical and anti-materialistic stance in the film celebrated, but Exception also has a product placement a year later in *24 City* as the provider of Zhao Tao's clothing (as well as the only wardrobe credit in the entire film), and is also listed as the sole "wardrobe provider" in *Mountains May Depart*. Furthermore, it is significant that the "Friends of Vuitton" are not discussing Ma's products, but foreign luxury items. Although these are hailed as being superior to "low quality" Chinese products by the shop assistant, the film contrasts this with Ma's patriotism and her desire to create a "Chinese" art. As argued in Chapter 4, this rhetoric appears to be part of a larger contemporary patriotic discourse regarding consumption, and specifically the "Chinese Elements" movement. Dating from 2006, the same year that the film was released, the "International Contest for Chinese Elements in Creative Work" was convened "to signify the formal campaign among China's marketing circle for gaining back the lost national culture in the modernizing consumer society."[58] This movement was a reaction to the earlier drive in the 1980s to "learn from the West," and echoes the 1905 "National Products Movement," in that both made "the consumption of national products a fundamental part of Chinese citizenship" by wedding patriotism and consumption.[59] Therefore, Ma's statements, the film's exploratory lens, and "Chinese Elements" are part of a much earlier narrative enabling her (and the film) to represent herself as a patriotic *rushang* working to enhance China's reputation abroad.

However, the second half of the film diverges from the focus on Ma to feature three rural tailors who are struggling. One left the profession and became a miner because he could not compete with cheap mass-produced clothing, and the businesses of the other tailors are similarly threatened. This second half reflects the current complicated relationship of the textile industry with contemporary Chinese society, whereas one "tailor" – Ma Ke – can become a millionaire, while another loses his business and must work in the mines to support his family. But this second half is not an ironic view of Ma's earlier interviews. Rather, it shifts the film from serving solely as a vehicle for Ma's work and philosophies to directly examining the materialist nature of clothing production and the impact of market reforms on the people. It does not contradict Ma's statements, but reinforces the idea of the *rushang* as an antidote for some of the problems of the market economy.

The final interview in *24 City* is with Su Na, a small business owner/operator born in 1982 and performed by the actress Zhao Tao. She represents another kind of *rushang*. Unlike Ma Ke, she does not speak about her philosophies

Figure 5.6 Su Na's face emerging from the debris in *24 City* (screenshot)

during her much shorter three and a half-minute interview. Instead, she narrates her memories of growing up in the factory and talks about her family, thus providing a friendly and emotional, rather than philosophical, facet to the contemporary *rushang* – a benign structure of feeling for this benevolent entrepreneur figure.

Su Na's interview serves as the finale for the film. Before it begins, a long take records a factory building's collapse, which causes a large cloud of dust to billow towards the camera and obfuscate the scene. This destruction is accompanied by a choir singing the "Internationale," and W.B. Yeats' poem "Spilt Milk" is projected across the screen: "Things we have thought and done must ramble and thin out like milk spilt upon a stone."[60] This composite metaphor for the fading of memory, the passing of time, and death synthesizes the film's larger theme of commemoration. This long take dissolves into the next, and from this grey cloud of destruction slowly emerges a face. As the image becomes clearer, it is revealed to be Su Na putting on her makeup in a mirror (Figure 5.6). She packs her bags, leaves her parent's apartment in the factory workers' neighborhood, and drives away in her Volkswagen New Beetle. During her commute, she is filmed talking to one of her clients on her cell phone, saying "The stuff you want is too expensive, who can afford it?" and "Who can afford to show off like you?." She laughs and teases yet, at the same time, compliments her clients on their expensive tastes and wealth. This scene cuts to a long shot of a woman posing for her photograph against a field of yellow flowers in bloom. The camera begins a slow pan to the right, finally stopping at Su's parked car (Figure 5.7). Su is sitting in the passenger seat and leaning out of the car's open window, resting on her folded arms. In the distance, a new high-rise development – perhaps 24 City – is being constructed. It then cuts to a medium close-up of her face. Like the woman posing by the field, she is smiling, as if waiting for a snapshot. This begins Su's friendly snapshot moving portrait, and in this duration of tensed time, she appears amiable and welcoming, the essence of the benign entrepreneur. This impression continues into the interview that follows.

During her interview, Su describes herself as being quite shallow as a teenager and young adult. After failing the college entrance exams, she just

Figure 5.7   Su Na in her car in *24 City* (screenshot)

socialized with her friends and went from boyfriend to boyfriend without any real ambition. She refused to work in the factory because the work did not appeal to her; rather, she describes it as menial and dehumanizing. She explains that she became a personal shopper (买手) who travels to Hong Kong every two weeks to buy for her rich clients in Chengdu, stating "Rich women with time on their hands . . . they like fashion but don't have the energy to buy it, so they hire me to buy for them." She gets paid a 1,000 Yuan "finders fee" per item, which, compared to the 2011 average monthly salary in Sichuan of 3,160 Yuan, is particularly impressive.[61] She also boasts about meeting a man on a plane who wants to hire her to manage his revolving restaurant on top of Chengdu's "Panda TV Tower," stating that, with this new job, she might become a "powerful woman" (女强人), a positive term used "to describe those women who have achieved success in the traditionally male-dominated professions such as politics, business, science and technology."[62] Hers is a tale of success through hard work, determination, and the opportunities provided by the Reform economy.

Although Su Na has become a successful middle-class entrepreneur who operates her own business as a personal shopper for wealthy clients, she was born into a worker family and remains emotionally connected to the worker class. This connection is emphasized not only by what she says during her interview but also its cinematography. As with the previous interviews in *24 City*, the director or cameraperson is not seen. But, unlike the other interviews, we hear a male voice from behind the camera that might be Jia Zhangke's. When she talks about the commission that she earns, this person interrupts her monologue with the exclamation "quite good!" (挺好的). She responds by laughing, and then asks him if he sees the Chengdu Radio and TV Tower in the distance, before segueing to her next memory. This exchange brings a sense of spontaneity and "realness" to this interview, because it makes this dialogue feel unscripted and as if we are experiencing a conversation taking place. Additionally, it is this intimate small talk about her life that makes her so likable, particularly when she starts talking about her feelings towards her family. For example, she explains how she did not want to go home after her father's retirement because she "felt the mood of failure and depression," and later underscores how she was once self-absorbed but that her final realization of her parents' sacrifice for her has inspired her to change her ways and assume her filial responsibilities. Thus, she has matured and become a *rushang*.

Although she makes her living as a personal shopper for Chengdu's nouveau riche, Su Na is not represented as materialistic. She does not drive a flashy car or wear ostentatious jewelry, and like Ma Ke in *Useless*, she is also dressed simply and is unadorned. In fact, as mentioned previously, the film credits indicate that her clothing is provided by Ma's Exception label, linking her to Ma's brand and philosophies. Furthermore, an anti-materialism similar to Ma's is emphasized during her interview, when she explains that she has the car only so that she can acquire clients and not feel embarrassed in front of the wealthy women for whom she works. Thus, although she may be a buyer for the shallow nouveau riche she, like Ma, is not shallow but is a *rushang* with more "depth."

Su Na also burnishes her image by expressing a filial desire to help her parents. During her interview, she describes how her mother was laid off from a factory that made telegraph poles. Su recalls how she had to go and look for her at work once, but had trouble finding her because everyone was dressed in the same uniforms. After speaking of her parents' struggles in the postsocialist era, she begins to cry, declaring: "The thing I want the most now is to make a lot of money and buy them an apartment in '24 City.'" Between sobs, she adds, "I know it will cost a lot, but I can do it; I'm the daughter of a worker" (我是工人的女儿). Her evocation of the Maoist past in her final statement connects with the earlier concept of "marketized nostalgia" that I discussed in Chapter 1, in that similar "nostalgic sentiments . . . regains harmony and continuity in the name of the individual, or consumerism."[63] In this final statement and the emotions it evokes, she connects the Maoist communal past of the factory with the individual capitalist present of the factory-turned-private-residential-complex of the film, which has been funded by the developer, thus using this marketized nostalgia to promote the development.

Su's tearful performance in this cathartic scene is amplified by the fading light, as if the sun is setting not only on the factory, but the past that is, in the Yeats quote that began Su's segment, the "milk spilt upon a stone." Similar to the change in light, emotions also vary with her memories of her childhood, the affable "small talk" with the person behind the camera, and her final remembrance of more painful memories. This complex range of emotions makes her feel like a "real" person, perhaps even a friend. As her story becomes increasingly intimate and melancholic, elements like her declaration of Confucian filial responsibility and her evocation of the Maoist Worker class spirit of hard work and determination build a moving cinematic experience that reportedly brought a Chinese audience to tears during a screening.[64] Catharsis is the "process of releasing,"[65] and this final scene provides such a "release." Tears are not only an index of suffering; rather, Béla Balázs equates watching tears fall like "the surgeon who holds a twitching heart in his hand, counting every last beat."[66] Thus, through these tears, the *rushang* figure of Su Na becomes the emotional bridge allowing the audience to mourn the passing of the Maoist worker.

In the film's final scene, Su is standing on top of a high building (Figure 5.8). Perhaps this is the revolving restaurant that she was offered a job managing, or one of 24 City's new buildings. She looks out at the city skyline in broad daylight, the wind ruffling her clothes and hair. Her brows are knit in concern as she looks into the distance. She takes a deep breath, and the camera slowly pans to follow her pensive gaze, revealing the cityscape and offering a reflective moment of tensed time to digest the interview's earlier emotional release. It also emphasizes Su's thoughtful determination. In the scene before Su's interview, the factory was being dismantled and the sun was setting over it, but now a new day has broken and construction has arisen from the destruction. As I argued in Chapter 1, *24 City* mourns the death of the Maoist state, but does not seek to

Figure 5.8 Su Na's gaze in *24 City* (screenshot)

reconstruct it. The film's final interview with Su Na presents this *rushang* as arising from the ashes of the socialist past – the construction from the destruction – a metaphor that is poignantly expressed in her face emerging from the cloud of dust as the factory is torn down at the beginning of the interview, her friendly look in her moving portrait, and finally her determined gaze over Chengdu's cityscape. Hers is the face of the new, benign entrepreneurial class in China that has been created through the process of the past's destruction, and is a symbol of how the socialist era is being reconstructed to serve another, noble purpose – the continuing development of the nation.

So far, I have examined the artist Ma Ke and the anti-materialistic and patriotic philosophies she advances, and the emotionally engaging interview with the daughter of workers-turned-entrepreneur Su Na, and have argued that they both construct a positive *rushang* figure and embody the positive structure of feeling associated with this group. Now I turn to *Words of a Journey* and argue that the interviews with the *rushang* in these films project them as inspirational figures. They evoke the sense of possibility that the era brings, emphasizing individual initiative and individual effort for individual success. Jia Zhangke was the executive producer of the project, and directed two of the film's interviews. The first is with the property developer and Small Office Home Office (SOHO) China Chief Executive Officer (CEO) Pan Shiyi, and the second is with Cao Fei, an e-commerce entrepreneur and founder of 371maicai.com. Both narrate stories of success through adversity, and stress the importance of Confucian filial piety, independence, hard work, perseverance, and self-improvement. Below, I examine what these entrepreneurs say, arguing that their stories of struggle and success are inspirational testimonies that urge the viewer to succeed in the Reform era, but that the Confucian attributes that they evoke also temper this financial success and represent them as *rushang*. Finally, I consider how they are not only representations of this *rushang* figure, but how they also advertise it because *Words of a Journey* originated as a series of television and web-based advertisements, each lasting approximately three and a half minutes.[67]

Words of a Journey was sponsored by the whiskey manufacturer Johnnie Walker as part of their Chinese advertisement campaign. It is composed of twelve television and online advertisements, consisting of interviews with "outstanding persons from the fields of finance, culture and social community," who discuss the "difficulties they have confronted and their wisdom and courage in overcoming the barriers."[68] The "Keep Walking" campaign was created for Johnnie Walker in 1999 by the firm Bartle Bogle Hegarty (BBH).[69] It was activated in more than 120 markets and, as of 2008, had been responsible for $2,210,000,000 USD in incremental sales.[70] The Chinese advertisement campaign was launched on 5 January 2011,[71] and began with a broadcast of Pan Shiyi's interview on Chinese national television, while the other eleven mini-documentaries that made up the campaign were later aired online.[72] "Keep Walking" was designed to appeal "to China's aspirational consumers," by "focusing on individuality and celebrating modern-day pioneers in China," and constructing "a brand associated with following one's dreams."[73] Therefore, they decided to base their marketing campaign on the idea of "personal progress,"[74] because according to a BBH report, "the most power [sic.] demonstration of masculine success was not material wealth but a thirst for self-improvement," because "A man was judged a success not by where he was, but where he was going."[75]

Pan is one of China's most famous billionaires. He is a social media guru, has written several books, and was nominated as deputy to Beijing's People's Congress in 2007. Born in 1963 in Tianshui, a poor area in Gansu province, he graduated from the Beijing Petroleum Institute in 1982, and then worked for the Ministry of the Petroleum Industry before quitting to work in real estate, first in Hainan and then later in Beijing. He co-founded SOHO China in 1995 with his wife Zhang Xin, the company's chairperson who was educated in Hong Kong and England, and appears briefly during his interview. They are a modern day "power couple," forming a marital and business union that is described by Forbes as "a fairy tale that combined Pan's grassroots as a native-born son of humble beginnings who became involved in developing modern housing projects . . . [with] Zhang's smarts and worldliness, drawn from her years of overseas experiences."[76] Similarly, the SOHO China website describes him as "a public role model and a star in the eyes of the media," and states:

> To many people in China, Pan Shiyi's life is a modern day success story of a young man who grew up in an impoverished area of Western China and who was able to advance to the forefront of an entire industry by following his dreams, exhibiting strong business savvy and entrepreneurial spirit, and seizing the opportunities made possible by China's Reform and Opening.[77]

Finally, Pan Shiyi was described by the *South China Morning Post* as "a sort of model worker for the new entrepreneur in China – a Lei Feng of the capitalist era, if you will,"[78] likening him to the aforementioned apocryphal model soldier who became famous for his selflessness, enthusiasm, and good deeds, and thus associating Pan with the structures of feeling of this noble figure.

In *Words of a Journey*, Pan's interview depicts him in multiple environments; first overseeing a construction site, then examining crops, and next in SOHO's glossy showroom, where the speaking part of his interview is filmed. These locations represent him as someone who is industrious and successful, but still attached to his rural roots. During his interview, he emphasizes his rags-to-riches story by stressing his poverty and his determination to succeed – structures of feeling of hard work and determination associated with this entrepreneur figure.

For example, he explains that before he moved to Hainan in 1988 for work, he would always go home for New Year with his parents. But in 1990 he did not have enough money to go back, so he spent the evening lonely, homesick, and poor. During his interview, he stresses his rural roots, stating "I did all kinds of work in the countryside," which is illustrated by shots of him walking through the fields, stopping to inspect the harvest by running his hand through a bag of grain, and visiting peasants in what is presumably his home village. This rural environment is juxtaposed with other scenes of him working with an iPad in the hyper-modern SOHO showroom, and various others depicting him as an urban cosmopolitan. This representation is even repeated when he visits the rural village, still clothed in his suit, and he incongruously wears it during this stroll through the fields. Overall, Pan appears as not just a peasant who has transformed into an entrepreneur in the Reform era, but also a *rushang*, who is benevolent, thoughtful, and modest. In the last part of his interview, he states, "material wealth is a kind of wealth, but it's certainly not everything," and in the final lines of the interview, he introduces himself and humbly describes his profession not as a real estate tycoon but simply as someone who builds housing in Beijing.

Although not a successful billionaire like Pan, Cao Fei is twenty years younger. He is represented as a heroic, adventurous, hard working, and driven e-commerce entrepreneur who, although he has faced failure, will ultimately prevail. Similar to Pan's interview, Cao Fei's segment also offers a multi-faceted view of his living and working environments, and records him in a market, on the street, at home, at work, and in his car. It begins with a shaky handheld shot as he walks through a vegetable market and stops to touch and smell the produce, offering an element of "realness" to his interview. Cao narrates that, after graduating from university, he and other graduates started a company selling vegetables online, called "Vegetable Life." This venture caused much excitement, and although it failed, it did not stop him from trying again. Like the film's English slogan "Keep Walking," (in Chinese "always onwards" (永远向前)), he has gone on to initiate yet another e-commerce venture, sagely declaring "I still have time to struggle, to keep moving forward until I gain success." Near the end of his interview, he is shown pushing his car on the highway after it stalls. He restates his commitment to persevere until he is successful, and then roars – a heroic finale that concludes his advertisement.

Cinematic Tropes: Advertisements and the Close-up

In order to analyze how the *rushang* are produced cinematically as the era's new model of emulation, I consider the use of facial close-ups to enhance intimacy with the viewer. They contribute to the structure of feeling of personal development associated with this figure by producing an inspirational quality through the use of facial close-ups of entrepreneurs to emphasize their positive characteristics and the homilies that they declare. These advertisements are similar to the promotion of class models during the Maoist era, because both deployed techniques intended to effect a certain reaction, be it a change in belief or interest in a product or service. For instance, as Christian Henriot and Wen-hsin Yeh point out, "advertising and propaganda represent two poles of mass communication that share the same purpose – to condition people to act and even think in a way that responds positively to the commercial or political interests behind the message."[79]

Words of a Journey is literally a series of TV and web-based advertisements. This is not Jia's only advertising work; he has also directed commercials for companies such as Olay and China Mobile.[80] Furthermore, although Jia's other films are not actual advertisements, some of them were co-produced or sponsored by various people, companies, and organizations that derive publicity benefits from them. For example, Ma Ke's business partner and co-founder of Exception de Mixmind, Mao Jihong, was one of the executive producers of *Useless*,[81] and the label has a product placement in *24 City*. Furthermore, *24 City* was sponsored and co-produced by China Resources Land Limited[82] – which was also the real estate developer of "24 City" – and the film is not named after the factory, but the luxury entertainment and residential complex that is replacing it.[83] In this light, the film also advertised the development. For example, one scene in the film is a news broadcast that eagerly reports that the site is being redeveloped into a "modern, living community" (一座现代的城市社区), and one of the interviewees is later filmed touring the development's showroom. Additionally, in her interview, Su Na also declares her intention to purchase a condo in *24 City* for her parents as proof of her filial piety and work ethic. Thus, the film records the factory's process of redevelopment into a private commercial and residential complex – the privatization (and, in this case, the condo-ization) of the Maoist past.[84]

As Jia Zhangke remarks regarding *Words of a Journey*, interviews with the entrepreneurs offer models for emulation: "Each film tells the unique story of one person, where they came from, how they got to where they are today and what it is that inspires them to do what it is they do. Our hope is that these stories will inspire people to reflect upon and tell their own stories."[85] Not only does this hearken back to the Maoist class models, but it also appears to be connected to the larger contemporary Chinese discursive "turn" towards bettering oneself through increasing one's *suzhi*, or "human quality," and thus evokes a structure of feeling associated with this figure and this era. This process has been intimately attached to the *rushang* figure. In her analysis of the *rushang*,

Carolyn Hsu states that the advent of the *suzhi* discourse allowed for the *rushang* to appear –"the educated, cultured, 'scientific,' and moral businessperson who served China's national interest through his or her success on the global market."[86] Thus, *suzhi* began to be used to demarcate the *rushang* who had "quality" from the rest, and "to be a person of quality also meant to be a person of culture (*wenhua*) in the Confucian sense."[87]

The interviews are inspirational not only because of what they say, but also because of how they are cinematically constructed. The interviews in *Words of a Journey* are very similar to those in *24 City*. They are each 3–5 minute-long pseudo-monologues in which the interviewer is never seen or heard and the only remaining trace of their presence is via the interviewees' eyelines and their address to the interviewer. As noted in the chapter on the intellectual, these elements position the viewer and interviewee seemingly "in direct relation" with one another, heightening the viewer's connection with the speaker. However, the interviews in *Words of a Journey* are much more fast-paced with frequent cuts and location changes, and the eye is constantly being engaged by this rapid movement. For instance, although Pan's segment is only two and a half minutes, there are 42 different cuts, and in Cao's three minute and twenty second segment, there are 40 cuts. Comparatively, the interviews with the workers in *24 City* are only slightly longer, but they are composed mostly of long takes interjected with intertitles, and they have between only four and seven cuts per interview. During the segments in *Words of a Journey*, the camera is continually shifting between close-ups, medium shots, and long shots, and alternating between being stationary and moving, sometimes making small motions even during these short takes. The overall effect of both Pan and Cao's interviews are that they are much more frenetic than those of the previous films, and the numerous cuts and the moving camera work to keep the viewer's eye engaged while the advertisement's "message" is punctuated with close-ups of the interviewees' faces which underscore what they are saying.

In Chapter 1, I wrote about the affective qualities of the moving portraits, arguing that they combined face, gaze, and time to enhance the intimacy and engagement with the viewer. This connects to the use of "emotionally effective" advertising, which is proffered as influencing the consumer through the belief in the alleged power of "emotional contagion" via facial expressions. For example, Dan Hill argues that "facial expressions are emotionally contagious," and when viewing advertising, "approximately 75 per cent of all gaze activity will be focused on faces when they're on screen . . . because they're the sensory centre of our lives, and a way to read another person's mood and intent."[88] Indeed, in *Words of a Journey*, the camera uses close-ups of Pan's and Cao's faces to punctuate certain things they are saying, then returning to observing them at a greater distance. For example, the camera returns to a close-up of Pan's face when he states that he wanted to amass wealth so that his mother would have medical care, again when he talks about not having enough money to return home for Spring Festival, a third time as he cautions that material wealth must be balanced by spiritual wealth, and, finally when he self-effacingly introduces himself as simply a man who builds houses. Similarly, there is a close-up of Cao's face when he humbly tells the interviewer that he considers himself to be a "failure" because he does not like a stable life and prefers freedom, next when, after telling the interviewer that others have told him that college students could not sell vegetables online, he asks, "Well, why *can't* college students sell vegetables, right?," and again to him standing in the market. Finally, when he instructs the viewer that everyone's mission "is simply to fight for one's dignity," it cuts to a close-up of his roar of triumph. These close-ups happen when they speak of their dreams and ambitions, when they give advice to the viewer, and when they emphasize their accomplishments through humble-sounding self compliments. When combined with the fast-paced editing of their commercials and the movement of the camera, these close-ups not only punctuate what they say, but also decrease the distance between the speaker and the viewer while simultaneously interjecting an abbreviated form of tensed time for the viewer to think about what is being said. Thus, the action of the frequent cuts keeps the eye engaged and the viewer's attention, while the close-ups and their proclamations ensure the memorability of their message and that the feeling is transmitted.

To conclude, in Jia's films, the Reform period is responsible for so much destruction. Workers have been dethroned and the class is soon to expire. Peasants have been made rootless and their existence is precarious. Soldiers are either corrupt or have simply disappeared. But the entrepreneur figure offers a glimmer of hope in its *rushang* form. This figure proves that one does not have to be vicious in order to survive, but can still inculcate moral values. It is a moral figure for the new era that combines the virtues of the Maoist era with an ability to adapt without losing these sentiments. This is not to say that this is state propaganda; rather, it is a structure of feeling that accompanies social change. What is being produced in the films is thus the valorization of this altruistic figure and the structures of feeling associated with it.

Thus, the *rushang* in Jia's films is not a figure of "New *Socialist* Human," but rather a new model for the Reform era – a "New *Reform* Human" – which has replaced the Maoist worker-peasant-soldier. Moreover, in Jia's films, these beneficial entrepreneur figures include members of other classes who have adapted and become entrepreneurs in the Reform era. They include members of the working class such as Su Na (the daughter of workers in *24 City*), peasants (Pan Shiyi in *Words of Journey*), and intellectuals (Ma Ke in *Useless*). Thus, they illustrate how the previous Maoist class figures can adapt and flourish in the Reform era as entrepreneurs. Although they are no longer of the classes that they were born into, they have "organically" emerged from these other class environments and their attachment to their former classes still remains, illustrating Raymond William's argument that structures of feeling are generational, and that previous affiliations are retained.[89] Successful, filial, philosophical, and emotional, they are altruistic *rushang* who are models of emulation that confirm that people can adapt but not lose their humaneness – the "construction from the destruction" for the Reform Era.

Notes

Introduction

1. Landsberger, "The 'Amazing' Series."
2. Huang, *Heroes and Villains in Communist China*, p. 212.
3. Evans and Donald, "Introducing Posters of China's Cultural Revolution," p. 20.
4. Wu, *The Cultural Revolution at the Margins*, pp. 48–49.
5. Barlow, "Zhishifenzi," p. 218; Liu, "Party-Building," p. 631.
6. Williams, *Marxism and Literature*, pp. 128–135.
7. Ibid. pp. 131, 134.
8. Ibid. pp. 131–134.
9. Ibid. pp. 132–133.
10. Ibid. pp. 134–135.
11. Anderson, *Encountering Affect*, p. 107.
12. Ibid. p. 116.
13. Harding and Pribram, "Losing Our Cool?," p. 870.
14. Flatley, *Affective Mapping*, p. 27.
15. Podalsky, "Affecting Legacies," p. 278.
16. Woodward, *Statistical Panic*, p. 14; citing Williams, *Politics and Letters*, p. 166.
17. Green, "Chinese Director Jia Zhangke."
18. Huang, *Heroes and Villains in Communist China*, p. 212.
19. Wortzel, *Class in China*, pp. 16–17.
20. Gernet, *Daily Life in China*, p. 71.
21. Wortzel, p. 18.
22. Mao, *Analysis of the Classes in Chinese Society*, p. 1.
23. Ibid. pp. 1–11.
24. Chen and Che, "The National Image of Chinese Movies Since 1949," p. 71.
25. So, "The Changing Pattern of Classes and Class Conflict in China," p. 365.
26. Wang, *Boundaries and Categories*, pp. 28–29.
27. Bian, *Work and Inequality in Urban China*, p. 13.
28. Ibid. p. 1.
29. Tang and Parish, *Chinese Urban Life Under Reform*, p. 29.
30. Solinger, *Contesting Citizenship in Urban China*, p. 27.
31. Naughton, *The Chinese Economy*, p. 124.
32. Ibid. pp. 114–115.
33. Ibid. p. 114.
34. Solinger, *Contesting Citizenship*, p. 4.

35. Bian, "Chinese Social Stratification and Social Mobility," p. 93.
36. Naughton, p. 120.
37. Watson, *Class and Social Stratification in Post-Revolution China*, p. 5.
38. Andreas, *Rise of the Red Engineers*, pp. 28–29.
39. Zhou, *The State and Life Chances in Urban China*, p. 59.
40. Unger, "The Class System in Rural China," pp. 130–131.
41. Florence, "Migrant Workers in the Pearl River Delta," p. 123.
42. American Consulate General (Hong Kong), "Study Chairman Mao's Works with a Profound Class Feeling," p. 61.
43. Unger, p. 127.
44. Huang, *Chinese Civil Justice*, p. 10.
45. Congress of Red Guards of Universities and Colleges in the Capital, "Declaration, 22 February 1967."
46. Anonymous, "Great Cultural Revolution in Progress."
47. American Consulate General (Hong Kong).
48. Ibid. p. 61.
49. Ibid. p. 61
50. Ibid. p. 61
51. "Class feelings" are referenced in several ethnographic studies of state factory workers. Lee, *Against the Law*, p. 143. See also: Sheehan, *Chinese Workers*; Hurst, *The Chinese Worker after Socialism*.
52. American Consulate General (Hong Kong), p. 61.
53. Mao, "Quotations from Mao Tse Tung."
54. Mao, *Mao Zedong's "Talks at the Yan'an Conference on Literature and Art,"* p. 65.
55. Huang, *Heroes and Villains in Communist China*, p. 212.
56. Landsberger, "Life as it Ought to Be," p. 26.
57. Landsberger, "Contextualising (Propaganda) Posters," p. 392.
58. Gittings, "Excess and Enthusiasm," p. 29.
59. Landsberger, "Contextualising (Propaganda) Posters," p. 381.
60. *Chinese–English Dictionary of Contemporary Usage*, 1977, s.v. "*mofan*."
61. Chen, *From the May Fourth Movement to Communist Revolution*, p. 3.
62. Landsberger, *Chinese Propaganda Posters*, p. 18.
63. Ibid. pp. 19, 27.
64. Anagnost, "The Polticized Body," p. 136.
65. Munro, *The Concept of Man in Early China*, p. 96. Cited by Burch, "Models as Agents of Change in China," p. 125.
66. Burch, p. 136.
67. Landsberger, "Contextualising (Propaganda) Posters," p. 379. Emphasis author's.
68. Landsberger, "Life as it Ought to Be," p. 26.
69. Burch, p. 122.
70. Anagnost, p. 147.
71. American Consulate General (Hong Kong), p. 61.
72. Evans and Donald, p. 20.
73. Burch, p. 127.

74. Laughlin, "The Revolutionary Tradition in Modern Chinese Literature," p. 228.
75. Trotsky, "Revolutionary and Socialist Art."
76. Landsberger, *Chinese Propaganda Posters*, p. 26.
77. Ibid. p. 18.
78. Ibid. p. 28.
79. Jia, "Speaking of the 'Sixth Generation'."
80. Evans, "'Comrade Sisters'," p. 64.
81. Anonymous, "Website of the Week."
82. Landsberger, "Contextualising (Propaganda) Posters," p. 396.
83. Ibid. p. 397.
84. Evans, p. 65.
85. Henriot and Yeh, "Introduction," xxiv. Emphasis authors'.
86. Pang, "The Dialectics of Mao's Images," p. 431.
87. Clark, *Chinese Cinema*, pp. 9, 57.
88. Yau, "Compromised Liberation," p. 139.
89. Zhu, *Chinese Cinema During the Era of Reform*, p. 6.
90. Clark, *Chinese Cinema*, p. 101.
91. Chen, "Propagating the Propaganda Film," pp. 162, 155.
92. Ibid. p. 162.
93. Ibid. p. 154.
94. Wang, *The Sublime Figure of History*, p. 14.
95. Yau, p. 139.
96. Clark, *Chinese Cinema*, p. 133.
97. Yu, "Make the Performance Stage Become the Mao Zedong Thought's Front Forever." cited by Pang, p. 414.
98. Xu, "Edification through Affection," p. 274.
99. Clark, *Chinese Cinema*, p. 136.
100. Unger, p. 139.
101. Whyte, "Destratification and Restratification in China," p. 325.
102. *Encyclopaedia Britannica*, s.v. "Special Economic Zone."
103. So, p. 366.
104. Goodman and Zang, "The New Rich in China," p. 1.
105. Hurst, *The Chinese Worker After Socialism*, p. 53.
106. Deng, *Selected Works by Deng Xiaoping*, p. 360; cited by Li, *The Structure and Evolution of Chinese Social Stratification*, p. 134.
107. Goodman and Zang, p. 2.
108. Wildau and Mitchell, "China Income Inequality Among World's Worst."
109. So, p. 367.
110. Fan, "China's Party Leadership Declares New Priority."
111. Chan, "Harmonious Society," pp. 821–822.
112. Hu, "Envisaging China's Grand Strategy," pp. 87–89; cited by Chan, "Harmonious Society," p. 821.
113. Dillon, *China*, p. 417.
114. Burch, p. 129.

Chapter 1

1. Mao, *Analysis of the Classes in Chinese Society*, p. 10.
2. Walder, *The Remaking of the Chinese Working Class*, pp. 5–10.
3. Ibid. p. 3.
4. Solinger, "The New Crowd of the Dispossessed," pp. 54–55; cited by Guo, "Class, Stratum and Group," p. 40.
5. Li, *The Structure and Evolution of Chinese Social Stratification*, p. 80.
6. Solinger, "The New Crowd of the Dispossessed," p. 50.
7. Guo, p. 43.
8. Sheehan, *Chinese Workers*, p. 197.
9. Landsberger, *Chinese Propaganda Posters*, p. 154.
10. Solinger, "The New Crowd of the Dispossessed," p. 55. Emphasis author's.
11. Jia, *A Collective Memory of Chinese Working Class*, p. 1.
12. Ibid. p. 2.
13. Hurst, *The Chinese Worker after Socialism*, p. 139.
14. Huang, *Heroes and Villains in Communist China*, p. 212.
15. Clark, *The Chinese Cultural Revolution*, p. 207.
16. Berry, "Jia Zhangke and the Temporality of Postsocialist Chinese Cinema," p. 115.
17. Berry, "Stereotypes and Ambiguities," p. 46.
18. Zhou, p. 307.
19. Abbott, "Against Narrative," p. 90.
20. Ibid. p. 86.
21. Solinger, "The New Crowd of the Dispossessed," p. 52.
22. Clark, *The Chinese Cultural Revolution*, p. 139.
23. Mao, "We Must Learn to Do Economic Work."
24. Translation of 不破不立, "There is no construction without destruction ... Put destruction first, and in the process you have construction." Rice, *Mao's Way*, p. 382.
25. I examine this further in Schultz, "Ruin in the Films of Jia Zhangke."
26. Wu, *Transience*, p. 80.
27. Wu, "Ruins, Fragmentation, and the Chinese Modern/Postmodern," p. 61.
28. Ibid. pp. 60–61.
29. Wu, *Transience*, p. 112.
30. There were three exit strategies: "bankruptcy, transfer to managers as a private firm, or sale to outside investors." Hurst, p. 53.
31. Ibid. pp. 1, 37.
32. Solinger, "The New Crowd of the Dispossessed," p. 53.
33. Trigg, *The Aesthetics of Decay*, xxvi.
34. Ibid. xxviii.
35. Berry, *Xiao Wu, Platform, Unknown Pleasures*, p. 138.
36. Wu, *Transience*, p. 112.
37. Debord, "Introduction to a Critique of Urban Geography," p. 23.
38. *New Oxford American Dictionary*, 2nd edn, s.v. "commemoration."
39. In an interview, Jia stated that more than one hundred interviews were conducted and over fifty were shot. Andrew, "Encounter," p. 81.

40. Anonymous, "The World Is Not Enough."
41. Hurst, p. 14.
42. Jia, *A Collective Memory of Chinese Working Class*, p. 4.
43. For an indepth analysis, see: Schultz, "Moving Portraits."
44. Andrew, p. 82.
45. Balázs, "Theory of the Film," p. 212.
46. Deleuze, *Cinema 1*, p. 97.
47. Kozloff, *The Theatre of the Face*, p. 59.
48. Deleuze, *Cinema 2*, p. 271.
49. Colebrook, *Gilles Deleuze*, p. 30.
50. Benjamin, *Illuminations*, p. 238.
51. Totaro, "Introduction to Andre Bazin, Part 1."
52. Schultz, "Portraits in Performance."
53. Anonymous, "The World is Not Enough."
54. Nora, "Between Memory and History," p. 7.
55. Ibid. pp. 7, 12.
56. Ibid. p. 19.
57. Nochimson, "Passion for Documentation," p. 413.
58. Cheah, "World as Picture and Ruination," p. 192.
59. Cui, "Negotiating In-Between," p. 99.
60. Berry, "Still Life," p. 4.
61. Chan, "Moving with the Times," p. 43.
62. Nora, p. 8.
63. Ibid. p. 8.
64. Xiao, "The Quest for Memory."
65. Boym, *The Future of Nostalgia*, p. 54.
66. Halbwachs, "The Collective Memory," p. 143.
67. Lee, "What Was Socialism to Chinese Workers?," p. 142.
68. Hershatter, *The Gender of Memory*, p. 30.
69. Mannheim, "The Sociological Problem of Generations," p. 95.
70. Jia, "24 City," p. 72.
71. Jia, *A Collective Memory of Chinese Working Class*, pp. 2–3.
72. Cheung, "Realisms within Conundrum," p. 18.
73. Wu, "Time, History, and Memory in Jia Zhangke's *24 City*," p. 13.
74. Ibid. p. 9. Emphasis author's.
75. Xu and Andrew, "The Lion's Gaze," p. 28.
76. Rugo, "Truth after Cinema," pp. 195, 206.
77. For a further discussion, see Schultz, "Memories in Performance."
78. Abbott, p. 67.
79. Ibid. p. 67
80. Ibid. pp. 70, 73, 76.
81. Ibid. pp. 76.
82. Xiao, "The Quest for Memory."
83. Lee, "What Was Socialism to Chinese Workers?," p. 163.
84. Dai, "Imagined Nostalgia," p. 160.

85. Chow, *Sentimental Fabulations*, pp. 51, 53.
86. Cooke, *Representing East Germany Since Unification*, p. 104.
87. Lu, *Chinese Modernity and Global Biopolitics*, pp. 17–18.
88. Huyssen, "Nostalgia for Ruins," p. 7.
89. Boym, p. 41.
90. Ibid. p. 49.
91. Dai, "Imagined Nostalgia," p. 147.
92. Ibid. p. 152.
93. Xstream Pictures, *24 City*, pp. 3, 9.
94. Unger, p. 131.
95. Lee, "What Was Socialism to Chinese Workers?," pp. 141–142.

Chapter 2

1. Feuerwerker, *Ideology, Power, Text*, p. 6.
2. Ibid. p.76. Referencing Lu Xun's "Preface to English Translation of 'Selected Short Stories'," p. 632.
3. Wemheuer, "Sexing the Body of the Peasant Workers in China's Cities," p. 3.
4. Feuerwerker, p. 11.
5. Ibid. p. 26.
6. Ibid. pp. 26, 32.
7. Mao, "Introducing a Co-operative."
8. Meisner, *Mao's China and After*, p. 299.
9. Chen, "Peasant and Woman in Maoist Revolutionary Theory," p. 55.
10. Pun and Lu, "Unfinished Proletarianization," p. 498.
11. Wang, "The Changing Situation of Migrant Labor," p. 186.
12. China Statistical Yearbook 2016, "2-3 Floating Population."
13. Florence, p. 133.
14. Ibid. p. 131.
15. Wang, "The Changing Situation of Migrant Labor," p. 185.
16. Nielsen and Smythe, *Migration and Social Protection in China*, pp. 3–5.
17. Yu, "The Riding the Train Effect," p. 38. Cited by Jacka, "Working Sisters Answer Back," p. 45.
18. So, p. 370.
19. Wemheuer, "Governing the Body of the Peasant Worker in Chinese Cities," 4–6.
20. Kochan, p. 291.
21. Pai, "China's Rural Migrant Workers Deserve More Respect from City Dwellers."
22. Kochan, p. 291.
23. Wang, "The Changing Situation of Migrant Labor," p. 193.
24. Wemheuer, "Governing the Body," p. 5.
25. Kochan, p. 295.
26. Naughton, p. 114.
27. Solinger, *Contesting Citizenship in Urban China*, p. 36.
28. Cohen, *Kinship, Contract, Community, and State*, p. 67.
29. Davies and Grant, "Righting Wrongs," p. 46.

30. Florence, pp. 139–140.
31. Unger, p. 131.
32. Landsberger, "New Year Prints."
33. *Chambers Dictionary of Quotations*, 1993, s.v. "It doesn't matter whether the cat is black or white, as long as it catches mice."
34. Powerhouse Museum, "Evolution and Revolution."
35. Ebrey, "Mao Suits."
36. Wu, *Chinese Fashion*, p. 3.
37. Andrew, pp. 82–83.
38. Berry, *Xiao Wu, Platform, Unknown Pleasures*, p. 134.
39. Yan, "Miner-Turned Director Shoots First Movie 'Little Angels'."
40. Wu, *Chinese Fashion*, pp. 8, 50.
41. Zhao, *The Chinese Fashion Industry*, p. 55.
42. Feuerwerker, pp. 53–54.
43. Florence, pp. 139–140.
44. Feuerwerker, pp. 53–54.
45. See: Lee, *Against the Law*.
46. Han, "The Era of *Blind Shaft* and the Fate of the Grassroots"; Lu, "Cultural Symbols in Jia Zhangke's Films"; Ma, "The Discourse of Powerless Groups in Media Images."
47. Lu, "Cultural Symbols in Jia Zhangke's Films," p. 70.
48. Han, "The Era of *Blind Shaft* . . ."
49. Ibid.
50. Ma, p. 150.
51. Landsberg, *Prosthetic Memory*, p. 149.
52. Spivak, "The New Subaltern," p. 324.
53. Ibid. p. 325.
54. Dhawan, "Can the Subaltern Speak German?"
55. Berry, *Speaking in Images*, p. 202.
56. Smith, "Imagining from the Inside," p. 417.
57. Fabe, *Closely Watched Films*, pp. 261–262.
58. Landsberg, p. 149.
59. Smith, p. 415.
60. Jia, "Xiao Wu," p. 40.
61. Nichols, *Introduction to Documentary*, p. xii.
62. Berry, *Xiao Wu, Platform, Unknown Pleasures*, p. 47.
63. Ibid. p.47.
64. McGrath, "The Independent Cinema of Jia Zhangke," p. 94.
65. Lee, "Jia Zhangke."
66. Cui, "Boundary Shifting," p. 179.
67. Berry, "Jia Zhangke . . .," p. 114.
68. Kang and Chen, "I Believe in the Cultural Value of My Films," p. 72. Cited by Berry, *Xiao Wu, Platform, Unknown Pleasures*, p. 52.
69. Mao, *Analysis of the Classes in Chinese Society*, p. 11.
70. Feuerwerker, p. 11.
71. Wu, *Chinese Fashion*, p. 15.

72. Chow, "China as Documentary," p. 5.
73. Fanon, *Black Skins and White Masks*, p. 170. Emphasis author's.
74. Monk, "Filmmaker Jia Zhangke Explores China's Dark Affair with Money in *Touch of Sin*."
75. Anonymous, "China Moves to Close All Unsafe Mines."
76. Virno, "The Dismeasure of Art."
77. Rayns, "Before the Deluge," p. 10.
78. Anonymous, "Han Sanming."
79. Chan, "The Culture of Survival," p. 180.
80. During, "From the Subaltern to the Precariat," p. 2.
81. Feuerwerker, p. 28.
82. Andrew, p. 82.
83. Berry, *Xiao Wu, Platform, Unknown Pleasures*, pp. 14–15. Emphasis author's.
84. Weil, *The Need for Roots*, pp. 44, 46.
85. Pun and Lu, p. 503.
86. Anderson, p. 129.
87. Debord, p. 23.
88. See also Schultz, "Ruin in the Films of Jia Zhangke."
89. Bauman, *Liquid Modernity*, pp. 5–6.
90. Bauman, *Liquid Times*, p. 17; *Liquid Modernity*, p. 161. Emphasis author's.
91. *Lumpenproletariat* definition: "the unorganized and unpolitical lower orders of society who are not interested in revolutionary advancement." *Oxford Dictionaries*, s.v. "Lumpenproletariat."
92. *The Free Dictionary*, s.v. "Lumpen."
93. Zhang, *Cinema, Space, and Polylocality* . . ., p. 86.
94. Lim, "In 'Touch of Sin', Jia Zhangke Changes His Style but Not Themes."
95. Nichols, *Introduction to Documentary*, pp. 59–61. Emphasis author's.

Chapter 3

1. Gernet, p. 71.
2. Landsberger, "People's Liberation Army."
3. Landsberger, "People's Liberation Army II."
4. Wei, "'Political Power Grows Out of the Barrel of a Gun'," p. 235.
5. Landsberger, "People's Liberation Army."
6. Shichor, "Demobilization," p. 74.
7. Blasko, "Always Faithful," p. 256.
8. Blasko, *The Chinese Army Today*, pp. 211–213.
9. Blasko, "Always Faithful," p. 256.
10. Landsberger, "PLA in 1954."
11. Ibid.
12. Luo, *The 1997 Criminal Code of the People's Republic of China*. Cited by Dobinson, "The Criminal Law of the People's Republic of China (1997)," p. 2.
13. Landsberger, *Chinese Propaganda Posters*, p. 158.
14. Ibid.

15. Wright, *The Promise of the Revolution*, p. 102.
16. Ibid.
17. Branigan, "China Invokes Spirit of Humble Soldier."
18. Blasko, "Always Faithful," p. 263.
19. Ibid. p. 265.
20. Landsberger, "The PLA's Self-Image in the 1980s."
21. Phelan, *Unmarked*, p. 146.
22. Blasko, "Always Faithful," p. 259.
23. Shichor, p. 77.
24. Ibid. p. 81.
25. Blasko, "Always Faithful," p. 264.
26. Landsberger, "The PLA's Self-Image in the 1980s."
27. Shichor, p. 81.
28. Landsberger, *Chinese Propaganda Posters*, p. 156.
29. Landsberger, "People's Liberation Army."
30. Landsberger, *Chinese Propaganda Posters*, p. 141.
31. Landsberger, "People's Liberation Army II."
32. *Pleco Chinese Dictionary*, s.v., "反省."
33. Nora, p. 7.
34. Phelan, p. 146.
35. Ibid. p. 147.
36. Peschel, "Structures of Feeling," p. 166.
37. Ibid. p. 167.
38. Berry and Farquhar, *China on Screen*, pp. 39–40.
39. Phelan, p. 152.
40. Lam, "Impulsive Scholars and Sentimental Heroes," p. 102.
41. Wei, p. 230.
42. Mackerras, "Music and Performing Arts," p. 258.
43. Mao, *The Writings of Mao Zedong*, p. 427.
44. Ibid.
45. Ibid.
46. Ibid.
47. Lam, pp. 89, 103.
48. Rose, "Insight."
49. Anonymous, "Hunting Tigers."
50. Liu, *The Chinese Knight-Errant*, pp. 4–6.
51. Olsen, "Filmmaker Jia Zhangke Gets Real in 'A Touch of Sin'."
52. Szeto, "A Moist Heart," p. 96.
53. Monk, "Filmmaker Jia Zhangke . . ."
54. Green, "Chinese Director Jia Zhangke."
55. Prince, "Graphic Violence in the Cinema," pp. 33–34.
56. Xstream Pictures, *A Touch of Sin*, p. 5.
57. Wei, p. 236.
58. Anonymous, "China's Red Winds of Nostalgia May Fan the Flames of Disdain."
59. Wu, "Tough Times Breed Nostalgia for Mao."

60. Anonymous, "China's Red Winds . . ."
61. Anonymous, "Profile: Bo Xilai."
62. Ibid.
63. Anonymous, "China's Red Winds . . ."
64. Dissanayake and Chen, "Sex, Lies and Videotapes."
65. Barmé, *In the Red*, p. 323.
66. Phelan, p. 147.

Chapter 4

1. Feuerwerker, p. 11.
2. Ibid.
3. Ibid. p. 174.
4. Ibid. p. 111.
5. Ibid. p. 243.
6. Mao, *Selected Works*, pp. 424–425.
7. Zhang, "Representations of Intellectuals," p. 284.
8. U, "Reification of the Chinese Intellectual," p. 605.
9. Mao, *Mao Zedong's "Talks at the Yan'an Conference on Literature and Art*, 521. Cited by Feuerwerker, p. 111.
10. Bian, *et. al.*, "Occupation, Class, and Social Networks in Urban China," p. 1446.
11. Ibid.
12. Landsberger, *Chinese Propaganda Posters*, pp. 78–79.
13. Ibid. pp. 152, 78.
14. Landsberger, "Models and Martyrs."
15. Landsberger, "Four Basic Principles."
16. Landsberger, "Socialist Spiritual Civilization (1980–2000)."
17. Rayns, "Challenges," p. 11.
18. Jia, "It's a Narrative as Well as a Documentary," p. 168.
19. Film Press Plus.
20. Ibid.
21. Pollack, "The Chinese Art Explosion."
22. Anonymous, "Full Cast and Crew for *Beijing Zazhong*."
23. Anonymous, "Full Cast and Crew for *Devils on the Doorstep*."
24. Rayns, "Nature and Creativity," p. 16.
25. Tsui, *China Fashion*, p. 164.
26. Wuyong, Wuyong webpage.
27. Memento Films International, *Still Life*, p. 20.
28. Shackleton, "Jia Zhangke Talks."
29. Anonymous, "Jia Zhangke Launches Yihui with Five-Project Slate."
30. Liu, "The Dual Roles of Jia Zhangke."
31. Anonymous, "Ancient City of Pingyao to Host Int'l Film Festival."
32. Anonymous, "Director Jia Zhangke."
33. Jia, "A People's Director," p. 119.
34. Lee, "Jia Zhangke."

35. Jia, "I Have More Headaches than the Monkey King," p. 81.
36. Anonymous, "Interview with Ma Ke."
37. Liu, "The Painting of Modern Life," p. 139.
38. Sans, "China Talks," p. 49.
39. Osnos, "A Reporter at Large."
40. Callahan, *China Dreams*, p. 36.
41. Berry, "Jia Zhangke . . .," p. 126.
42. Feuerwerker, pp. 111, 39.
43. Ibid. pp. 255, 96.
44. Sheng, "Liu Xiaodong," p. 68.
45. Dal Lago, "The Voice of the 'Superfluous People'," p. 29.
46. Zhang, "Building on the Ruins," p. 116. Cited by Robinson, "From 'Public' to 'Private'," p. 182.
47. Lu, "Rethinking China's New Documentary Movement," p. 18.
48. Davies, *Worrying About China*, p. 7.
49. Ibid. p. 21.
50. Szeto, p. 104.
51. Wu, "A Conversation between Liu Xiaodong and Wu Hung," p. 122.
52. Sans, p. 47.
53. Tsui, p. 166.
54. Wuyong, Wuyong webpage.
55. Bourne, "Jia Zhang-ke's 'Useless'."
56. Rayns, "Nature and Creativity," p. 16.
57. Zhang, *Encyclopedia of Chinese Film*, p. 283.
58. Ibid.
59. Wang, "Contemporary Chinese Thought and the Question of Modernity," p. 10.
60. Wu, "Contemporary Chinese Social and Political Thought," p. 369.
61. Ibid. pp. 361, 369. Emphasis author's.
62. Tsui, p. 182.
63. Wuyong, Wuyong webpage.
64. Ibid.
65. Wu, "Corner of the World," p. 35. "今天中国所谓的现代化,是一个运动式的现代化,我们在那么短的时间内有了现代化的物质,但现代化远远不是物质本身."
66. Havis, "Illusory Worlds," p. 58. Emphasis author's.
67. Boym, p. xviii.
68. Albrecht, "Solastalgia," p. 46.
69. Tsui, pp. 177–178.
70. Ibid. p. 182.
71. Davies, p. 54.
72. Nichols, *Representing Reality*, p. 54.
73. Ibid.
74. Ibid. p. 56.
75. Grimshaw and Ravetz, *Observational Cinema*, p. 68.
76. Dolar, *A Voice and Nothing More*, p. 14.
77. Nichols, *Introduction to Documentary*, p. 189.

78. In his analysis of observational French New Wave cinema, Young writes that it left the viewer "to our imagination . . . They left us space to fill and we participated," because "the difference is between TELLING a story and SHOWING us something." Young, "Observational Cinema," p. 103.
79. Nichols, *Representing Reality*, p. 42.
80. Grimshaw and Ravetz, pp. xiv, 23.
81. Lury writes: "In adopting/adapting a prosthesis, the person creates (or is created by) a self-identity that is no longer defined by the edict 'I think, therefore I am'; rather, he or she is constituted in the relation 'I can, therefore I am.'" Lury, *Prosthetic Culture*, p. 3.
82. Grimshaw and Ravetz, 23, p. xiv.
83. Feuerwerker, p. 77.
84. Zhang, *Cinema, Space, and Polylocality* . . ., pp. 150–151.
85. *Miriam Webster Dictionary*, s.v. "create."
86. *Miriam Webster Dictionary*, s.v. "make."
87. Wu, "The Three Gorges Dam and Contemporary Chinese Art," p. 72.
88. Jones, Jones, and Woods, *An Introduction to Political Geography*, p. 174, referencing the work of Edward Said.
89. McGrath, *Postsocialist Modernity*, p. 225.
90. Landsberg, p. 149.
91. Agustín, "Forget Victimization," 30. Emphasis author's.
92. Said, *Orientalism*, p. 1.
93. Marx, "The Eighteenth Brumaire of Louis Bonaparte, 1852."
94. Feuerwerker, p. 76. Referencing Lu Xun's "Preface to English Translation of 'Selected Short Stories'," p. 632.
95. Wuyong, Wuyong webpage.
96. Shanin, *Defining Peasants*, p. 6.
97. Feuerwerker, p. 96.
98. Chan, "Chinese Brand Exception . . ."

Chapter 5

1. Translation of the idiom *bupo buli*, 不破不立. Rice, p. 382.
2. *Nciku Dictionary*, s.v. "儒商."
3. Williams, *Marxism and Literature*, pp. 134–135.
4. *Pleco Chinese Dictionary*, s.v. "entrepreneur."
5. Brook, *The Confusions of Pleasure*, p. 72.
6. Hsu, *Creating Market Socialism*, p. 6.
7. Wortzel, pp. 16–17.
8. Gates, *China's Motor*. Cited by Hsu, p. 138.
9. Kraus, *Class Conflicts in Chinese Socialism*, pp. 185–187.
10. Hsu, p. 17.
11. Ibid. p. 7.
12. Ibid. p. 17.
13. Ibid. p. 141.

14. Guo, 42.
15. Hsu, 20.
16. Ibid. pp. 18–19.
17. McGrath, "The Independent Cinema of Jia Zhangke," p. 91.
18. Hsu, p. 124.
19. Yueh, "China's Entrepreneurs," p. 15
20. *The People's Daily*, 17 February and 25 April, 2001. Cited by Guo, p. 42.
21. Lu, *Chinese Modernity*, p. 210.
22. Landsberger, "Jiang Zemin Theory."
23. Landsberger, "Lei Feng: Part Two."
24. Mees and Zhang, "Chinese Worker Heroes," p. 3.
25. He, "China's New Model of 'Model Workers'."
26. Confucius, *The Analects*, pp. 146–147.
27. Sun, "Re-accumulation of Resources," pp. 61–62.
28. Hust, *The Chinese Worker After Socialism*, p. 53.
29. Berry, "Jia Zhangke and the Temporality . . .," p. 115.
30. Anonymous, "International Dialogue on Chinese Dream Held in Shanghai."
31. Phillips, "China Launches Global 'Fox Hunt' for Corrupt Officials."
32. Hollingsworth, "The Hong Kong Luxury Hotel . . ."
33. Guo, p. 42.
34. Hsu, pp. 127, 139.
35. Ibid. pp. 189, 141.
36. He, "China's New Model . . ."
37. Ibid.
38. Anonymous, "Liu Yonghao and Family."
39. He, "China's New Model . . ."
40. Anonymous, "2012 Forbes Celebrity List."
41. Tsui, *China Fashion*, p. 165.
42. Ibid. p. 164.
43. Ibid. p. 187.
44. Chan, "Chinese Brand Exception de Mixmind . . ."
45. Ibid.
46. Wuyong, Wuyong webpage.
47. Rayns, "Challenges," p. 13.
48. Wuyong, Wuyong webpage.
49. Ibid.
50. Rayns, "Challenges," p. 13.
51. Huang, *Post-Material*, pp. 13–14. Cited by Lu, *Chinese Modernity and Global Biopolitics*, pp. 181–182.
52. Dai, *Cinema and Desire*, pp. 221–222.
53. Marx, *Karl Marx*, pp. 458–467.
54. Chan, "Chinese Brand Exception . . ."
55. Tsui, p. 186. Emphasis author's.
56. Chan, "Chinese Brand Exception . . ."
57. Liu, "The Dual Roles of Jia Zhangke."

58. Wang and Lin, "Migration of Chinese Consumption Values," p. 405.
59. Gerth, "Consumption and Politics in Twentieth-Century China," pp. 38, 42.
60. This is the film's English subtitle, but the original poem is actually "We that have done and thought, that have thought and done, must ramble, and thin out like milk spilt on a stone." Yeats, "Spilt Milk," p. 240.
61. Anonymous, "China's 2011 Average Salaries Revealed."
62. Chen, "Nüqiangren, Chiruanfan," p. 612.
63. Dai, "Imagined Nostalgia," p. 152.
64. Lee, "24 City," p. 46.
65. *New Oxford American Dictionary*, s.v. "catharsis."
66. Balázs, *Early Film Theory*, p. 90.
67. For an analysis of the series' interviews, please see: Schultz, "The Rise of the Entrepreneur in Jia Zhangke's *Words of a Journey*."
68. Anonymous. "Renowned Directors Gather at 35th Hong Kong International Film Festival."
69. Brook, "Johnnie Walker Strolls Off with Three IPA Awards."
70. Ibid.
71. Ogilvy and Mather Group, "Johnnie Walker to Launch 12 Film Campaign."
72. Sokolowski, "Johnnie Walker Celebrates Chinese Pioneers."
73. Ibid.
74. Wright, "APG Creative Strategy Awards."
75. Brook, "Johnnie Walker Strolls Off with Three IPA Awards."
76. SOHO China, "Zhang Xin," citing Forbes.com
77. SOHO China, "Pan Shiyi."
78. Ibid.
79. Henriot and Yeh, xxii.
80. Osnos, "A Reporter . . ."
81. Film Press Plus, *Useless*, p. 23.
82. Xstream Pictures, *24 City*.
83. Yu, "CR Land . . ."
84. Schultz, "Worker, Peasant, Soldier . . .," p. 57.
85. Ogilvy and Mather Group, "Johnnie Walker . . ."
86. Hsu, p. 141.
87. Ibid. pp. 22, 175.
88. Hill, *About Face*, pp. 59, 69.
89. Williams, *Marxism and Literature*, pp. 134–135.

Filmography

24 City (二十四城记). Directed by Jia Zhangke. 2008. Hong Kong: CN Entertainment Ltd., 2009. DVD.
A Touch of Sin (天註定). Directed by Jia Zhangke. 2014. Shenley: Arrow Films, 2014. DVD.
Dong (东). Directed by Jia Zhangke. 2006. Beijing: Xstream Pictures, 2006. DVD.
I Wish I Knew (海上传奇). Directed by Jia Zhangke. 2010. Beijing: Xstream Pictures, 2010. DVD.
Mountains May Depart (山河故人). Directed by Jia Zhangke. 2015. Beijing: Xstream Pictures, 2015. DVD.
Platform (站台). Directed by Jia Zhangke. 2000. London: Artificial Eye, 2003. DVD
Still Life (三峡好人). Directed by Jia Zhangke. 2006. Beijing: Zhongguo Luyin Luxiang Chuban Zongshe, 2006. DVD.
Unknown Pleasures (任逍遥). Directed by Jia Zhangke. 2002. Beijing: Zhongguo Yinyuejia Yinxiang Chubanshe, 2004. DVD.
Useless (无用). Directed by Jia Zhangke. 2007. Beijing: Xstream Pictures, 2007. DVD.
The World (世界). Directed by Jia Zhangke. 2004. New York: Zeitgeist Films, 2005. DVD.
Words of a Journey (语路). Produced by Jia Zhangke. 2011. Beijing: Johnnie Walker, 2011. Accessed March 4, 2012. https://www.youtube.com/watch?v=YSVMpfZA6ys&list=PLAAAAE4C15D9A2A75
Xiao Shan Going Home (小山回家). Directed by Jia Zhangke. 1995. Hong Kong: Ying E Chi, 2007. DVD.
Xiao Wu (小武). Directed by Jia Zhangke. 1997. London: Artificial Eye, 2004. DVD.

Shorts

One Day in Beijing (有一天，在北京, 1994).
Du Du (嘟嘟, 1996).
In Public (公共场所, 2001).
La Condition Canine (狗的状况, 2001).
Our Ten Years (我们的十年, 2007).
Cry Me a River (河上的爱情, 2008).
Black Breakfast (2008).
Venezia 70 Future Reloaded: Jia Zhangke (2013).

Works Cited

Abbott, Andrew. "Against Narrative: A Preface to Lyrical Sociology." *Sociological Theory* 25, no. 1 (March 2007): 67–99.
Agustín, Laura M. "Forget Victimization: Granting Agency to Migrants." *Development* 46, no. 3 (2003): 30–36.
Albrecht, Glenn. "'Solastalgia': A New Concept in Health and Identity." *PAN: Philosophy, Activism, Nature* 3 (2005): 44–59.
American Consulate General (Hong Kong). "Study Chairman Mao's Works with a Profound Class Feeling." *Current Background*, no. 739 (24 August 1964): 59–61.
Anagnost, Ann. "The Politicized Body." In *Body, Subject & Power in China*, edited by Angela Zito and Tani E. Barlow, 131–156. Chicago: University of Chicago Press, 1994.
Anderson, Ben. *Encountering Affect: Capacities, Apparatuses, Conditions*. Farnham: Ashgate, 2014.
Andreas, Joel. *Rise of the Red Engineers: The Cultural Revolution and the Origins of China's New Class*. Stanford: Stanford University Press, 2009.
Andrew, Dudley. "Encounter: Interview with Jia Zhang-Ke." *Film Quarterly* 62, no. 4 (Summer 2009): 80–83.
Anonymous. "2012 Forbes Celebrity List" (福布斯2012中国名人榜). Accessed December 9, 2013.
Anonymous. "Ancient City of Pingyao to Host Intn'l Film Festival." *China Daily*, October 13, 2017. Accessed October 19, 2017. http://www.china.org.cn/arts/2017-10/13/content_41725966.htm
Anonymous. "China Moves to Close All Unsafe Mines." *BBC News*, April 5, 2006. Accessed April 13, 2010.
Anonymous. "China's 2011 Average Salaries Revealed." *China Daily*, July 6, 2012. Accessed October 3, 2013. http://www.chinadaily.com.cn/china/ 2012-07/06/content_15555503.htm
Anonymous. "China's Red Winds of Nostalgia May Fan the Flames of Disdain." *Want China Times*, June 6, 2011. Accessed May 24, 2014. http://www.wantchinatimes.com/news-subclass-cnt.aspx?id=20110624000108&cid=1701
Anonymous. "Director Jia Zhangke: True to Life." *China.org.cn*, December 5, 2003. Accessed March 22, 2010.
Anonymous. "Full Cast and Crew for *Beijing Zazhong*." Accessed February 10, 2014. http://www.imdb.com/title/tt0106378/fullcredits#cast

Anonymous. "Full Cast and Crew for *Devils on the Doorstep*." Accessed February 10, 2014. http://www.imdb.com/title/tt0245929/fullcredits#cast

Anonymous. "Great Cultural Revolution in Progress: Workers' Mao Tse-tung's Thought Propaganda Teams in Colleges and Schools." *Peking Review* 11, no. 43 (October 25, 1968). Accessed May 5, 2014. https://www.marxists.org/subject/china/peking-review/1968/PR1968-43g.htm

Anonymous. "Han Sanming," *CriEnglish.com*, September 14, 2009. Accessed March 1, 2013. english.cri.cn/4406/2009/09/11/1942s515161.htm

Anonymous. "Hunting Tigers." *The Economist*, September 7, 2013. Accessed May 24, 2014. http://www.economist.com/news/leaders/21585004-cracking-down-corrupt-officials-xi-jinping-must-not-forget-fundamental-reforms-hunting

Anonymous. "International Dialogue on Chinese Dream Held in Shanghai." *China Daily*, December 7, 2013. Accessed April 27, 2014. http://africa.chinadaily.com.cn/china/2013-12/07/content_17159570.htm

Anonymous. "Interview with Ma Ke." *Eco Fashion World* (2008). Accessed October 24, 2012.

Anonymous. "Jia Zhangke Launches Yihui with Five-Project Slate." *Screen Daily*, June 19, 2012. Accessed March 20, 2014. http://www.screendaily.com/ jia-zhangke-launches-yihui-with-five-project-slate/5043469.article

Anonymous. "Liu Yonghao and Family." *Forbes*. Accessed December 8, 2013. http://www.forbes.com/profile/liu-yonghao/

Anonymous. "Profile: Bo Xilai." *BBC News*, September 22, 2013. Accessed May 26, 2014. http://www.bbc.co.uk/news/world-asia-china-19709555

Anonymous. "Renowned Directors Gather at the 35th Hong Kong International Film Festival: Master Class – Jia Zhangke, Retrospective of Abbas Kiarostami and Kuei Chih-hung." *35th Hong Kong International Film Festival*, February 1, 2011. Accessed November 20, 2013. http://35.hkiff.org.hk/eng/info/press/press_release/20110202.html

Anonymous. "The World is Not Enough: Has Jia Zhangke Permanently Left the Art House?" *China Film Journal*, March 26, 2008. Accessed May 5, 2010. http://chinafilmjournal.com/2008/03/26/the-world-is-not-enough-has-jia-zhangke-permanently-left-the-art-house/

Anonymous. "Website of the Week: This Week: Stefan Landsberger's Chinese Propaganda Poster Pages." *PopCultMag.Com*. Accessed June 10, 2014. http://www.popcultmag.com/passingfancies/websiteoftheweek/chineseposters/chinese1.html

Balázs, Béla. *Early Film Theory*. New York: Berghahn Books, 2010.

Balázs, Béla. "Theory of the Film." In *Film: An Anthology*, edited by Daniel Talbot, 201–215. Berkeley: University of California Press, 1959.

Barlow, Tani. "Zhishifenzi [Chinese Intellectuals] and Power." *Dialect Anthropology* 16, nos. 3–4 (1991): 209–232.

Barmé, Geremie R. *In the Red: On Contemporary Chinese Culture*. New York: Columbia University Press, 1999.

Bauman, Zygmunt. *Liquid Modernity*. Cambridge: Polity, 2000.

Bauman, Zygmunt. *Liquid Times: Living in an Age of Uncertainty*. Cambridge: Polity, 2007.
Benjamin, Walter. *Illuminations*. Translated by Hannah Arendt. New York: Schocken Books, 1968.
Berry, Chris. "Jia Zhangke and the Temporality of Postsocialist Chinese Cinema: In the Now (And Then)." In *Futures of Chinese Cinema: Technologies and Temporalities in Chinese Screen Cultures*, edited by Olivia Khoo and Sean Metzger, 113–128. Bristol: Intellect, 2009.
Berry, Chris. "Stereotypes and Ambiguities: An Examination of the Feature Films of the Chinese Cultural Revolution." *Journal of Asian Culture* 6 (1982): 37–72.
Berry, Chris. "*Still Life*." In *Still Life* [DVD booklet], 3–6. London: BFI, 2006.
Berry, Chris. "*Xiao Wu*: Watching Time Go By." In *Chinese Films in Focus II*, edited by Chris Berry, 250–257. Basingstoke: Palgrave Macmillan, 2008.
Berry, Chris and Mary Farquhar. *China on Screen: Cinema and Nation*. New York: Columbia University Press, 2006.
Berry, Michael. *Speaking in Images: Interviews with Contemporary Chinese Filmmakers*. New York: Columbia University Press, 2005.
Berry, Michael. *Xiao Wu, Platform, Unknown Pleasures: Jia Zhangke's 'Hometown Trilogy.'* London: British Film Institute, 2009.
Bian, Yanjie. "Chinese Social Stratification and Social Mobility." *Annual Review of Sociology* 28 (2002): 91–116.
Bian, Yanjie. *Work and Inequality in Urban China*. Albany: State University of New York Press, 1994.
Bian, Yanjie, Ronald Breiger, Deborah Davis and Joseph Galaskiewicz. "Occupation, Class, and Social Networks in Urban China." *Social Forces* 83, no. 4 (June 2005): 1443–1468.
Blasko, Dennis J. "Always Faithful: The PLA from 1949 to 1989." In *A Military History of China*, edited by David A. Graff and Robin Higham, 249–266. Lexington: University Press of Kentucky, 2012.
Blasko, Dennis J. *The Chinese Army Today: Transition and Transformation for the 21st Century*. London: Routledge, 2012.
Bourne, Christopher. "Jia Zhang-ke's '*Useless*' – 2007 New York Film Festival Review." *Meniscus Magazine*, November 6, 2007. Accessed October 24, 2012. http://www.meniscuszine.com/articles/20071106792/documentary-review-jia-zhang-kes-useless/
Boym, Svetlana. *The Future of Nostalgia*. New York: Basic Books, 2001.
Branigan, Tania. "China Invokes Spirit of Humble Soldier in Effort to Improve Social Harmony." *The Guardian*, March 4, 2013. Accessed March 4, 2013. http://www.theguardian.com/world/2013/mar/04/china-humble-soldier-social-harmony (date accessed 4 March 2014).
Brook, Stephen. "Johnnie Walker Strolls Off with Three IPA Awards." *The Guardian*, November 4, 2008. Accessed January 26, 2013. www.guardian.co.uk/media/2008/nov/04/advertising-marketingandpr1
Brook, Timothy. *The Confusions of Pleasure: Commerce and Culture in Ming China*. Berkeley: University of California Press, 1998.

Burch, Betty B. "Models as Agents of Change in China." In *Value Change in Chinese Society*, edited by Richard W. Wilson, Amy Auerbacher Wilson, and Sydney L. Greenblatt, 122–137. New York: Praeger, 1979.

Callahan, William A. *China Dreams: 20 Visions of the Future*. Oxford: Oxford University Press, 2013.

Chan, Andrew. "Moving with the Times." *Film Comment* (March–April 2009): 40–43.

Chan, Anita. "The Culture of Survival: Lives of Migrant Workers Through the Prism of Private Letters." In *Popular China: Unofficial Culture in a Globalizing Society*, edited by Perry Link, Richard P. Madsen, and Paul G. Pickowicz, 163–188. Lanham: Rowman and Littlefield, 2002.

Chan, Jenny. "Chinese Brand Exception de Mixmind Gets Moment of Glory as First Lady Fashion." *Campaign Asia Pacific*, March 26, 2013. Accessed March 27, 2013. http://www.campaignasia.com/Article/337680,chinese-brand-exception-de-mixmind-gets-moment-of-glory-as-first-lady-fashion.aspx

Chan, Kin-man. "Harmonious Society." In *International Encyclopedia of Civil Society*, edited by Helmut K. Anheier and Stefan Toeper, 821–825. New York: Springer, 2010.

Cheah, Pheng. "World as Picture and Ruination: On Jia Zhangke's *Still Life* as World Cinema." In *The Oxford Handbook of Chinese Cinemas*, edited by Carlos Rojas and Eileen Cheng-Yin Chow, 190–206. Oxford: Oxford University Press, 2013.

Chen, Lily. "Nüqiangren, Chiruanfan." In *Encyclopedia of Contemporary Chinese Culture*, edited by Edward L. Davis, 612. London: Routledge, 2005.

Chen, Tina Mai. "Peasant and Woman in Maoist Revolutionary Theory, 1920s–1950s." In *Radicalism, Revolution, and Reform in Modern China*, edited by Catherine Lynch, Robert B. Marks and Paul G. Pickowicz, 55–56. Lanham: Lexington Books, 2011.

Chen, Tina Mai. "Propagating the Propaganda Film: The Meaning of Film in Chinese Communist Party Writings, 1949–1965." *Modern Chinese Literature and Culture* 15, no. 2 (Fall 2003): 154–193.

Chen, Xiaoming. *From the May Fourth Movement to Communist Revolution: Guo Moruo and the Chinese Path to Communism*. Albany: State University of New York Press, 2007.

Chen, Xuguang, and Che Lin (陈旭光, 车琳). "The National Image of Chinese Movies Since 1949" (新中国电影 60 年:社会阶层变迁与银幕主流形象的流变). *Contemporary Cinema* (当代电影) 1 (2010): 70–75.

Cheung, Esther M.K. "Realisms within Conundrum: The Personal and Authentic Appeal in Jia Zhangke's Accented Films." *China Perspectives* 1 (2010): 11–20.

China Statistical Yearbook 2016. "2-3 Floating Population." Accessed June 18, 2017. http://www.stats.gov.cn/tjsj/ndsj/2016/indexeh.htm

Chow, Rey. "China as Documentary: Some Basic Questions (Inspired by Michelangelo Antonioni and Jia Zhangke)." *European Journal of Cultural Studies* 17, no. 1 (2013): 1–15.

Chow, Rey. *Sentimental Fabulations, Contemporary Chinese Films: Attachment in the Age of Global Visibility*. New York: Columbia University Press, 2007.

Clark, Paul. *Chinese Cinema: Culture and Politics Since 1949*. Cambridge: Cambridge University Press, 1987.

Clark, Paul. *The Chinese Cultural Revolution: A History*. Cambridge: Cambridge University Press, 2008.

Cohen, Myron L. *Kinship, Contract, Community, and State: Anthropological Perspectives on China*. Stanford: Stanford University Press, 2005.

Colebrook, Claire. *Gilles Deleuze*. London: Routledge, 2002.

Confucius. *The Analects*. Ware: Wordsworth Editions Ltd., 1996.

Congress of Red Guards of Universities and Colleges in the Capital. "Declaration of the Congress of Red Guards of Universities and Colleges in Peking, 22 February 1967." Accessed June 10, 2014. http://www.wengewang.com/simple/ index.php?t18559.html

Cooke, Paul. *Representing East Germany Since Unification: From Colonization to Nostalgia*. Oxford: Berg, 2005.

Cui, Shuqin. "Boundary Shifting: New Generation Filmmaking and Jia Zhangke's Films." In *Art, Politics, and Commerce in Chinese Cinema*, edited by Ying Zhu and Stanley Rosen, 175–194. Hong Kong: Hong Kong University Press, 2010.

Cui, Shuqin. "Negotiating In-Between: On New-Generation Filmmaking and Jia Zhangke's Films." *Journal of Modern Chinese Literature and Culture* 18, no. 2 (2006): 98–130.

Dai, Jinhua. *Cinema and Desire: Feminist Marxism and Cultural Politics in the Work of Dai Jinhua*. Edited by Jing Wang and Tani E. Barlow. London: Verso, 2002.

Dai, Jinhua. "Imagined Nostalgia." Translated by Judy T. H. Chen. In *Boundary 2* 24, no. 3 (Autumn 1997): 143–161.

Dal Lago, Francesca. "The Voice of the 'Superfluous People': Painting in China in the Late 1980s and Early 1990s." In *Writing on the Wall: Chinese New Realism and Avant-Garde in the Eighties and Nineties*, compiled by Cees Hendrikse, 21–32. Rotterdam: Groninger Museum, NAI Publishers, 2008.

Davies, Gloria. *Worrying About China: The Language of Chinese Critical Inquiry*. Cambridge, MA: Harvard University Press, 2007.

Davies, Gloria, and Scott Grant. "Righting Wrongs: The Language of Policy Reform and China's Migrant Workers." In *Migration and Social Protection in China*, edited by Ingrid Nielsen and Russell Smythe, 31–48. Singapore: World Scientific, 2008.

Debord, Guy. "Introduction to a Critique of Urban Geography." In *Critical Geographies: A Collection of Readings*, edited by Harald Bauder and Salvatore Engel-Di Mauro, 23–27. Kelowna, BC: Praxis, 2008.

Deleuze, Gilles. *Cinema 1: The Movement-Image*. Translated by Hugh Tomlinson and Barbara Habberjam. London: Continuum, 1986.

Deleuze, Gilles. *Cinema 2: The Time-Image*. Translated by Hugh Tomlinson and Robert Galeta. London: The Athlone Press, 1985.

Deng, Xiaoping. *Selected Works of Deng Xiaoping, Volume III: (1982–1992)*. Beijing: Foreign Languages Press, 1994.

Dhawan, Nikita. "Can the Subaltern Speak German? And Other Risky Questions." *Translate.eipc.net*, April 25, 2007. Accessed March 3, 2012. http://translate.eipcp.net/strands/03/dhawan-strands01en#redir

Dillon, Michael. *China: A Modern History*. London: I. B. Tauris, 2010.

Dissanayake, Samanthi and Zhuang Chen. "Sex, Lies and Videotapes: A Year in Chinese Microblogs." *BBC News China*, December 29, 2012. Accessed May 18, 2014. http://www.bbc.co.uk/news/world-asia-china-20765530

Dobinson, Ian. "The Criminal Law of the People's Republic of China (1997): Real Change or Rhetoric?" *Pacific Rim Law & Policy Journal* 11, no. 1 (January 2002): 1–62.

Dolar, Mladen. *A Voice and Nothing More.* Cambridge, MA: The MIT Press, 2006.

During, Simon. *"From the Subaltern to the Precariat."* Accessed February 12, 2014. https://www.academia.edu/4547447/From_the_subaltern_to_the_precariat

Ebrey, Patricia Buckley. "Mao Suits." In *A Visual Sourcebook of Chinese Civilization.* Accessed July 7, 2013. http://depts.washington.edu/chinaciv/clothing/11maosui.htm

Encyclopaedia Britannica. "Special Economic Zone." Accessed February 10, 2012. http://www.britannica.com/EBchecked/topic/558530/special-economic-zone-SEZ

Evans, Harriet. "'Comrade Sisters': Gendered Bodies and Spaces." In *Picturing Power in the People's Republic of China: Posters of the Cultural Revolution*, edited by Harriet Evans and Stephanie Donald, 63–100. Lanham: Rowman and Littlefield, 1999.

Evans, Harriet and Stephanie Donald. "Introducing Posters of China's Cultural Revolution." In *Picturing Power in the People's Republic of China: Posters of the Cultural Revolution*, edited by Harriet Evans and Stephanie Donald, 1–26. Lanham: Rowman and Littlefield, 1999.

Fabe, Marilyn. *Closely Watched Films: An Introduction to the Art of Narrative Film Technique.* Berkeley: University of California Press, 2004.

Fan, Maureen. "China's Party Leadership Declares New Priority: 'Harmonious Society'." *Washington Post*, October 12, 2006. Accessed July 30, 2013. http://www.washingtonpost.com/wp-dyn/content/article/2006/10/11/AR2006101101610.html

Fanon, Franz. *Black Skins and White Masks.* London: Pluto Press, 1967.

Feuerwerker, Yi-tsi Mei. *Ideology, Power, Text: Self-Representation and the Peasant "Other" in Modern Chinese Literature.* Stanford: Stanford University Press, 1998.

Film Press Plus. *Useless: A Film by Jia Zhangke.* Paris: Film Press Plus, Richard Lormand, 2007.

Flatley, Jonathan. *Affective Mapping: Melancholia and the Politics of Modernism.* Cambridge, MA: Harvard University Press, 2008.

Florence, Eric. "Migrant Workers in the Pearl River Delta: Discourse and Narratives about Work as Sites of Struggle," *Critical Asian Studies* 39, no. 1 (2007): 121–150.

Gates, Hill. *China's Motor: A Thousand Years of Petty Capitalism.* Ithaca: Cornell University Press, 1996.

Gernet, Jacques. *Daily Life in China, On the Eve of the Mongol Invasion, 1250–1276.* Stanford: Stanford University Press, 1962.

Gerth, Karl. "Consumption and Politics in Twentieth-Century China." In *Citizenship and Consumption*, edited by Kate Soper and Frank Trentmann, 34–50. Basingstoke: Palgrave Macmillan, 2008.

Gittings, John. "Excess and Enthusiasm." In *Picturing Power in the People's Republic of China: Posters of the Cultural Revolution*, edited by Harriet Evans and Stephanie Donald, 27–46. Lanham: Rowman and Littlefield, 1999.

Goodman, David S. G., and Xiaowei Zang. "The New Rich in China: The Dimensions of Social Change." In *The New Rich in China: Future Rulers, Present Lives*, edited by David S. G. Goodman, 1–20. London: Routledge, 2008.

Green, Sue. "Chinese Director Jia Zhangke Lets Characters Vent Their Rage in Latest Film." *South China Morning Post*, November 19, 2013. Accessed November 20, 2013. https://www.scmp.com/user/login?destination=lifestyle/arts-culture/article/1359417/chinese-director-jia-zhangke-lets-his-characters-vent-their

Grimshaw, Anna, and Amanda Ravetz. *Observational Cinema: Anthropology, Film, and the Exploration of Social Life*. Bloomington: Indiana University Press, 2009.

Guo, Yingjie. "Class, Stratum and Group: The Politics of Description and Prescription." In *The New Rich in China: Future Rulers, Present Lives*, edited by David S. G. Goodman, 38–52. London: Routledge, 2008.

Halbwachs, Maurice. "The Collective Memory." In *The Collective Memory Reader*, edited by Jeffrey K. Olick, Vered Vinitzky-Seroussi, and Daniel Levy, 139–149. Oxford: Oxford University Press, 2011.

Han, Chen (韩琛). "The Era of *Blind Shaft* and the Fate of the Grassroots: Class Consciousness and Sixth Generation Films' Imagery of the Lowest Level of Society" (时代的 "盲井" 与草根的命运－论阶级自觉与 "第六代" 电影的底层影像). *Frontiers* (天涯) 1 (2007): unpaged.

Harding, Jennifer, and E. Deidre Pribram. "Losing Our Cool? Following Williams and Grossberg on Emotions," *Cultural Studies* 18, no. 6 (Nov. 2004): 863–883.

Havis, Richard J. "Illusory Worlds: An Interview with Jia Zhangke." *Cineaste* (Fall 2005): 58–59.

He, Na. "China's New Model of 'Model Workers'." *China Daily*, 28 September, 2009. Accessed April 22, 2013. http://www.chinadaily.com.cn/china/2009-09/28/content_8744702.htm

Henriot, Christian and Wen-hsin Yeh. "Introduction: China Visualised: What Stories Do Pictures Tell?" In *Visualising China, 1845–1965: Moving and Still Images in Historical Narratives*, edited by Christian Henriot and Wen-hsin Yeh, vii–xxvi. Leiden: Brill, 2013.

Hershatter, Gail. *The Gender of Memory: Rural Women and China's Collective Past*. Berkeley: University of California Press, 2011.

Hill, Dan. *About Face: The Secrets of Emotionally Effective Advertising*. London: Kogan Page, 2010.

Hollingsworth, Julia. "The Hong Kong Luxury Hotel Turned Tycoon Hideout Away from Prying Mainland Chinese Eyes." *South China Morning Post*, 2 February 2017. Accessed 21 June 2017. http://www.scmp.com/news/hong-kong/law-crime/article/2067271/hong-kong-luxury-hotel-turned-tycoon-hideout-away-prying

Hsu, Carolyn L. *Creating Market Socialism: How Ordinary People are Shaping Class and Status in China*. Durham, NC: Duke University Press, 2007.

Hu, Angang. "Envisaging China's Grand Strategy: The Ambitious Goal of a Prosperous People and a Powerful Nation." *Social Sciences in China* 26, no. 4 (2005): 87–99.

Huang, Du, editor. *Post-Material: Interpretations of Everyday Life by Contemporary Chinese Artists*. Beijing: World Chinese Arts Publication Co., 2000.

Huang, Joe C. *Heroes and Villains in Communist China: The Contemporary Chinese Novel as a Reflection of Life*. London: C. Hurst and Co., 1973.

Huang, Philip C.C. *Chinese Civil Justice, Past and Present*. Plymouth: Rowman and Littlefield, 2010.

Hurst, William. *The Chinese Worker after Socialism*. Cambridge: Cambridge University Press, 2009.

Huyssen, Andreas. "Nostalgia for Ruins." *Grey Room* 23 (Spring 2006): 6–21.

Jacka, Tamara. "Working Sisters Answer Back: The Representation and Self-Representation of Women in China's Floating Population." *China Information* 13, no. 1 (Sept. 1998): 43–75.

Jia, Zhangke. *A Collective Memory of Chinese Working Class* (中国工人访谈录). Jinan: Shandong Huabao Chubanshe (山东华宝出版社), 2009.

Jia, Zhangke. "Speaking of 'the Sixth Generation': I Don't Believe that You Can Predict Our Ending." *DGenerateFilms.Com*, November 10, 2010. Accessed November 19, 2010. http://dgeneratefilms.com/academia/full-translation-of-jia-zhangkes-essay-on-sixth-generation-cinema-now-available/#more-4378

Jia, Zhangke. "*24 City*." In *Jia Zhangke Speaks Out: The Chinese Director's Texts on Film*, translated by Alice Shih, 71–72. Los Angeles: Bridge 21 Publications, 2015.

Jia, Zhangke. "A People's Director from the Grassroots of China." In *Jia Zhangke Speaks Out: The Chinese Director's Texts on Film*, translated by Claire Huot, 89–121. Los Angeles: Bridge 21 Publications, 2015.

Jia, Zhangke. "I Have More Headaches than the Monkey King." In *Jia Zhangke Speaks Out: The Chinese Director's Texts on Film*, translated by Claire Huot, 79–83. Los Angeles: Bridge 21 Publications, 2015.

Jia, Zhangke. "It's a Narrative as Well as a Documentary." In *Jia Zhangke Speaks Out: The Chinese Director's Texts on Film*, translated by Alice Shih, 161–173. Los Angeles: Bridge 21 Publications, 2015.

Jia, Zhangke. "*Xiao Wu*." In *Jia Zhangke Speaks Out: The Chinese Director's Texts on Film*, translated by Claire Huot, 35–40. Los Angeles: Bridge 21 Publications, 2015.

Jones, Martin, Rhys Jones, and Michael Woods. *An Introduction to Political Geography: Space, Place and Politics*. London: Routledge, 2004.

Kang, Xingxuan and Chen Fang (康杏旋, 陈芳). "I Believe in the Cultural Value of My Films" (我相信自己的电影文化价值). *Ming Pao Monthly* (明报) (December 2006): 70–75.

Kochan, Dror. "Visual Representation of Internal Migration and Social Change in China." *China Information* XXIII, no. 2 (2009): 285–316.

Kozloff, Max. *The Theatre of the Face: Portrait Photography Since 1900*. London: Phaidon, 2007.

Kraus, Richard Curt. *Class Conflict in Chinese Socialism*. New York: Columbia University Press, 1981.

Lam, Joseph. "Impulsive Scholars and Sentimental Heroes: Contemporary *Kunqu* Discourses of Traditional Chinese Masculinities." In *Gender in Chinese Music*, edited by Rachel Harris, Rowan Pease, and Shar E. E. Tan, 87–106. Rochester: University of Rochester Press, 2013.

Landsberg, Alison. *Prosthetic Memory: The Transformation of American Remembrance in the Age of Mass Culture*. New York: Columbia University Press, 2004.

Landsberger, Stefan. *Chinese Propaganda Posters: From Revolution to Modernization*. Amsterdam: Pepin Press, 1995.

Landsberger, Stefan. "Contextualising (Propaganda) Posters." In *Visualising China, 1845–1965: Moving and Still Images in Historical Narratives*, edited by Christian Henriot and Wen-hsin Yeh, 379–405. Leiden: Brill, 2013.

Landsberger, Stefan. "Four Basic Principles (1979)." *ChinesePosters.Net*. Accessed November 20, 2013. http://chineseposters.net/themes/four-basic-principles.php

Landsberger, Stefan. "Jiang Zemin Theory." *ChinesePosters.Net*. Accessed November 20, 2013. http://chineseposters.net/themes/jiangzemin-theory.php

Landsberger, Stefan. "Lei Feng: Part Two." *ChinesePosters.Net*. Accessed January 10, 2014. http://chineseposters.net/themes/leifeng-2.php

Landsberger, Stefan. "Life as it Ought to Be." *IIAS Newsletter* 48 (Summer 2008): 26–27.

Landsberger, Stefan. "Models and Martyrs." *ChinesePosters.Net*. Accessed March 3, 2011. http://chineseposters.net/themes/models.php

Landsberger, Stefan. "New Year Prints." *ChinesePosters.Net*. Accessed February 10, 2010. http://chineseposters.net/themes/new-year-prints-2.php

Landsberger, Stefan. "People's Liberation Army." *ChinesePosters.Net*. Accessed January 10, 2014. http://chineseposters.net/themes/pla.php

Landsberger, Stefan. "People's Liberation Army II." *ChinesePosters.Net*. Accessed January 10, 2014. http://chineseposters.net/themes/pla-2.php

Landsberger, Stefan. "PLA in 1954." *ChinesePosters.Net*. Accessed January 10, 2014. http://chineseposters.net/themes/pla-1954.php.

Landsberger, Stefan. "Socialist Spiritual Civilization (1980–2000)." *ChinesePosters.Net*. Accessed November 8, 2013. http://chineseposters.net/ themes/socialist-spiritual-civilization.php

Landsberger, Stefan. "The PLA's Self-Image in the 1980s." *ChinesePosters.Net*. Accessed November 10, 2014. http://chineseposters.net/themes/pla-1980s.php

Landsberger, Stefan. "The Amazing Series." (August 15, 2013). *ChinesePosters.Net*. Accessed January 23, 2014. http://chineseposters.net/themes/amazing.php

Laughlin, Charles. "The Revolutionary Tradition in Modern Chinese Literature." In *The Cambridge Companion of Modern Chinese Culture*, edited by Kam Louie, 218–234. Cambridge: Cambridge University Press, 2008.

Lee, Ching Kwan. *Against the Law: Labor Protests in China's Rustbelt and Sunbelt*. Berkeley: University of California Press, 2007.

Lee, Ching Kwan. "What Was Socialism to Chinese Workers? Collective Memories and Labor Policies in an Age of Reform." In *Re-envisioning the Chinese Revolution: The Politics and Poetics of Collective Memories in Reform China*, edited by Ching Kwan Lee and Guobin Yang, 141–165. Stanford: Stanford University Press, 2007.

Lee, Kevin B. "24 City." *Cineaste* 34, no. 4 (Fall 2009): 44–46.

Lee, Kevin B. "Jia Zhangke," *Senses of Cinema*, 25 (March 21, 2003). Accessed July 9, 2011. http://sensesofcinema.com/2003/great-directors/jia/

Li, Yi. *The Structure and Evolution of Chinese Social Stratification*. Lanham: University Press of America, 2005.

Lim, Dennis. "In 'Touch of Sin,' Jia Zhangke Changes His Style but Not Themes." *Los Angeles Times*, May 25, 2013. Accessed September 6, 2013. http://articles.latimes.com/2013/may/25/entertainment/la-et-mn-cannes-film-festival-touch-sin-20130526

Liu, Alan. "Party-Building," in *Encyclopedia of Contemporary Chinese Culture*, edited by Edward L. Davis. 631–632. London: Routledge, 2005.

Liu, James. *The Chinese Knight-Errant*. London: Routledge and Kegan Paul, 1967.

Liu, Xiaodong. "Liu Xiaodong." In *The Painting of Modern Life, 1960s to Now*. Curated by Ralph Rugoff, organized by Caroline Hancock, 139. London: Southbank Centre, Hayward Publishing, 2007.

Liu, Xiaojing. "The Dual Roles of Jia Zhangke." *Caixin Online*, June 15, 2016. Accessed June 20, 2017. http://www.caixinglobal.com/2016-06-15/101011610.html

Lu, Sheldon H. *Chinese Modernity and Global Biopolitics: Studies in Literature and Visual Culture*. Honolulu: University of Hawai'i Press, 2007.

Lu, Xinyu. "Rethinking China's New Documentary Movement: Engagement with the Social." In *The New Chinese Documentary Film Movement: For the Public Record*, edited by Chris Berry, Xinyu Lu, and Lisa Rofel, 15–48. Hong Kong: Hong Kong University Press, 2010.

Lu, Zhaoxu (卢兆旭). "Cultural Symbols in Jia Zhangke's Films" (贾樟柯电影的文化符号). *Journal of Hulunbeier College* (呼伦贝尔学院学报) 17, no. 4 (August 2009): 68–70.

Luo, Wei, translator. *The 1997 Criminal Code of the People's Republic of China*. Buffalo: W. S. Hein and Co., 1998.

Lury, Celia. *Prosthetic Culture: Photography, Memory and Identity*. London: Routledge, 1998.

Ma, Haoying (马昊莹). "The Discourse of Powerless Groups in Media Images: From the Films of Jia Zhangke" (影像媒介中弱势群体的话语表达 – 从贾樟柯电影说起). *News World* (新闻世界) 9 (2010): 149–150.

Mackerras, Colin. "Music and Performing Arts: Tradition, Reform and Political and Social Relevance." In *The Cambridge Companion to Modern Chinese Culture*, edited by Kam Louie, 253–271. Cambridge: Cambridge University Press, 2008.

Mannheim, Karl. "The Sociological Problem of Generations." In *The Collective Memory Reader*, edited by Jeffrey K. Olick, Vered Vinitzky-Seroussi, and Daniel Levy, 92–98. Oxford: Oxford University Press, 2011.

Mao, Zedong. *Analysis of the Classes in Chinese Society*. Peking: Foreign Languages Press, 1965.

Mao, Zedong. "Introducing a Co-operative." *Marxists.Org*. Accessed June 10, 2014. Available: https://www.marxists.org/reference/archive/mao/selected-works/volume-8/mswv8_09.htm

Mao, Zedong. *Mao Zedong's "Talks at the Yan'an Conference on Literature and Art": A Translation of the 1943 Text with Commentary*. Translated by Bonnie S. McDougall. Ann Arbor: Center for Chinese Studies, The University of Michigan, 1980.

Mao, Zedong. "Quotations from Mao Tse Tung." Accessed October 10, 2014. Available: https://www.marxists.org/reference/archive/mao/works/ red-book/ch32.htm

Mao, Zedong. *Selected Works: The Period of the Socialist Revolution and Socialist Construction*. Beijing: Foreign Languages Press, 1977.

Mao, Zedong. *The Writings of Mao Zedong, 1949–1976: Vol II, January 1956-December 1957*. Edited by John K. Leung and Michael Y. M. Kau. New York: M. E. Sharpe, Inc, 1992.

Mao, Zedong. "We Must Learn to Do Economic Work." Accessed February 14, 2010. http://www.marxists.org/reference/archive/mao/selected-works/volume- 3/mswv3_22.htm

Marx, Karl. *Karl Marx: Selected Writings*. Edited by David McLellan. Oxford: Oxford University Press, 2000.

Marx, Karl. "The Eighteenth Brumaire of Louis Bonaparte, 1852." *Marxists.Org*. Accessed February 14, 2010. http://www.marxists.org/archive/marx/works/1852/18th-brumaire/ch07.htm

McGrath, Jason. *Post-Socialist Modernity: Chinese Cinema, Literature, and Criticism in the Market Age*. Stanford: Stanford University Press, 2008.

McGrath, Jason. "The Independent Cinema of Jia Zhangke: From Postsocialist Realism to a Transnational Aesthetic." In *The Urban Generation: Chinese Cinema and Society at the Turn of the Twenty-First Century*, edited by Zhen Zhang, 81–114. Durham, NC: Duke University Press, 2007.

Mees, Bernard and Jiaying Zhang. "Chinese Worker Heroes: Between Patriotism and Nostalgia." In Challenges for International Business in a Turbulent Global Environment: Proceedings of the ANZIBA Annual Conference 2011, Melbourne, Australia, 28–30 April 2011, edited by Cherrie Zhu, 1–7. Mulgrave: Australia and New Zealand International Business Academy, 2011.

Meisner, Maurice. *Mao's China and After: A History of the People's Republic*. New York: The Free Press, 1999.

Memento Films International. *Still Life: A Film by Jia Zhangke*. Paris: Memento Films International, 2006.

Monk, Katherine. "Filmmaker Jia Zhangke Explores China's Dark Affair with Money in *Touch of Sin*." *The Edmonton Journal*, October 3, 2013. Accessed October 3, 2013. http://www.edmontonjournal.com/entertainment/movie-guide/Filmmaker+Zhangke+explores+China+dark+affair/8989010/story.html

Munro, Donald J. *The Concept of Man in Early China*. Stanford: Stanford University Press, 1968.

Naughton, Barry. *The Chinese Economy: Transitions and Growth*. Cambridge, MA: The MIT Press, 2007.

Nichols, Bill. *Introduction to Documentary*, 2nd ed. Bloomington: Indiana University Press, 2010.

Nichols, Bill. *Representing Reality: Issues and Concepts in Documentary*. Bloomington: Indiana University Press, 1991.

Nielsen, Ingrid, and Russell Smythe. "The Rhetoric and the Reality of Social Protection for China's Migrant Workers." In *Migration and Social Protection in China*, edited by Ingrid Nielsen and Russell Smythe, 3–13. Singapore: World Scientific, 2008.

Nochimson, Martha P. "Passion for Documentation: An Interview with Jia Zhangke." *New Review of Film and Television Studies* 7, no. 4 (2009): 411–419.

Nora, Pierre. "Between Memory and History: Les Lieux de Mémoire." *Representations* 26 (Spring 1989): 7–24.

Ogilvy and Mather Group. "Johnnie Walker to Launch 12 Film Campaign." January 13, 2011. Accessed November 20, 2013. http://www.ogilvy.com/News/Press-Releases/January-2011-Johnnie-Walker-Keep-Walking.aspx

Olsen, Mark. "Filmmaker Jia Zhangke Gets Real in 'A Touch of Sin'." *Los Angeles Times*, October 12, 2013. Accessed March 5, 2014. http://articles.latimes.com/ 2013/oct/12/entertainment/la-et-mn-jia-zhangke-touch-of-sin-20131012

Osnos, Evan. "A Reporter at Large: The Long Shot." *The New Yorker* 85, no. 13 (May 11, 2009). Accessed May 15, 20110. http://www.newyorker.com/magazine/2009/05/11/the-long-shot

Pai, Hsiao-Hung. "China's Rural Migrant Workers Deserve More Respect from City Dwellers." *The Guardian*, August 25, 2012. Accessed May 4, 2013. www.guardian.co.uk/commentisfree/2012/aug/25/china-rural-migrants-more-respect

Pang, Laikwan. "The Dialectics of Mao's Images: Monumentalism, Circulation and Power Effects." In *Visualising China, 1845–1965: Moving and Still Images in Historical Narratives*, edited by Christian Henriot and Wen-hsin Yeh, 407–438. Leiden: Brill, 2013.

Peschel, Lisa. "'Structures of Feeling' as Methodology and the Re-emergence of Holocaust Survivor Testimony in 1960s Czechoslovakia." *Journal of Dramatic Theory and Criticism* 26, no. 2 (Spring 2012): 161–172.

Phelan, Peggy. *Unmarked: The Politics of Performance*. London, Routledge, 2002.

Phillips, Tom. "China Launches Global 'Fox Hunt' for Corrupt Officials." *The Telegraph*, July 25, 2014. Accessed June 19, 2017. http://www.telegraph.co.uk/news/worldnews/asia/china/10991255/China-launches-global-fox-hunt-for-corrupt-officials.html

Podalsky, Laura. "Affecting Legacies: Historical Memory and Contemporary Structures of Feeling in *Madagascar* and *Amores Perros*," *Screen* 44, no. 3 (Autumn 2003): 277–294.

Pollack, Barbara. "The Chinese Art Explosion." *ARTnews* (September 2009). Accessed July 9, 2012. www.artnews.com/2008/09/01/the-chinese-art-explosion/

Powerhouse Museum. "Evolution and Revolution: Chinese Dress 1700s-1900s – Mao Suit." Accessed July 8, 2013. www.powerhousemuseum.com/hsc/evrev/ mao_suit.htm.

Prince, Stephen. "Graphic Violence in the Cinema: Origins, Aesthetic Design, and Social Effects." In *Screening Violence*, edited by Stephen Price, 1–44. London: The Athlone Press, 2000.

Pun, Ngai, and Lu Huilin. "Unfinished Proletarianization: Self, Anger, and Class Action Among the Second Generation of Peasant-Workers in Present-Day China." *Modern China* 36, no. 5 (Sept. 2010): 493–519.

Rayns, Tony. "Before the Deluge." *Sight and Sound* 18, no. 2 (February 2008): 10.

Rayns, Tony. "Challenges: An Interview with Jia Zhangke." In *Useless: A Film by Jia Zhangke*, 10–13. Paris: Film Press Plus, Richard Lormand, 2007.

Rayns, Tony. "Nature and Creativity: An Interview with Ma Ke." In *Useless: A Film by Jia Zhangke*, 14–17. Paris: Film Press Plus, Richard Lormand, 2007.

Rice, Edward Earl. *Mao's Way*. Berkeley: University of California Press, 1972.
Robinson, Luke. "From 'Public' to 'Private': Chinese Documentary and the Logic of *Xianchang*." In *The New Chinese Documentary Film Movement: For the Public Record*, edited by Chris Berry, Lu Xinyu, and Lisa Rofel, 177–194. Hong Kong: Hong Kong University Press, 2010.
Rose, Adam. "Insight: China's Xi Fails to Earn Stripes as Antigraft 'Tiger' Hunt Underwhelms," *Reuters*, November 23, 2013. Accessed May 24, 2014. http://uk.reuters.com/article/2013/11/23/uk-china-corruption-insight-idUKBRE9AM0CQ20131123
Rugo, Daniele. "Truth after Cinema: The Explosion of Facts in the Documentary Films of Jia Zhangke." *Asian Cinema* 24, no. 2 (2013): 195–208.
Said, Edward W. *Orientalism*. London: Penguin, 1991.
Sans, Jérôme. "China Talks: Liu Xiaodong." In *China Talks: Interviews with 32 Contemporary Artists*, edited by Chen Yun and Michelle Woo, 46–52. Hong Kong: Timezone 8, 2009.
Schultz, Corey K. N. "Memories in Performance: Commemoration and the Commemorative Experience in Jia Zhangke's *24 City*." *Film-Philosophy* 20, nos. 2–3: 265–282.
Schultz, Corey K. N. "Moving Portraits: Portraits in Performance in Jia Zhangke's *24 City*." *Screen* 55, no. 2 (2014): 276–287.
Schultz, Corey K. N. "The Rise of the Entrepreneur in Jia Zhangke's *Words of a Journey*." In *Contemporary Cinema and Ideology: Neoliberal Capitalism and Its Alternatives in Filmmaking*, edited by Ewa Mazierska and Lars Kristensen, 91–104. London: Routledge, 2018.
Schultz, Corey K. N. "Ruin in the Films of Jia Zhangke." *Visual Communication* 15, no. 4 (2016): 439–460.
Schultz, Corey K.N. "Worker, Peasant, Soldier . . . Middle Class? Class Figures in Jia Zhangke's *24 City*." *Asian Cinema* 26, no. 1 (2015): 43–59.
Shackleton, Liz. "Jia Zhangke Talks New Projects, Arthouse Distribution." *Screen Daily*, October 25, 2016. Accessed November 22, 2016. https://www.screendaily.com/news/jia-zhangke-talks-new-projects-arthouse-distribution/5110605.article
Shanin, Teodor. *Defining Peasants: Essays Concerning Rural Societies, Expolary Economies, and Learning from Them in the Contemporary World*. Oxford: Basil Blackwell, Ltd., 1990.
Sheehan, Jackie. *Chinese Workers: A New History*. London: Routledge, 1998.
Sheng, Hao. "Liu Xiaodong." *Orientations* 41, no. 7 (October 2010): 66–69.
Shichor, Yitzhak. "Demobilization: The Dialectics of PLA Troop Reduction." In *China's Military in Transition*, edited by David Shambaugh and Richard H. Yang, 72–95. Oxford: Clarendon Press, 1997.
Smith, Murray. "Imagining from the Inside." In *Film Theory and Philosophy*, edited by Richard Allen and Murray Smith, 412–430. Oxford: Clarendon Press, 1997.
So, Alvin Y. "The Changing Pattern of Classes and Class Conflict in China." *Journal of Contemporary Asia* 33, no. 3 (2003): 363–376.
SOHO China. "Pan Shiyi." Accessed October 3, 2013. http://eng.sohochina.com/about/en/panshiyi.html
SOHO China. "Zhang Xin." Accessed October 3, 2013. http://eng.sohochina.com/about/en/zhangxin.html

Sokolowski, Jennifer. "Johnnie Walker Celebrates Chinese Pioneers." *BrandChannel. Com*, February 3, 2011. Accessed January 26, 2013. www.brandchannel.com/home/post/2011/02/03/Johnnie-Walker-Celebrates-Chinese-Pioneers.aspx

Solinger, Dorothy J. *Contesting Citizenship in Urban China: Peasant Migrants, the State, and the Logic of the Market*. Berkeley: University of California Press, 1999.

Solinger, Dorothy J. "The New Crowd of the Dispossessed: The Shift of the Urban Proletariat from Master to Mendicant." In *State and Society in 21st-Century China: Crisis, Contention, and Legitimation*, edited by Peter Hays Gries and Stanley Rosen, 50–66. New York: Routledge, 2004.

Spivak, Gayatri Chakravorty. "The New Subaltern: A Silent Interview." In *Mapping Subaltern Studies and the Postcolonial*, edited by Vinayak Chaturvedi, 324–340. London: Verso, 2012.

Sun, Liping. "Re-accumulation of Resources: The Background of Social Stratification in China in the 1990s." *Social Sciences in China* (Spring 2002): 59–68.

Szeto, Kin-Yan. "A Moist Heart: Love, Politics, and China's Neoliberal Transition in the Films of Jia Zhangke." *Visual Anthropology* 22, no. 2 (2009): 95–107.

Tang, Wenfang, and William L. Parish. *Chinese Urban Life Under Reform*. Cambridge: Cambridge University Press, 2000.

Totaro, Donato. "Introduction to Andre Bazin, Part 1: Film Style Theory in Its Historical Context." *Offscreen* 7, issue 7 (July 2003). Accessed February 25, 2010. http://www.horschamp.qc.ca/new_offscreen/bazin_intro.html

Trigg, Dylan. *The Aesthetics of Decay: Nothingness, Nostalgia, and the Absence of Reason*. New York: Peter Lang Publishing, 2009.

Trotsky, Leon. "Revolutionary and Socialist Art." *Marxists Internet Archive*, January 6, 2007. Accessed June 10, 2014. http://www.marxists.org/archive/trotsky/1924/lit_revo/ch08.htm

Tsui, Christine. *China Fashion: Conversations with Designers*. Oxford: Berg, 2009.

U, Eddy. "Reification of the Chinese Intellectual: On the Origins of the CCP Concept of Zhishifenzi." *Modern China* 35, no. 6 (November 2009): 604–631.

Unger, John. "The Class System in Rural China: A Case Study." In *Class and Social Stratification in Post-Revolution China*, edited by James L. Watson, 121–141. Cambridge: Cambridge University Press, 2010.

Virno, Paolo. "The Dismeasure of Art: An Interview with Paolo Virno." *Open* 17 (2009). Accessed January 15, 2014. http://classic.skor.nl/id.php/GIELENENLAVAERTOPEN17.html

Walder, Andrew G. "The Remaking of the Chinese Working Class, 1949–1981. *Modern China* 10, no. 1 (January 1984): 3–48.

Wang, Ban. *The Sublime Figure of History: Aesthetics and Politics in Twentieth-Century China*. Stanford: Stanford University Press, 1997.

Wang, Cheng Lu and Xiaohua Lin. "Migration of Chinese Consumption Values: Traditions, Modernization, and Cultural Renaissance." *Journal of Business Ethics* 88 (2009): 399–409.

Wang, Chunguang. "The Changing Situation of Migrant Labor." *Social Research* 73, no. 1 (Spring 2006): 185–196.

Wang, Feng. *Boundaries and Categories: Rising Inequality in Post-Socialist Urban China.* Stanford: Stanford University Press, 2008.

Wang, Hui. "Contemporary Chinese Thought and the Question of Modernity." Translated by Rebecca E. Karl. *Social Text* 55 (1998): 9–44.

Watson, James L., editor. *Class and Social Stratification in Post-Revolution China.* Cambridge: Cambridge University Press, 2010.

Wei, William. "'Political Power Grows Out of the Barrel of a Gun': Mao and the Red Army." In *A Military History of China*, edited by David A. Graff and Robin Higham, 229–248. Lexington: University Press of Kentucky, 2012.

Weil, Simone. *The Need for Roots: Prelude to a Declaration of Duties Towards Mankind.* London: Routledge Classics, 2002.

Wemheuer, Felix. "Governing the Body of the Peasant Worker in China's Cities." Accessed October 20, 2010. http://public.univie.ac.at/fileadmin/user_upload/ proj_ faminesoc/ wemheuerchina.pdf.

Wemheuer, Felix. "Sexing the Body of the Peasant Workers in China's Cities: Dangerous Sexual Desires of the 'Other' in the Official Discourse." Paper presented at the Association for Asian Studies (AAS) Annual Meeting, Philadelphia, March 25-28, 2010.

Whyte, Martin King. "Destratification and Restratification in China." In *Social Inequality: Comparative and Developmental Approaches*, edited by Gerald D. Berreman, 309–335. New York: Academic Press, 1981.

Wildau, Gabriel and Tom Mitchell. "China Income Inequality Among World's Worst," *Financial Times*, January 14, 2016. Accessed June 10, 2017. https://www.ft.com/content/3c521faa-baa6-11e5-a7cc-280dfe875e28?mhq5j=e3

Williams, Raymond. *Marxism and Literature.* Oxford: Oxford University Press, 1977.

Williams, Raymond. *Politics and Letters: Interviews with the New Left Review.* London: New Left Books, 1979.

Woodward, Kathleen. *Statistical Panic: Cultural Politics and the Poetics of the Emotions.* Durham, NC: Duke University Press, 2009.

Wortzel, Larry M. *Class in China: Stratification in a Classless Society.* New York: Greenwood, 1987.

Wright, Daniel B. *The Promise of the Revolution: Stories of Fulfillment and Struggle in China's Hinterland.* Lanham: Rowman and Littlefield, 2003.

Wright, Jacob. "APG Creative Strategy Awards: Johnnie Walker 'Keep Walking' by BBH Asia." *CampaignLive.co.uk*, August 18, 2009. Accessed January 6, 2013. www.campaignlive.co.uk/features/927734/

Wu, Guanjun. "Contemporary Chinese Social and Political Thought." In *Routledge Handbook of Contemporary Social and Political Theory*, edited by Gerard Delanty and Stephen P. Turner, 361–373. Abingdon: Routledge, 2011.

Wu, Guanping (吴冠平). "Corner of the World" (世界的角落). *Dianying Yishu* (电影艺术) 1 (2005): 32–36.

Wu, Hung. "A Conversation Between Liu Xiaodong and Wu Hung." In *Displacement: The Three Gorges Dam and Contemporary Chinese Art*, edited by Wu Hung, 122–137. Chicago: Smart Museum of Art, University of Chicago, 2008.

Wu, Hung. "Ruins, Fragmentation, and the Chinese Modern/Postmodern." In *Inside Out: New Chinese Art*, edited by Minglu Gao, 59–66. Berkeley: University of California Press, 1998.

Wu, Hung. "The Three Gorges Dam and Contemporary Chinese Art." *Orientations* 40, no. 1 (January/February 2009): 67–73.

Wu, Hung. *Transience: Chinese Experimental Art at the End of the Twentieth Century*. Chicago: The David and Alfred Smart Museum of Art, The University of Chicago, 1999.

Wu, Juanjuan. *Chinese Fashion: From Mao to Now*. Oxford: Berg, 2009.

Wu, Shu-chin. "Time, History, and Memory in Jia Zhangke's *24 City*." *Film Criticism* 36, no. 1 (Fall 2011): 3–23.

Wu, Yiching. *The Cultural Revolution at the Margins: Chinese Socialism in Crisis*. Cambridge, MA: Harvard University Press, 2014.

Wu, Zhong. "Tough Times Breed Nostalgia for Mao." *Asia Times Online*, May 6, 2009. Accessed May 24, 2014. http://www.atimes.com/atimes/ China/KE06Ad02.html

Wuyong. Wuyong webpage. Accessed February 12, 2012. http://www.wuyonguseless.com

Xiao, Jiwei. "The Quest for Memory: Documentary and Fiction in Jia Zhangke's Film." *Senses of Cinema* 59 (2011). Accessed February 10, 2012. http://sensesofcinema.com/2011/feature-articles/the-quest-for-memory-documentary-and-fiction-in-jia-zhangke%E2%80%99s-films/

Xstream Pictures. *24 City: A Film by Jia Zhangke*. Beijing: Xstream Pictures Ltd., 2008.

Xstream Pictures. *A Touch of Sin: A Film by Jia Zhangke*. Beijing: Xstream Pictures Ltd., 2013.

Xu, Gary. "Edification Through Affection: The Cultural Revolution Films, 1974–1976." In *The Oxford Handbook of Chinese Cinemas*, edited by Carlos Rojas and Eileen Cheng-yin Chow, 269–280. Oxford: Oxford University Press, 2013.

Xu, Jing and Dudley Andrew. "The Lion's Gaze: Truth and Legend in *I Wish I Knew*," *Film Criticism* 36 (2011): 24–43.

Yan, Yan. "Miner-Turned Director Shoots First Movie '*Little Angels*'," *People's Daily Online*, July 4, 2011. Accessed March 13, 2014. en.people.cn/90001/90783/91324/7428604.html

Yau, Esther. "Compromised Liberation: The Politics of Class in Chinese Cinema of the Early 1950s." In *The Hidden Foundation: Cinema and the Question of Class*, edited by David E. James and Rick Berg, 138–171. Minneapolis: University of Minnesota Press, 1996.

Yeats, William Butler. "Spilt Milk." In *The Collected Works of William Butler Yeats Volume 1: The Poems*, edited by Richard J. Finneran, 240. New York: Simon and Schuster, 1996.

Young, Colin. "Observational Cinema." In *Principles of Visual Anthropology*, edited by Paul Hockings, 99–113. The Haag: Mouton de Gruyter, 2003.

Yu, Depeng. "The 'Riding the Train Effect' in Relations between the City and the Countryside." *Shehui* 3: 37–39.

Yu, Huiyong (于会泳). "Make the Performance Stage Become the Mao Zedong Thought's Front Forever" (让文艺舞台永远成为毛泽东思想的阵地). *Shanghai Wenhui Daily*, May 23, 1968.

Yu, Sen-Lun. "CR Land, Shanghai Film Group Invest in Jia Zhangke's *24 City*," *Screen-Daily.Com*, April 2, 2007. Accesed October 21, 2017. https://www.screendaily.com/cr-land-shanghai-film-group-invest-in-jia-zhangkes-24-city/4031741.article

Yueh, Linda. "China's Entrepreneurs." *CentrePiece* (Spring 2008): 15–18.

Zhang, Yingjin. *Cinema, Space, and Polylocality in a Globalizing China*. Honolulu: University of Hawai'i Press, 2010.

Zhang, Yingjin. "Representations of Intellectuals." In *The Encyclopedia of Chinese Film*, edited by Yingjin Zhang and Zhewei Xiao, 283–284. London, Routledge, 1998.

Zhang, Yingjin and Zhewei Xiao. *The Encyclopedia of Chinese Film*. London: Routledge, 1998.

Zhang, Zhen. "Building on the Ruins: The Exploration of New Urban Cinemas of the 1990s." In *Reinterpretation: A Decade of Experimental Chinese Art, 1990–2000*, edited by Wu Hung, Wang Huangsheng, and Feng Boyi, 113–120. Guangzhou: Guangzhou Museum of Art, 2002.

Zhao, Jianhua. *The Chinese Fashion Industry: An Ethnographic Approach*. London: Bloomsbury, 2013.

Zhou, Xueguang. *The State and Life Chances in Urban China: Redistribution and Stratification, 1949–1994*. Cambridge: Cambridge University Press, 2004.

Zhu, Ying. *Chinese Cinema During the Era of Reform: The Ingenuity of the System*. Westport: Praeger, 2003.

Index

Note: *italic* page numbers indicate illustrations

24 City (2008), 3, 16–17, 20, 21, 159
  and entrepreneurs, 151–6
  and generations, 40–1
  and interviews, 42–3, 120
  and memory, 39–40
  and migrant workers, 60
  and nostalgia, 43–4, 45
  and portraits, 68, 80–1
  and ruin, 29–30, 31
  and soldier, 84, 87, 92, 93–6, 106
  and workers, 26, 33–9, 46–7

A Touch of Sin (2013), 3, 18
  and entrepreneurs, 143–4
  and gaze, *81*, 82–3
  and migrant workers, 51, 56, 59, 74
  and peasants, 53, 55
  and sex workers, 75, 76
  and soldier, 85, 87, 90, *91*, 97–108
Abbott, Andrew, 25, 42
advertising, 12, 156–7, 158–9
agriculture, 24
Albrecht, Glenn, 118
All-China Federation of Trade Unions (ACFTU), 51
altruism, 18, 19, 61, 117
"Amazing Educational Propaganda Posters," 1
Analysis of the Classes in Chinese Society (Mao Zedong), 7
Anderson, Ben, 5, 77
anxiety, 18, 25, 117–18
art, 10, 13, 14–15, 30; *see also* posters
athletes, *1*, 2
Augustín, Laura, 133

Balázs, Béla, 35, 155
Bartle Bogle Hegarty (BBH), 156–7
Bauman, Zygmunt, 78
Beijing Bastards (Zhang Yuan, 1993), 113
Benjamin, Walter, 36

Bergson, Henri, 25
Berry, Chris, 24, 68, 96
Berry, Michael, 67, 77
Bo Xilai, 107
boats, 78–9
body, the, 70–6
bourgeoisie, 7, 8
Boym, Svetlana, 40, 44–5
bravery, 17
business people *see* entrepreneurs; *rushang*

cadres, 8, 110–11
Cai Mingzhao, 143
Calle, Sophie, 95
camera, 18, 124–9; *see also* close-ups; observational shot; point-of-view (POV) shot
Cao Fei, 156, 158, 160–1
capitalism, 8, 15, 137
CCP *see* Chinese Communist Party
Chan, Anita, 76
Chen, Joan, 94
chengfen (family background), 8–9
children, 8, 25
China, 30, 116–17, 143
  and class, 6–10
  and history, 69, 88–9
  and intellectuals, 115–16
  and nostalgia, 43, 44
  see also Maoist period; Reform era
China Resources Land Limited, 34, 45, 159
"Chinese are Amazing!" poster, 1–2, 138, *139*
Chinese Communist Party (CCP), 1, 13, 14, 16, 107
  and class, 7–8, 9
  and entrepreneurs, 138, 146
  and PLA, 92
  and workers, 21, 27, 28
"Chinese Elements" movement, 151
chorus, 24

196 Moving Figures

Chow, Rey, 43, 72
Chung Kuo (Antonioni, 1972), 72
cinematography, 19
cities, 51–2
class, 4–10
class figures, 1, 2–4, 11–16; *see also* entrepreneurs; intellectuals; peasants; soldiers; workers
close-ups, 19, 28, 34, 35–8
    and entrepreneurs, 158–9, 160–1
    and intellectuals, 124
    and violence, 101–6
Collective Memory of Chinese Working Class, A (Jia Zhangke), 22
collectivization, 7–8
communism, 44; *see also* Chinese Communist Party; Communist Revolution
Communist Revolution, 7, 21, 86, 107
Confucianism, 6–7, 11, 12, 61, 140–1
    and businesspersons, 18–19
    and intellectuals, 117
    and scholar gentry, 110
consumerism, 45, 148–9
Cooke, Paul, 44
coolies, 69–70
corruption, 90–1, 99–100, 107–8; *see also* criminals
craftsmen, 2, 6, 7
criminals, 18, 86, 138–40
Cry Me a River (2008), 112
Cui, Shuqin, 67
Cultural Revolution, 2, 10, 14–15, 22, 111

Dai Jinhua, 43, 45, 150
Dal Lago, Francesca, 115
danwei (work unit), 8, 22, 34
Davies, Gloria, 115–16, 119
Days, The (Wang Xiaoshuai, 1993), 113
death, 74, 104
Debord, Guy, 78
Deleuze, Gilles, 35–6
Deng Xiaoping, 15, 54, 92, 111
Devils on the Doorstep (Jiang Wen, 2000), 113
Dhawan, Nikita, 62
dingti policy, 25
documentaries, 115; *see also 24 City; Dong; I Wish I Knew; Useless*
Dong (2006), 18, 125–9, 131–2
    and intellectuals, 112
    and interviews, 119–21, 123–4
    and migrant workers, 48, 59, 62, 68–9
    and nationalism, 116–17
    and nudity, 71, 72–3
    and peasants, 53, 55
    and sex workers, 129–30
During, Simon, 76

economic reforms, 3, 6, 15–16, 30, 118
education, 34
elderly, 55–6
emotion, 3, 4, 34, 35, 45–6; *see also* feeling; nostalgia
empathy, 17, 49
employment, 21, 51, 137–8; *see also* unemployment
Engels, Friedrich, 32, 142
entertainers, 17
entrepreneurs, 1, 2–3, 6, 18–19, 136–7
    and *24 City*, 151–6
    and corruption, 138–46
    and history, 137–8
    and Ma Ke, 146–51
    and *Words of a Journey*, 156–62

Fabe, Marilyn, 63, 65
factories, 16, 17, 20–1, 130–1
    and closure, 22, 25, 26
    and migrant workers, 60
    and ruin, 28–31
    and workers, 31–3
Factory 420, 21, 26, 33–4, 38–9, 92, 93–4
family, 8–9, 46
Fanon, Franz, 73
Farquhar, Mary, 96
fashion *see* Ma Ke
feeling, 3, 4–6, 14, 17
    and class, 9–10
    and hopelessness, 49
    and the past, 96
    and precariousness, 78
    and ruin, 20–1, 33
    and workers, 22
    see also emotion; nostalgia
Feuerwerker, Yi-tsi Mei, 49, 61, 77, 110
    and intellectuals, 115, 128, 134, 135
fiction, 42
film, 4, 13, 14–15, 39
Five-Year Plans, 16
Flatley, Jonathan, 5–6
food rations, 22
Four Cleanups Campaign, 2, 9, 92

Gates, Bill, 146
gaze, 24, 28, 38, 160
    and migrant workers, 49, 67–8, 79–83
generations, 4–5, 40–1, 43
German Democratic Republic (GDR), 44

getihu (self-employed), 137–8
Goodman, David, 15
Grimshaw, Anna, 125
Gu Kailai, 107

Halbwachs, Maurice, 40
Han Chen, 61
Han Sanming, 48, 57–8, 59–60, 62, 73–5, 76
Harding, Jennifer, 5
haunted time, 96
He Xikun, 36–8, 39, 41
healthcare, 21, 34
Hershatter, Gail, 40
Heywood, Neil, 107
history, 34, 39–40, 42
home, 77–8
Hometown Boy (Yao Hung-I, 2012), 113
honor, 17
hopelessness, 49
Hou Hsaio-Hsien, 113
Hou Lijun, 46, 47
household registration system, 8
housing, 16, 21, 22, 25, 29–30, 34
Hsu, Carolyn, 137, 159–60
Hu Jintao, 16
Huang Baomei, 26–7, 28–9, 146
Huang Baomei (Xie Jin, 1958), 27, 28, 29
Huang Du, 149–50
hukou (household registration), 8
humanitarianism, 18, 132–3
Hurst, William, 22
Huyssen, Andreas, 44

I Wish I Knew (2010), 20, 26–9, 120
  and migrant workers, 60, 69–70
  and soldier, 84–5, 88–9
Iacocca, Lee, 146
idealization, 12, 22
identity, 22, 41
illiteracy, 11
Imperial Examination, 7
income, 7, 8, 9, 15–16, 22
individualism, 45, 47
industry, 21, 24; *see also* factories
inequality, 15–16
intellectuals, *1*, 2–3, 6, 8, 18, 114–16
  and anxiety, 117–18
  and history, 110–12
  and peasants, 9–10, 125–9, 132–5
  and tradition, 118–19
  and voice, 109–10
"Internationale, The," 31, 152
interviews, 38–9, 40, 41–3, 46

  and entrepreneurs, 160–1
  and intellectuals, 119–24

Jia Zhangke, 2, 4, 6, 82, 113–14
  and advertising, 159
  and art, 13
  and camera, 18
  and economics, 118
  and entrepreneurs, 138–9, 150–1, 161–2
  and intellectuals, 109, 110, 112, 114–15
  and long-take shots, 69
  and memory, 38–9
  and migrant workers, 56
  and workers, 20, 22, 24–5
  and *wuxia* genre, 100–1
  see also *24 City*; *A Touch of Sin*; *Cry Me a River*; *Dong*; *I Wish I Knew*; *Mountains May Depart*; *Platform*; *Still Life*; *Unknown Pleasures*; *Useless*; *Words of a Journey*; *World, The*; *Xiao Shan Going Home*; *Xiao Wu*
Jiang Wen, 113
Jiang Zemin, 138
Jinhua Zhao, 58
Jiwei Xiao, 40, 43
Johnnie Walker, 156

"Keep Walking" campaign, 156–7
Kozloff, Max, 35

land reforms, 8–9
landlords, 6, 7
Landsberg, Alison, 61, 65, 133
Landsberger, Stefan, 13, 88, 112
Lee, Ching Kwan, 40
Lee, Kevin, 67
Lei Feng, 89–90, 138
Lenin, Vladimir, 7, 32, 142
Leninism, 13
Li Zhubin, 143
Lin Biao, 92
"Lin Chong Flees in the Night," 78–9, 98–9
literacy, 11, 14
literature, 10, 13, 14–15
"Little Red Book," 24
Liu Shaoqi, 11, 14
Liu Xiaodong, 18, 53, 55, 59, 112–13
  and creation, 131–2
  and entrepreneurship, 135
  and intellectuals, 109, 114
  and interviews, *119*, 120–1, 123–4
  and nationalism, 116–17
  and nudity, 71–2, 73
  and the past, 118
  see also *Dong*

Liu Yonghao, 146
Louis Vuitton, 148–9
Lu, Sheldon, 44
Lu Huilin, 77
Lü Liping, 46, 47
Lu Xun, 49, 115, 128
Lu Zhaoxu, 61
lumpenproletariat, 7, 80
Lury, Celia, 125
lyrical sociology, 42

Ma Haoying, 61
Ma Ke, 18, 109, 112, 113, 130–1
   and *24 City*, 154
   and advertising, 159
   and anxiety, 117–18
   and entrepreneurship, 135, 146–51
   and intellectuals, 114
   and interviews, 120–4
   and nationalism, 116–17
   and the past, 118–19
   and peasants, 134
McGrath, Jason, 67, 132
Mannheim, Karl, 40
Mao Jihong, 159
Mao suit, 55–6, 58
Mao Zedong, 7, 9–10, 32, 142
   and class figures, 11, 12, 69
   and intellectuals, 111
   and the military, 92
   and peasants, 50
   and ruins, 136
   and *Water Margin*, 99
   and workers, 21, 28
Maoist period (1949–76), 2, 9–10, 30
   and peasants, 50
   and soldiers, 86, 92, 108
   and workers, 20, 21
market economy, 2, 15, 18, 21–2, 41, 43–4
Marx, Karl, 7, 32, 134, 142, 150
Marxism, 13
materialism, 148–50
May Fourth period (1915–21), 50, 61, 110, 115
media, the, 52, 59–60
memory, 34, 38–40, 45–6, 95–6
   and environments of memory, 39
   and sites of memory, 39, 95
   see also nostalgia
Mencius, 12, 49–50, 70, 110
merchants, 2, 6, 7, 10, 137
migrant workers, 2, 16, 17, 20, 26
   and the body, 70–6
   and films, 53, 56–62

   and gaze, 79–83
   and intellectuals, 114
   and Jia Zhangke, 48–9
   and observational shots, 68–70
   and prejudice, 51–2
   and Reform era, 50–1
   and uprootedness, 76–9
   and Xiao Wu, 62–3, *64*, 65–8
mingong see migrant workers
model worker, 27, 28, 140, 146, 157
"model worker" awards, 146
models, 11–13, 14, 26–8
mofan see models
money, 73–4
morality, 12, 33, 137
Mountains May Depart (2015), 3, 18, 113, 151
   and entrepreneurs, 143, 144–6
   and migrant workers, 56
   and soldier, 87, 96
moving portraits, 43, 44, 65, 68–9, 80–1, 130, 160
   and *24 City*, 21, 34, 35–8, 95, 152, 156

nationalism, 45, 116–17
New Documentary Movement, 115
"New Man" concept, 13
   and New Reform/Socialist Human, 19, 160
Ngai, Pun, 77
Nichols, Bill, 66, 83, 119, 122, 125
Nora, Pierre, 39–40, 95
Northern Wei dynasty, 118
nostalgia, 17, 21, 43–5, 106–8, 118
   and marketized nostalgia, 45, 154
   see also Ostalgie
nudity, 70–3

observational shot, 17, 68–70, 125–6
Ostalgie, 44, 118
Othering, 18, 73, 132–5

Pan Shiyi, 156, 157–8, 160–1
patriotism, 9, 10, 14, 18, 115–16
peasants, *1*, 2, 6, 7, 8, 17
   and class, 15
   and films, 52–3
   and history, 49–52
   and intellectuals, 114, 115, 125–9, 132–5
   and Jia Zhangke, 48–9
   and Mao suit, 55–6
   and models, 11, 13
   and representation, 24
   and rootedness, 77
   and suffering, 9
   and Xiao Wu, 53–5

Peng Liyuan, 148
People's Liberation Army (PLA), 2, 84, 86, 87, 92
    and Lei Feng, 89–90
    and nostalgia, 106
    and Shanghai, 88–9
People's Republic of China (PRC) *see* China
performance, 13, 15
Peschel, Lisa, 96
Phelan, Peggy, 92, 95, 96, 108
PLA *see* People's Liberation Army
Platform (2003), 48, 112, 140–1
    and migrant workers, 59, 60, 62, 73–5
Podalsky, Laura, 6
point-of-view (POV) shot, 17, 62–3, *64*, 65–8
police officers, 17, 84, 87–8
politics, 115–16, 146
Popular Cinema (journal), 14
portraits 28, 32, 34, 35–6, 38, 72, 80–1, 142;
    see also moving portraits
posters, 1–2, 11, 13–14
    and entrepreneurs, 138, *139*
    and soldiers, 97–8
    and workers, 22, *23*, 24
POV *see* point-of-view shot
poverty, 54–5
precarity, 76–7, 78
Pribam, E. Deidre, 5
Prince, Stephen, 104
profiteering, 141–2
proletariats, 7, 10, 21
propaganda, 1–2, 6, 10, 34–5
    and intellectuals, 111
    and PLA, 87
    and posters, 11, 13–14
    and workers, 22, *23*, 24, 28
psychogeography, 78

Qin dynasty, 7

racism, 73
Ravetz, Amanda, 125
reality, 12
"red culture," 107
Red Guards, 10, 86
Reform era, 2–4, 6, 15
    and entrepreneurs, 19, 136–7, 141–2, 161–2
    and intellectuals, 18, 111–12
    and migrant workers, 49
    and nostalgia, 44
    and peasants, 50
    and soldiers, 92–3
    and workers, 20, 21–2, 24, 32–3

"Remember the Bitterness" campaigns, 9, 45–6
retirement, 25
role models, 12
roots, 77
rubble, 47
ruin, 16, 20–1, 28–33, 44, 47
rural-to-urban migration *see* migrant workers
rushang (scholar-businessperson), 3, 18–19, 136, 143, 156–62
    and Ma Ke, 148, 149, 150, 151

sacrifice, 46, 52, 59–60
Said, Edward, 134
scholar gentry, 2, 6, 7, 110
science, 2, 138, 153, 160
security guards, 17, 84, 89
self-cultivation, 12, 13
self-employed, 137–8
sex workers, 17, 51, 70, 75–6, 90
    and intellectuals, 114
    and Liu Xiaodong, 129–30
Shanghai Battle, The (Wang Bing, 1959), 84–5, 89
Shanin, Teodor, 134
Sheng Hao, 115
"Singing for our Nation," 34
Smith, Murray, 63, 65
social experience, 4–5
social status, 22
socialism, 2, 12–13, 24, 43–4, 45
society, 114–16
SOHO China, 157, 158
soldiers, *1*, 2, 6, 7, 8, 17–18
    and *24 City*, 93–6
    and *A Touch of Sin*, 97–108
    and corruption, 91–2
    and decline, 92–3
    and films, 84–5, 87–91
    and history, 86
    and models, 11, 13
    see also police officers; security guards
solidarity, 9, 10, 41, 43
Solinger, Dorothy, 22, 33
Soviet Union, 13
"Special Economic Zones," 15
"Spilt Milk" (Yeats), 152, 154
Spivak, Gayatri, 62
Stalin, Joseph, 32, 142
State Owned Enterprises (SOEs), 32, 34, 142
Still Life (2006), 3, 20
    and entrepreneurs, 140, 141–2
    and migrant workers, 48, 56, 57–8, 59–60, 62, 68–9, 73–4, 78–9
    and nudity, 70–1

Still Life (2006) (*cont.*)
   and politics, 116
   and ruin, 29–31
   and sex workers, 75
   and soldier, 84, 89–90
   and workers, 26, 31–3
"Stinking Ninths," 18, 111, 134
Su Na, 41, 45, 151–6
subaltern, 62
sympathy, 17, 18, 49, 61–2, 133
Szeto, Kin-Yan, 116

Taoism, 119
technology, 2, 21, 111, 146
tensed time, 25–6, 60, 74–5, 103, 130, 161
   and *24 City*, 35, 36, 94, 155
Thailand, 129–30
"Three Prominences," 14–15
Tiananmen Square, 90, 91–2, 112
time *see* haunted time; tensed time
tomatoes, 107
Totaro, Donato, 36
tradition, 118–19
Trigg, Dylan, 33
Tsui, Christine, 148

unemployment, 15, 21–2, 25–6
Unger, Jonathan, 45
uniforms, 41, 55–6, 90
Unknown Pleasures (2004), 20, 25–6, 112, 141
   and ruin, 29–30, 33
   and sex workers, 75
   and soldier, 84, 88
uprootedness, 76–8
Useless (2007), 3, 18, 116, 117, 130–1
   and camera, 125
   and entrepreneurship, 146–51
   and intellectuals, 112
   and interviews, 119–24
   and migrant workers, 48, 60
   and nudity, 70, 71

violence, 101–6
Virno, Paolo, 76
voice, 18, 109–10, 115, 121–2

Walder, Andrew G., 21
Wang, Master, 39, 41
Wang Hongwei, 48, 57–8, 60, 144
Wang Hui, 117
Wang Lijun, 107

Wang Qingsong, 125–9
Wang Xiaoshuai, 113
water, 78–9
Water Margin (Shi Nai'an), 98–9
wealth, 7, 15, 45, 47, 54
Weil, Simone, 77
Wemheuer, Felix, 52
Williams, Raymond, 3, 4–5, 6, 136–7
Woodward, Kathleen, 6
Words of a Journey (2011), 3, 53, 156–62
work units *see* danwei
workers, 1, 2, 6, 8, 16–17, 20–1
   and *24 City*, 33–9, 46–7
   and documentaries, 26–9
   and generations, 40–1
   and history, 21–2
   and Jia Zhangke, 24–5
   and memory, 39–40
   and models, 11, 13
   and nostalgia, 43–4
   and representation, 22, *23*, 24
   and ruin, 29–31
   and *Still Life*, 31–3
   and *Unknown Pleasures*, 25–6
World, The (2005), 48, 52–3, 113, 140
   and migrant workers, 56, 62, 74, 75, 80
   and security guards, 84, 89
Wu Guanjun, 117
Wu Hung, 30, 33
wuxia genre, 100–6

Xi Jinpeng, 148
Xiao Hua, *37*
Xiao Shan Going Home (1995), 3, 48, 56, 75, 77
Xiao Wu (1997), 3, 75, 139–40
   and migrant workers, 48, 57–9, 62–3, *64*, 65–8
   and nudity, 71
   and peasants, 52–5, 56
   and police, 84, 87–8
Xiaowei Zang, 15
xiushen (fix the self), 12, 13

Yao Hung-I, 113
Yao Ming, 146
Yingjin Zhang, 80
Yuanming Yuan (Old Summer Palace), 30

Zhang Xin, 157
Zhang Yuan, 113
Zhao Gang, 41, 45, *94*, 95
Zhao Tao, 144, 151

EU representative:
Easy Access System Europe
Mustamäe tee 50, 10621 Tallinn, Estonia
Gpsr.requests@easproject.com

www.ingramcontent.com/pod-product-compliance
Lightning Source LLC
Chambersburg PA
CBHW051117230426
43667CB00014B/2618